Sri Ramana Maharshi's Moksha

A Hindu Astrological Pilgrimage into the Life and Moksha of Sri Ramana Maharshi

Sankara Bhagavadpada

YogiImpressions®

YogiImpressions®
SRI RAMANA MAHARSHI'S MOKSHA
First published in India in 2008 by
Yogi Impressions Books Pvt. Ltd.
1711, Centre 1, World Trade Centre,
Cuffe Parade, Mumbai 400 005, India.
Website: www.yogiimpressions.com

First Edition, December 2008
Second Reprint, January 2014

Cover design: Priya Mehta

ISBN 978-81-88479-40-5

Śrī Ramaṇa Maharṣi on Aruṇācala, the Sacred Hill

"I have discovered a new thing! This hill, the lodestone of lives, arrests the movements of anyone who so much as thinks of it, draws him face to face with it, and fixes him motionless like itself, to feed upon his soul thus ripened. What (a wonder) is this! Oh souls! beware of It and live! Such a destroyer of lives is this magnificent Aruṇācala, which shines within the Heart!"

DEDICATION

My position in Hindu society as a householder who is also concomitantly a spiritual seeker has given me an 'amphibious' existence in two distinct worlds – *Artha* and *Kāma* on the one hand and *Dharma* and *Mokṣa* on the other. Therefore, my *Dharma* dictates that I make this dedication two-fold:

In the Sphere of Family Life

To my beloved grandparents *Śrīmatī* Niraghatam Yamini Poorna Tilakamma and *Śrī* Niraghatam Ramakotayya, for being noble and selfless *karmayogis,*

To my beloved parents *Śrīmatī* Kanaka Durga Ramachandran and *Śrī* Anantha Ramachandran, for their lifelong unconditional love and support,

To the beloved Dr. N. Sivakamu for her self-effacing compassionate support of my Master's and my spiritual work during its inceptional stages,

And to my beloved younger brother *Śrī* Sriram, for having been an adorable being of loving innocence, in spite of the handicap of Down's syndrome.

In the Sublime Spheres of Dharma and Mokṣa

To my beloved philosopher-friend and compassionate Master *Śrī Śrī Bhagavān,* now in our midst, for his magnanimous blessings for my Hindu Astrological Pilgrimage in the spheres of *Dharma* and *Mokṣa,*

To my three other beloved departed *advaitic* Masters, *Śrī J. Krishnamurti, Śrī Nisargadatta Maharaj,* and especially *Śrī Ramaṇa Maharṣi,* into whose life and *Mokṣa* I have undertaken this Hindu Astrological Pilgrimage,

To my beloved *Jyotiṣācāryas* Professor Vinod Kumar Choudhry and Pandit Vamadeva Shastri, now in our midst, without the light of whose knowledge this Hindu Astrological Pilgrimage would not have been possible,

And to my fellow pilgrims travelling on diverse spiritual paths: *Brahma-jijñāsus* and *Mumukṣus,* English-educated Hindus, Hindu astrologers, as well as kindred spiritual seekers and astrologers from all other climes and cultures of the world.

V. K. CHOUDHRY
M.B.A.
Author & Astrologer
Founder & Chairman
International Institute of Predictive Astrology
Fairfield, IA, U.S.A.

A-105, South City-II
Gurgaon- 122101 (INDIA)
Ph. : 91-124-2219240, 5360240, 2060021
Fax. : 91-124-2219102
www.YourNetAstrologer.com
E-mail : siha@vsnl.com

FOREWORD

I am extremely grateful to the Almighty for having blessed me with an opportunity for writing a few words about the esteemed work of Sri Sankara Bhagavadpada, who continuously dedicates his time and energy for promoting an understanding of the state of Hindu society and *Sanatana Dharma,* in view of Hindu society being the soil from which Hindu astrology springs.

As Hindu society has been fighting to survive disintegration for nearly the full span of the bygone millennium, the majority of Hindus are, by and large, not deeply anchored at all to the spiritual ethos of *Sanatana Dharma.* Some Hindus have been enchanted by the glitter of materialistic pursuits, but are still indecisive on adapting to them in totality. There is, thus, either a complete apathy on the part of Hindus allured by materialism towards all things bound up with the Hindu religion (*Sanatana Dharma*), or at best, only a superficial adherence to the outer symbols and manifestations of the religion, without the curiosity and faith to go into deeper waters. What is more, all

---

Author of :
• SELF LEARNING COURSE IN ASTROLOGY • SYSTEMS' APPROACH FOR INTERPRETING HOROSCOPES
• HOW TO STUDY DIVISIONAL CHARTS • HOW TO IDENTIFY SIGNIFICANT EVENTS
• IMPACT OF ASCENDING SIGNS • HOW TO ANALYSE MARRIED LIFE • PREDICTIVE TECHNIQUES

Hindu *vidyas*, especially Hindu astrology, are either not recognized or are given only a secondary or tertiary position in a world that is becoming increasingly materialistic and unspiritual to that corresponding degree.

The author, through this serious interdisciplinary Hindu astrological work in the spiritual spheres of *Dharma* and *Moksha*, has attempted to stir the hearts of Hindus in a gentle but persuasive manner, thereby sensitizing them to the highest aspect of *Moksha* in their *Sanatana Dharma*. Simultaneously, he has also attempted to raise Hindu astrology, which has undeservedly been beaten too hard by so-called rationalists, to the highest levels of appreciation and veneration through its capacity to throw new astounding light on the *Moksha* and life of one of *Sanatana Dharma's* greatest Sages of all time.

In the last nine years, his labours of learning have been in the spheres of *Vedic* astrology and the Systems Approach to *Vedic* astrology, not only in the spheres of *Artha* and *Kama*, but also in the spiritual spheres of *Dharma* and *Moksha*. Using a harmonious combination of *Vedic* astrology and the Systems Approach, he has thrown abundant astrological light on the theme of his present work, brings into full view a number of new astrological *sutras* governing *Moksha* and the spiritual life, and illustrates them through the life and Self-Realization of Sri Ramana Maharshi.

Taking into account the author's background as a former researcher in the field of theoretical nuclear physics as well as his vast experience as an *acharya* [spiritual teacher] who dedicated his labours to his Master's spiritual mission for many years, one is able to appreciate his special advantages, which he has fully utilized in this fascinating interdisciplinary work.

As per *Ramacharithramanas*, in *Kaliyuga* one can attain *Moksha* while in *grihasthashrama* through one's *karma* and devotion to God. It is therefore my cherished wish that Sri Sankara Bhagavadpada, who happens to be a householder, should secure this highest blessing of *Moksha* through his dedication and devotion to his beloved Masters, as well as to the *vidya* of Hindu astrology — which is so very evident in this work.

I would like to place on record my deep appreciation of the dedicated work of Sri Sankara Bhagavadpada, and I am sure this work will successfully achieve its objective and be enjoyed by readers in its true spirit.

I wish the author all the very best.

V. K. Choudhry
26 June 2008

PUBLISHER'S PREFACE

When Sankara approached me with this manuscript, I wondered, as I leafed through it, whether just one horoscope warranted an entire book being published about it. But that doubt was promptly dispelled when I realized that his work was a detailed study of the birth chart of none other than Sri Ramana Maharshi, with a view to understanding the astrological significance of the Sage's *Moksha* or Liberation.

According to Sankara, Ramana's personality was 'blown away' at the young age of sixteen and, thereafter, it was the 'Presence of *Arunachala Siva*' living through the bodily form of Ramana. In the pantheon of India's illustrious Sages, Ramana's teaching shines bright as it carries the Divine Light of *Arunachala's Deepam* to the far corners of the earth.

There was nothing more to be said. No further conviction was needed, nor sought. The book had to happen for the purpose the Divine had willed it.

While this book is a serious study in *Vedic* astrology of Ramana Maharshi's birth chart, its intention is to use this ancient science to shed light on the most eventful aspect of life — the quest for Self-Realization. The book provides a qualitative understanding of what *Moksha* is all about, in terms of the loss of the 'self'. Its purpose is to 'show the way' by which the stage was set for Ramana's *Moksha*. Taking your hand, Sankara guides you along this adventurous road of self-discovery. The Sage of *advaita,* Nisargadatta Maharaj could not have put it better when he said, *"The road is the goal."*

Indeed, Sankara lights up the road as he brings his skill-sets and experience in the astrological deciphering of the mystery of enlightenment. In a lighter vein, talking of Nisargadatta reminds me of an amusing anecdote I heard. When a seeker asked him if there was any difference between *Bhagavan* and him, Maharaj replied, *"There is none. Perhaps the only difference is I am slightly better dressed!"*

We hope you enjoy the 'pilgrimage' that Sankara has pains-takingly mapped out, making the light of *Vedic* astrology shine on such a luminous, spiritual figurehead as Ramana Maharshi. And, to guide you along your life's journey, here is a sparkler from Ramana himself: *"There is no need to rush about anything; everything happens at the appointed hour as per the Divine Will."*

Sri Gautam Sachdeva
25 September 2008
Mumbai

PREFACE

Hindu Society in the Last Millennium

This is essentially a spiritual-astrological Pilgrimage in the spheres of Dharma and Mokṣa that has been set a-going by the challenge of a long-standing and ongoing collective crisis in Hindu society, and the repercussions of this crisis in my individual life as a Hindu in particular. As discerning Hindus, we should know that our society has been in *a pathetic state of civilizational debility and darkness* for practically a greater part of the last millennium. Though it is not my intention here to adduce irrefutable evidence for the above premise, we may note in passing that the observations of the keen-sighted Arab traveller Alberuni in 1030 CE, in fact, offered testimony to Hindu society having entered into a state of breakdown even by that date.

If we take for the time-span of a single generation a modest estimate of one quarter of a century, this would mean that such an age of civilizational debility and darkness [*Kaliyuga?*] has continued for at least forty successive generations, spanning some ten centuries in the process. These considerations are intended to be no more than preliminary conservative estimates of the age of debility and darkness to which Hindu society seems to have succumbed on account of *the inevitable slow turning of the wheel of Time, with the consequent coming and going of the cyclical seasons* [*yugas*] *of civilizations.*

It now comes to us as a soothing consolation that though we are standing on the shaky ground of a comparatively unresearched and nebulous area of Hindu *Purāṇic* history, it is our immense good fortune that the illustrious Hindu Spiritual Master, *Śrī Swāmi Yukteśwar Giri* (1855-1936 CE) has, in a single master stroke, done away with the long-persisting absurd *Purāṇic* chronology of *yugas* (*Śrī Swāmi Yukteśwar Giri* 8-24); he has given us in its place a reliable new model based on the pertinent *precessional cycle of equinoxes* (roughly 24,000 years).

Śrī Yukteśwar Giri's model for the chronology of Yugas, based on the Precessional Cycle of the Equinoxes of roughly 24,000 years		
	Yuga	Extent in Time
Descending Half of the Cycle	*Satya*	11501 BCE to 6701 BCE = 4800 years, inclusive of *sandhis*
	Treta	6701 BCE to 3101 BCE = 3600 years, inclusive of *sandhis*
	Dwapara	3101 BCE to 701 BCE = 2400 years, inclusive of *sandhis*
	Kali	701 BCE to 499 CE = 1200 years, inclusive of *sandhis*
Ascending Half of the Cycle	*Kali*	499 CE to 1699 CE = 1200 years, inclusive of *sandhis*
	Dwapara	1699 CE to 4099 CE = 2400 years, inclusive of *sandhis*
	Treta	4099 CE to 7699 CE = 3600 years, inclusive of *sandhis*
	Satya	7699 CE to 12499 CE = 4800 years, inclusive of *sandhis*

With *Śrī Yukteśwar Giri's* model of the chronology of the *yugas*, we will find to our satisfaction that we get our bearings right, at least insofar as the *Vedic* astronomical observations of the continuously shifting *vernal equinox* are concerned. In Section 8 of Chapter III, we shall have occasion to dwell at greater length on the whole question of the movement of the *vernal equinox* on the *zodiacal belt* with the slow progression of the ages, or *yugas*.

Another immediately apparent consequence of the new model is that according to it, with effect from 1899 CE, Hindu society has entered the true *Dwāparayuga* (beyond the transitional zone or *sandhi*), and this civilizational season is expected to endure for the ensuing two millennia. Insofar as the ingredient of *Dharma*, or virtue, in the *Dwāparayuga* is concerned, Hindu *Purāṇas* maintain that while it is at an all time low of only 25% in *Kali*, it enjoys the much more blessed level of 50% in the succeeding *Dwāpara*.

In fact, we find that the significant milestone developments in Indian history in the last century in spheres of life ranging from political to spiritual offer unmistakable testimony for a radical upward shift in *Dharma* (from *Kali* to *Dwāpara*, in the ascending cycle) to have actually occurred in our Hindu society. Thus, having provisionally satisfied ourselves with the results of using this new model for the chronology of the *yugas*, we may now turn our attention once more in the direction of the *civilizational debility and darkness in Hindu society* with which we actually started.

Śrī Yukteśwar Giri's model also implies that the age of civilizational debility and darkness, which preceded the commencement of *Dwāparayuga* (1899 CE), had actually come into existence as far back as 701 BCE, thus extending the bygone season of *Kali* to no less a span than 2,400 years. For lack of thorough and conclusive research into Indian history of this period, we shall not touch upon the important question of the actual tenure of *Kaliyuga*, but shall now move on to consider the underlying essence of the civilizational debility and darkness that continues to haunt us, even after Hindu society has decisively entered into the ascending *Dwāpara* season.

Though Hindu society in the course of the last five centuries – when *Kali* was still very much the dominant *yuga* — had been struggling to follow in the footsteps of its two illustrious predecessors, the Indic and the *Vedic,* which were religious to the core, it has nevertheless had to suffer the misfortune of an even greater dissociation from its spiritual and cultural roots on account of its having come under mounting pressure from changing forms of Westernization from the time of the landfall of *Vasco da Gama* at Calicut (on the West coast of India) in 1498 CE.

Repercussions of the Hindu Crisis for Hindu Astrology

A tragic repercussion of this long-drawn-out Hindu crisis is seen in the apathy and derision of English-educated Hindus towards all things connected in one way or the other with our spiritual and cultural ethos of *Sanātana Dharma.* Thus, our attitude to Hindu astrology has also necessarily been only one of contempt and disdain. *This has been one of the challenges that has made me embark on this Hindu astrological Pilgrimage, for it gives me the opportunity to unveil the original intelligent face of Hindu astrology — before it came to be mutilated and disfigured during the course of the age of civilizational debility and darkness.*

There is assuredly one manifestation of the crisis in Hindu astrology in the outer realms of Hindu society: though the rank and file of Hindus still rely on the guidance and wisdom that Hindu astrology offers as a means of coping with the baffling problems of their existence, when it comes to English-educated Hindus and our modern intelligentsia, one sees nothing but insolence and indifference for this ancient and profound system of Hindu spiritual learning [*vidyā*].

Such a sorry state of affairs has continued because there has not been sufficiently intense light thrown, time and again, on the foundations of Hindu astrology from just the right angles; so that what has appeared up to this point as something irrational and incomprehensible — from the point of view of modern science – may now, under new intense illumination, suddenly begin to light up and glow with the profound meaning of *God-centred spiritual insights and a remarkable spiritual vision of life. In the past, there has been an insufficient emphasis on the spiritual and God-centred nature of Hindu astrology.*

The Way to Approach and Understand Hindu Astrology

We cannot understand and appreciate Hindu astrology, much less Hindu *Dharma,* if we attempt to illuminate these ancient disciplines with the light of the modern sciences. Hindu astrology, and surely, Hindu *Dharma* (or going back further to their source, the *Vedas*) do have a profound system of *darśana* [philosophical world view] and *nyāya* [a system of spiritual logic] of their own; this system of logic and understanding is entirely different from the logic of the modern physical sciences. *Thus, if we wish to understand and appreciate Hindu astrology, we cannot begin by throwing the light of science upon it, which is what we inadvertently tend to do in an attempt to grasp this discipline.*

Rather, we must be more discriminating in the kind of light we deem appropriate to illuminate Hindu astrology in order to bring out its hidden mysteries and beauties. The absurdity of judging and attempting to understand Hindu astrology from the point of view of the modern sciences may be brought home through the following telling analogy: Imagine what the outcome of our efforts would be if we sought to understand disciplines that are entirely alien to the sciences such as history, economics, or politics, by throwing the light of modern science upon them. Or better still, think of the inevitable confusion in which we enmesh ourselves if we undertake to understand physics by throwing the light of history or religion upon it. *The derision and disdain that has been hurled at Hindu astrology is the unfortunate result of attempting to approach this ancient discipline with the inappropriate light of modern science.*

English-Educated Hindus and their Spiritual Predicament

Having undergone a 'cultural conversion' to a western outlook on life — *of which we are largely unconscious* — we, the English-educated Hindus, are still following and imitating our materially powerful, yes, but nonetheless, spiritually sterile western role models, little realizing that this has not brought lasting contentment to our souls, which have been spiritually sick and starving right through the course of this continuing process of Westernization. By 'role models', we are not to understand the genuine Spiritual Masters from the West, but only those who, with a purely materialistic orientation, dictate all the norms in that society in the form of the gross pursuit of pleasure and success to the exclusion of all other higher spiritual aspirations of the human soul. These cultural trends are based on purely body-centred physical considerations, without even the faintest glimmer of recognition that a human is fundamentally a being of light in the image of God, rather than a puny bio-physical organism, albeit with self-consciousness.

As modern English-educated Hindus who have had to make *an unconscious break with the traditional spiritual heritage* given to us by our wise forefathers, we have been inwardly succumbing to that dreadful spiritual malady of inner desolation and despair, which we have had to inherit from the West as an unfortunate concomitant of their *apotheosis* of science and technology. This spiritual malady in our Hindu consciousness is so strange an affliction that it is even difficult to discover the exact nature of this sickness in our souls, precisely because this malady has, so to speak, struck at the hearts of vast numbers of English-educated Hindus, sparing in the process, no more than, perhaps, a handful of fortunate individuals.

The nearly universal nature of the spiritual malady and the continuing process of civilizational debility and darkness, both at macrocosmic as well as at microcosmic levels, has made the healing of this malady a slow and painful process. Therefore, there is indeed a continuing sickness in Hindu souls that may not have been identified as something spiritually unhealthy as such, but which, nevertheless, will continue to haunt Hindus in the form of a certain never-subsiding restlessness so long as they refuse to heed the recurring inner call to return 'home', either to the sanctuary of their *Vedic*/Hindu heritage or directly into the bosom of their own inner consciousness.

My concern has been, in the first instance for my 'tribesmen' — English-educated Hindus, whose predicament I can well imagine. They constitute an important segment of the creative minority of our society and have had to suffer this colossal loss of our spiritual and cultural ethos, and with it, the loss of their spiritual well-being as well. *This was the most fundamental challenge confronting India on the verge of her Independence, though the gravity of this Hindu tragedy largely went unnoticed at that nascent stage.*

A Spiritual Resolution of the Hindu Crisis is the Only True Resolution

The crisis in which Hindu society finds itself is fundamentally a spiritual one, *for whether it is domination by alien powers or Westernization, all these are only its outer manifestations*. This means that the crisis has come into the foreground of our personal and social lives on account of individual Hindus having lost the blessings and grace of God in the microcosm of our souls and as a result, in the field of our social and political life. As Hindu society has always been a spiritual and religious one, this loss of grace in the lives of individual Hindus had already profoundly weakened this society even as far back as the early eleventh century, when it entered into its time of troubles.

In studying the historical rhythms of Hindu society and its predecessor, the Indic society, I have had to follow the insights given to us in this field by the British historian Arnold J. Toynbee, as I have found him to be philosophically and spiritually insightful to a degree that is far beyond the ken of other historians of modern times.

God's Grace for 'Seeing'

If we look at the whole process of the onset of the crisis and its cessation at some later date, we shall find that it comes to be precipitated only when members of Hindu society lose touch with the grace of God or *with their own souls*, if we wish to put it that way. Finding again that lost grace, they are able to emerge from the crisis into the fullness of a new life that is now based either on a constant awareness of God and His ways or *on abidance in their Self.*

For a civilization to flourish and grow, it is very important that its members be blessed with the grace of God or *what tantamounts to the same thing: for its members to be centred in their being-nature and in their souls*; for it is this grace, throughout the whole course of human history, that has been behind all great inspired works in every conceivable field of human endeavour. It has always been grace that has given humans that higher spiritual and creative faculty of *seeing*, and it has only been this higher faculty of seeing that created all the great civilizations of the past. When this grace departs from our lives, it takes away from us that precious spiritual faculty of seeing as well.

Thus, one of the effects of our spiritual crisis is our being deprived of the spiritual faculty of seeing what is actually going on, both within our consciousness as well as out there, in the world at large. 'Deprivation' implies that we had this spiritual faculty well intact, until a day came in our lives, either suddenly or gradually, when we simply lost this spiritual faculty of seeing things as they actually are. For many, there is even the definitive grimmer possibility that they may not have suffered the deprivation of anything; for they might have entered into the centre stage of their life as perfect strangers to that spiritual faculty and continue in that spiritually blinded condition till the time of awakening arrives and opens up that spiritual vision, probably for the first time in their lives. Thus, deprivation is not quite the question. *One of the concomitants of our spiritual crisis is our inability to have the grace for seeing.*

If, through the bounty of grace, we are able to see, this reveals things to us as they actually are. And in those lucid moments of seeing, when there is inner stillness, there is a sudden flash of insight into the nature of what has been seen, and this insight creates understanding or learning. Conversely, when individuals and their society have lost the spiritual faculty of seeing because of the denial of God's grace, then all learning comes to an end. *We thus reach the startling conclusion that in our Hindu society, which is currently not entirely free of the state of civilizational debility and darkness, the denial of God's grace has not only taken away from us the spiritual faculty of seeing, it has also denied us the possibility of learning about life and the fruits thereof.*

'Hindu Medicine' and Hindu Homecoming

Through this Pilgrimage into *Śrī Ramaṇa Maharṣi's* life and *Mokṣa,* I am attempting to draw the attention of my fellow Hindus to a certain efficacious *Hindu medicine,* for on a previous occasion, a similar application of such a Hindu medicine had had a most salutary spiritual effect upon my own life. In fact, it even had the potency to sober me and wean me away from that dangerous tendency of approaching all things in life through the cold, unfeeling intellect. And what is more, it made my passage back home – my Hindu homecoming to *Sanātana Dharma* – so much more easier and filled with delight. *In my case, however, the Hindu medicine was administered to me by my beloved Master Śrī Śrī Bhagavān when I was just setting foot into the mainstream of my adult life as a lost Hindu soul in the wilderness of a spiritually debilitated Hindu society.*

Satsaṅg with Aruṇācala Śiva and My Beloved Masters

In the ensuing Pilgrimage, we will have an opportunity on practically every one of its pages to take a draught of this sobering Hindu medicine, for what can this be other than the words of *upadeśa* [spiritual instruction] of *Śrī Ramaṇa Maharṣi* himself or one of my three other beloved Masters? As we shall discover for ourselves, this Hindu medicine is only available when there is a *satsaṅg* [an occasion to soak in the radiation of the Master's grace] with the Masters, and fortunately for us, the entire Pilgrimage affords us a continuous unbroken stream of *satsaṅg* either with that *advaitic* Master *Śrī Ramaṇa Maharṣi,* who is an embodiment of *Aruṇācala Śiva,* or if not with him, then definitely with one of my three other Masters, beginning with *Śrī Śrī Bhagavān.*

A potent medicine that has worked for one can work equally well for all — since the spiritual malady is more in the nature of a universal affliction. Readers can therefore feel reassured that though their intellects may rebel against the repugnant idea of the administration of a Hindu medicine for the alleviation of some alleged spiritual malady, at least insofar as their thirsting souls are concerned, this medicine cannot be construed as anything other than a drink fit for the gods. Thus, the Hindu medicine, in real terms, is nothing but the flowing nectar of grace coming from that transcendental God of the Hindu world *Aruṇācala Śiva,* as also from my Spiritual Masters.

As soon as I took the first draught of this medicine after the same was prescribed for me by my Master *Śrī Śrī Bhagavān,* it had the spiritual effect of making me turn inwards and start looking at myself. Thereafter, there was no looking back! May this miracle of the Hindu homecoming, which happened to me in the course of a personal crisis, also happen to all my fellow Hindus. Not that I wish them to be engulfed in personal crises, although a crisis may well be mandatory as an important factor serving to trigger the Hindu homecoming!

Readers may well ask, "If it is simply the Hindu homecoming that is the goal of this Pilgrimage, what is the compelling necessity to scale the highest peak of *Sanātana Dharma,* namely, Self-Realization?" My lifelong spiritual association with my Master *Śrī Śrī Bhagavān* and with the *advaitic* teachings of my other Masters, including *Śrī Ramaṇa Maharṣi,* did not give me any other option in this regard, as I have tried to make clear in Chapter I.

Aruṇācala Śiva as Śrī Ramaṇa Maharṣi

It is against this vast backdrop of the Hindu heritage and Hindu spiritual predicament that we embark on this astrological Pilgrimage into the life story of the boy *Ramaṇa,* who, when he was only sixteen years, was destined to undergo a Divine metamorphosis into *Aruṇācala Śiva,* the transcendental God of the Hindu world. Conversely, it is also the story of how *Aruṇācala Śiva* came to wear a human body and live the life of *Śrī Ramaṇa Maharṣi* to remind His creation of the highest blessings of *Mokṣa,* which had been so beloved to His devotees in the ages past but which had been lost sight of for a greater part of the last millennium. That *Aruṇācala Śiva* was indeed the *Mokṣapradāta* [giver of *Mokṣa*] for the boy *Ramaṇa* was adequately acknowledged by the *Maharṣi* himself:

> *From my home Thou didst entice me, then stealing into my Heart didst draw me gently into Thine, [such is] Thy Grace Oh Arunachala!...*
>
> *Watching like a spider to trap me in the web [of Thy Grace], Thou didst entwine me and when imprisoned feed upon me, Oh Arunachala!* (Sri Ramana Maharshi, qtd. in Sri Ramanasramam 93-94)

A Hindu Astrological Pilgrimage

This Pilgrimage will give us rare astrological insights into this absolutely unheard-of metamorphosis as well as into the strange human life of *Aruṇācala Śiva.* Like astronomers use the powerful tool of the telescope or microbiologists use the microscope as the instrument of their skilled perception, in this Pilgrimage, we shall use the Hindu astrological horoscope as our magical 'magnifying glass' in order to see deeply and clearly into the life and *Mokṣa* of the *Maharṣi.*

In fact, *Jyotiṣa* [Hindu astrology] has been held by Hindus since ancient times to be 'the eye of wisdom'. Though the horoscope of Hindu astrology is no physical and technological instrument of perception but is more in the nature of *a mystic yantra, portraying the mood of God at the time and place of birth,* yet, insofar as its capacity to make us *see* deeply into human lives is concerned – how the forces of the grace and wrath of God govern our lives – *there is hardly another discipline of human knowledge, ancient or modern, that can surpass it as an instrument of seeing and as a source of consummate wisdom, capable of teaching us to understand duality within ourselves as well as in others, thus enabling us to live our lives fully and wisely on both the material and the spiritual planes.*

Therefore, the first half of our Pilgrimage will be devoted to learning the skills of *astrological seeing*; that is, through the magnifying glass of the horoscope. As there are many different systems of Hindu and *Vedic* astrology, I am obliged to specify the systems of astrology that I relied upon for this Pilgrimage: I have used for the most part the remarkable theoretical framework of the Systems Approach to *Vedic* astrology (henceforth SA) developed by one of the illustrious living Masters of *Vedic* astrology, Professor V. K. Choudhry. To strengthen my emphasis on the spiritual spheres of *Dharma* and *Mokṣa* in *Vedic* astrology, I have had to invoke another inspirational source, the spiritual system of *Vedic* astrology (henceforth VA) developed by the renowned *Vedācārya* Pandit Vamadeva Shastri.

The SA gives us predictive accuracy and analytical clarity into all the four spheres of life whereas the VA of Vamadeva Shastri gives us valuable spiritual insights into the spheres of *Dharma* and *Mokṣa.* On the basis of a number of well-attested milestone events from the *Maharṣi's* life, a rectification of the *Maharṣhi's* birth chart has been done. It is probably for the first time that the *Maharṣi's* life and *Mokṣa* are being presented comprehensively from a Hindu astrological perspective. *Without the powerful analytical tools of the SA, there was no way in which one could have attempted the birth rectification of the Maharṣi's horoscope, much less undertaken this astrological Pilgrimage in the spiritual spheres of Dharma and Mokṣa.*

In the enunciation of the principles of Hindu astrology, emphasis has been placed on astrological wisdom and insights into the paradoxes of our earthly life, maintaining that these are important fruits of Hindu astrology — at least insofar as the spiritual life is concerned. Many astrological principles, especially those governing the colossal spiritual blessings of *Mokṣa,* have also been cast in a new thought-provoking and inspiring form so that they may kindle our philosophical wonder and give us that much needed impetus to get on with the Pilgrimage. In addition, the subjective nature of astrological time has also been given special importance, as the significance of 'subjective time' in Hindu astrology has not usually been explained in such clear terms.

Mokṣa and the Mahānirvāṇa of the Maharṣi

While every moment of the Pilgrimage may well give us some kind of a soul-satisfying astrological insight or other, two very momentous and memorable milestones in the second half of the Pilgrimage that are highly evocative of the Hindu ethos — one, the *Mokṣa* or Immortality of the *Maharṣi,* and the other, his *Mahānirvāṇa* [passing away] — will stand out as the most overwhelming moments, serving to impact upon our sensibilities and sensitizing us to the eternal truths of Immortality and death. We astrologically see these two important milestones in the *Maharṣi*'s life through what astrologers call transit significant events (TSEs).

The 'Distributaries' of the Pilgrimage

After I had completed writing the text of this Pilgrimage, I found to my consternation that in the course of the narration, as many as four distinct paths on which the Pilgrimage was simultaneously advancing had unexpectedly emerged, with each path continuously criss-crossing the others to such an extent that if readers were not made aware of these paths, they would run the risk of not knowing at all what the author was actually attempting to convey!

Thus, to lay at rest my own fears as well as to give readers a clearer picture of the terrain on which I shall be advancing, I decided to add to the Preface this additional section in the form of an instructive analogy, hoping that it would be sufficient to throw into full relief the manifold nature of the Pilgrimage. Through such a perspective, it will also be easier for readers to have not only a wide-angled vision of the Pilgrimage in its comprehensive reach, but also a little foretaste of what I am intending to convey through its ensuing long stretches.

In the well-known geographical phenomenon of delta formation, which occurs in the penultimate stage at the mouth of any river before it peacefully flows into the sea, there is always a spontaneous slowing down and a concomitant breaking up of the one gigantic flowing river mass into its many branches or tributaries. If you like, we may think of the sea as the final destination of the Pilgrimage, namely, the *Mokṣa* of *Śrī Ramaṇa Maharṣi,* whereas the river itself may be likened to the Pilgrimage proper.

The kindred spontaneous breaking up of the Pilgrimage was not something that I had anticipated or even contrived in any way in the beginning. On the contrary, it was simply a thing I had to come to terms with as soon as I started reviewing the finished work — but now only in the capacity of a dispassionate reader. I could identify in all, four distinct 'distributaries' of the original river of the Pilgrimage.

It might be worthwhile for us at this stage to note that though the waters of these distributaries are all undeniably alike in a fundamental sense, yet, as they also now enjoy distinctive functions — in their newer roles as *individualized distributaries* rather than as the *self-same streams of the original river* — it becomes necessary for us to keep track of their *individualized identities* as they in the course of their advancement work out their respective roles and destinies, but of course, only within the larger context of the destiny of the Pilgrimage as a whole.

The four distributaries of the Pilgrimage appear below along with their individualized destinies:

(i) The first distributary concerns itself with *the nature of the civilizational debility and darkness in which Hindu society has been engulfed in the last millennium and the way out of this darkness through the miracle of the Hindu medicine.* Its waters can be seen to be steadily flowing in the Preface as well as in Chapters I and II. The potent *Hindu medicine,* which seeks to alleviate the still widely prevalent spiritual malaise in Hindu souls even in our own day, is readily available *in the form of grace for seeing* for all spiritually hungry souls who are prepared to turn inwards.

(ii) *The second distributary's essence is the satsaṅg with the beloved Spiritual Masters and the Jyotiṣācāryas, which actually constitutes the life blood or the vitalizing inspiration for the entire Pilgrimage.* It is seen flowing in the Preface as well as in all four chapters. The potent *Hindu medicine,* which is one of the powerful blessings that become available to all who undertake this Pilgrimage, is available in liberal quantities all along this second distributary as guidance from the beloved Masters in the form of their rare utterances and admonitions.

(iii) The third distributary deals with *Hindu astrology in the spiritual spheres of Dharma and Mokṣa, with an emphasis on the underlying philosophical foundations.* It can be seen coursing all through Chapters II, III, and IV. The waters of this distributary acquire a dynamic living quality by intermingling with the living waters of the adjacent fourth distributary, namely, the life and *Mokṣa* of *Śrī Ramaṇa Maharṣi.* The potent *Hindu medicine* is equally available everywhere in these blended waters of the third distributary – but especially more easily for astrologers, who happen to be placed in a more advantageous position than the other readers – in the form of calming astrological insights into *Dharma* and *Mokṣa* as well as blessings from the beloved Masters.

(iv) *The life and Mokṣa of one of the greatest Avatārs of Aruṇācala Śiva, Śrī Ramaṇa Maharṣi,* constitutes the fourth distributary, whose clear and luminous waters are visible all along Chapters I, II, III, and IV. These waters are inextricably mingled with those of the third, as this is in the very nature of this Pilgrimage. The potent *Hindu medicine* is available in its pristine form through the life and *upadeśa* of *Śrī Ramaṇa Maharṣi* in particular as well as through several astrological insights into spiritual life in general. *In addition, in this last distributary readers also secure parting blessings from all the Spiritual Masters and Aruṇācala Śiva as well.*

The Role of Western Seekers of the Hindu Medicine

If at all I have inadvertently given the impression that the present Hindu medicine is a formula that has been put together only for the express purpose of healing the spiritual debility in Hindu consciousness, I must hasten to add that this was never my original intention. For, though this is indeed a medicine from the Hindu stock, it nevertheless has the same time-tested quality of *universality* that every one of its predecessors has had in times past. Thus, it now comes happily within the reach of all earnest non-Hindu seekers as well. Especially those, who have been in search of such a healing balm of Hindu dispensation for giving them that lasting relief from the one and only spiritual fever from which, not one among us can claim to have been exempt. *Namely, from the pain of duality and separation, which is an unfortunate nemesis of our individual and separative existence — when the same is carried to its farthest limits of self-centredness.*

If in a spirit of magnanimity, we turn a blind eye for the time being, to the unspeakable horrors of political subjugation, economic exploitation, and religious proselytization, perpetrated on the rest of the world by the western civilization, ostensibly in the name of their 'civilizing mission and progress', without that rankling sense of hurt; we will find to our great relief that there has also been, in the midst of this adversity of the 'cultural invasion' by the West, a redeeming compensation. Since the landfall of *Vasco da Gama* in 1498 CE, numberless missionaries, explorers, merchants, scholars and spiritual seekers, have all been coming to India, in search of this Hindu medicine (in one form or the other), at least out of a compelling intellectual curiosity if not as a sure means for achieving their spiritual salvation.

It is reasonable to suppose that every one of these earnest seekers (predominantly from the West, but also in lesser measure from the other world civilizations: Arabic, Chinese, Japanese, Eurasian, etc.) whose forlorn souls must have been enraptured and made beatific by the spiritual blessings of this ancient civilization, has conscientiously and devotedly rendered selfless service to *Sanātana Dharma*. They have done this by firstly securing that lasting relief through that Hindu medicine and what is more, walking many steps further down the same road, they have also served as Divine messengers, who brought either the news of this medicine, or in very many cases, the medicine itself directly to the doorsteps of vast numbers of kindred fellow-seekers, in the spirit of Hindu *karmayogis* and *jñānayogis*.

As the steady stream of these seekers from the West and other distant lands is still continuing in our own day, without showing the slightest signs of their spiritual appetites dwindling, my conscience impels me to take cognizance of their noteworthy contributions and thus reckon them also as my kindred fellow pilgrims. Indeed, I have known through direct first-hand experience on many a memorable occasion that their passionate single-minded dedication and intellectual acumen in this field, has often been commensurate with that of their Hindu counterparts, who have been devotedly labouring in the very same fields, but from the more comfortable positions of their own cultural home grounds.

If one were to take a dispassionate view of things, one must even go so far as to say that in a number of noteworthy cases, the seminal contributions of these western and non-Hindu savants and seekers have even surpassed the creative works of indigenous Hindus, springing from the cultural matrix of their own homeland — to such an extent that these rising new waves of a Hindu or *Vedic* awakening, have often resulted in entirely new spurts of growth in *Sanātana Dharma,* but now coming to flower from the 'still-fertile' soil of the western civilization.

Whenever and wherever this cross-cultural seeding has happily come to pass, we must see in this phenomenon of the 'reversal of roles', a happy marriage between intrinsically two widely-different civilizations, creating in the process of this intermingling, an opportunity to discover the unity of all mankind, through the transcending of the divisive categories of 'East and West', to which our minds have grown so accustomed.

This 'reversal of roles' has implied a greater 'Hindu or *Vedic* calling' and correspondingly a greater measure of Divine grace, for 'Hindu homecoming', as well as for the *prasāda* of Hindu *Mokṣa,* paradoxically, falling to the lot of western seekers, rather than to their Hindu counterparts. In much the same way, the more gifted among the Hindus, in the wake of that tragic loss of their religious and cultural moorings, have also reciprocally turned to the West, in admiration of its material and intellectual achievements and have already come upon greener material and intellectual pastures for the fulfilment of their appetites and are still in that process of securing for themselves a material and intellectual salvation in the spheres of *Artha* and *Kāma.*

Fellow Pilgrims and the Fruits of the Pilgrimage

I have taken homecoming Hindus, astrologers, and spiritual seekers travelling on diverse paths, as my fellow pilgrims. In telling them how in the course of my own pilgrimage this touching story of *Aruṇācala Śiva* found its way into my heart, I am not only securing for myself that much needed contentment that comes from *being faithful to the actual yearnings in one's heart,* but more importantly, I also have the opportunity to bring together all the necessary articles of faith on the basis of which my fellow pilgrims might feel impelled to embark on this Pilgrimage without any contrary perceptions to hold them back. In this way, I hope the waves of grace from *Aruṇācala Śiva* as well as from my four beloved Masters are received in the form of that Hindu medicine for the alleviation of our collective Hindu spiritual malady.

If we begin with the conviction that in reading and taking this story greedily into our hearts, we shall be opening ourselves up to the blessings of *Aruṇācala Śiva,* we shall certainly not be mistaken at all. For indeed, this is truly an awe-inspiring story of His grace and life on planet earth.

It seems to be only fair to make it known that the Pilgrimage is likely to be of far greater value to two special categories of readers. For *astrologers* who have already felt the first inner stirrings of the need to catch a first-hand glimpse of the unfamiliar spiritual shores of *Dharma* and *Mokṣa* as well as for *spiritual seekers* who, standing upon the terrain of *Dharma* or *Mokṣa,* have had the first surges of a calling to travel to the yonder shore of Hindu astrology, the 'vessel' of this Pilgrimage will undoubtedly provide a safe and reliable passage either way. *In this sense, this is certainly a work that will have a special attraction for astrologers and spiritual beings alike, especially when they have persistently been on the lookout for a comprehensive world view that bridges the chasm between their unintelligible spiritual life on the one hand, and a Hindu astrological understanding and insight into the same, on the other.*

In the spheres of *Dharma* and *Mokṣa,* if modern Hindus, astrologers, and spiritual seekers find the Pilgrimage delivering that efficacious Hindu medicine for creating a happy Hindu homecoming, nothing more can be asked for! But if, in addition, the Pilgrimage also succeeds in kindling our yearning for *Mokṣa* and our devotion, not only towards *Aruṇācala Śiva* but also towards my four beloved Masters, then I shall certainly feel honoured beyond my wildest expectations. In this event, I shall naturally be profoundly grateful to my perceptive readers for having been magnanimous enough in reposing their trust in an author who, for them, has been nothing more than a perfect stranger.

Śaṅkara Bhagavadpāda
1 May 2008
Chennai

ACKNOWLEDGEMENTS

In traditional Hindu society, it is inculcated in childhood that one's parents are the closest and the most beloved of all of God's manifestations. This spiritual perception in fact constitutes the bedrock of Hindu society and the Hindu ethos. Even before one pours out a salutation of love to one's beloved Masters and to God, one offers the very same salutation to one's beloved parents.

The non-verbal teachings of my late beloved father, *Śrī* Anantha Ramachandran and my late beloved mother, *Śrīmatī* Kanaka Durga Ramachandran, shall forever remain as the foundational blessings of my whole life. From father I learnt honesty, frankness, fearlessness, kindness towards the working class, and the virtue of being able to stand up for what one felt to be the truth. It has been my extreme good fortune – through the blessings of my beloved Master *Śrī Śrī Bhagavān* – that in my life, I never had to contend with those human failings and sufferings which I repeatedly witnessed in the life of my beloved father. The value of such profound lessons of destiny is often lost upon us. From mother I imbibed character, compassion, and inculcation of the spiritual life. She not only bequeathed the spiritual legacy of her Master's grace in her life to me but also showed me my Master *Śrī Śrī Bhagavān* when I was still only a school boy. If today, I worship my parents on a daily basis as beloved manifestations of God, I do this only out of devotional adoration in an attempt to discharge my colossal debt of gratitude.

Profound gratitude, in the same spirit is also due to the beloved, late Dr. N. Sivakamu, who had been a very concerned and benevolent patron of my Master's and my educational-spiritual work, which had its humble beginnings in 1984 in a very remote corner of Chittoor District in Andhra Pradesh.

This is a good place also to record my sincere gratitude to Professor R. Ramakrishna Iyer, a learned *Sanskrit* Pandit from whom I had the good fortune of learning the rudiments of this ancient language between 1994 and 1997.

Thanks to the magnanimity of Prof. V. K. Choudhry, the founder of the Systems Approach to *Vedic* astrology, there have emerged two internet fraternities (SATVA and SAMVA) of dedicated SA astrologers whose main concern has been the learning and sharing of their astrological knowledge within the framework of the Systems Approach and under the guidance of the founder. It has been a real blessing to belong to these fraternities and learn, practically on a day-to-day basis, from the many ongoing dialogues between these astrologers and Prof. V. K. Choudhry. Needless to say, one is at a loss to satisfactorily discharge one's debt of gratitude to the *Jyotiṣācārya* Prof. Choudhry as well as to these fraternities of SA astrologers.

I do not want to play that dangerous game of self-deception by pretending to be detached from my family – something that can become a veritable pitfall for spiritual people – but shall record here my whole-hearted appreciation of the constant encouragement and co-operation extended to me by my small loving family: my wife Dr. Prema and daughter *Śrī* Gayatri. They have, on many an occasion, had to forego even the simple pleasure of holding an impromptu conversation with me, just because I couldn't so much as raise my head from these engulfing astrological waters! For critical comments, useful suggestions, for being exceedingly swift in identifying typographical errors and omissions, and for being ever-willing to read several times over, sometimes at three- or four-day intervals, various sections that had to be modified, Dr. Prema deserves my heartfelt appreciation.

Where continued dedicated service has been concerned, my whole-souled appreciation goes to *Śrī* Kannanji, who has provided me with dependable, spiritual-secretarial support, and excellent co-operation in patiently typing, reading, and checking several drafts of this work, as well as in the efficient preparation of the *Sanskrit* [*Saṁskṛta*] glossary. He has managed most affairs of my office in the course of the last nine years, including maintaining my accounts, archives, and files. He thereby made it possible for me to take my mind off these burdens and devote my energies entirely to my astrological study and research. I honestly think it has been my Master's grace that I have had *Śrī* Kannanji to stand by me these last nine years when I was working practically only from the seclusion of my home.

I wish to record my gratitude also to other loving family members: my sister *Śrīmatī* Geetha Balakrishna and her husband *Śrī* Madduri Balakrishna for their generous hospitality and support at various times in the course of my life. I thank GB and two of her perceptive friends for having made some useful suggestions that helped to rephrase and clarify some paragraphs of the book. I am happy to record my heartfelt gratitude to my loving niece *Śrīmatī* Nandini Balakrishna for her dedicated, painstaking, and meticulous editorial work during the last eighteen months. She was the first of the highly skilled and self-effacing God-sent *devatās,* who came in as an important teammate for this project and executed the editorial work to perfection, down to the smallest details. *Śrī* Anand Balakrishna Madduri, my sensitive nephew and *Śrī* S. M. Kumar sent me important books from overseas, as the same were not available in the Indian book market. They both deserve my sincere thanks for having willingly obliged me every time I placed a request before them.

I am also grateful to a compassionate enlightened Master in Mumbai, *Śrī* Ramesh Balsekar, who unhesitatingly granted me a personal interview in October 2004 and was kind enough to give me his birth details when I declared to him that I was engaged in astrological research into enlightenment. To *Śrīmatī* Santosh Sachdeva of Mumbai, an author and Spiritual Teacher, I am equally beholden for making her birth details available to me, and above all, for her wonderful kindness in sharing some spiritual life events with my wife and myself. Her recent works on *Kuṇḍalinī* Awakening provided me with ample data for my research in the spheres of *Dharma* and *Mokṣa*. In no smaller measure am I grateful to Dr. Jimmy Modi, a psychiatrist and a 'Master of crystalline energies' in Mumbai, who also put his birth details and a fund of very unusual spiritual and psychic information at my disposal. *I take up the study of the lives of many of these spiritual beings from the astrological point of view in my larger work, which is currently under preparation.*

It has been a rewarding experience to work closely with *Śrī* Gautam Sachdeva, who struck me as an unusually perceptive publisher with a balanced and modern spiritual orientation. I am happy to record my heartfelt gratitude to him for a number of valuable suggestions he made for enhancing the readability of this work, for all the consideration shown to me from time to time, and for giving me the much needed exposure to the harsh realities of publishing. When I first approached him to have my book (then still under preparation) published by his concern, he made me aware of market realities by raising the pertinent question, *"for whom was I writing my book?"* at which I was initially taken aback! However, upon reflection, I was able to regain my composure, as I found substantial evidence that even truly great authors, when they were writing their works for the first time under the inspiration from some muse, did not actually know for whom they intended their writing!

I wish to record here my sincere gratitude to *Śrī* M. Raghu, *Sanskrit* lecturer and librarian of the Madras *Sanskrit* College.

He came like a God-sent self-effacing *devatā* at the final stages of this work to skillfully finish the task of incorporating *Saṁskṛta* [*Sanskrit*] diacritical marks throughout the text, as well as to initially format the entire manuscript in the layout required by the publisher. Thanks are also due to the directors of Anugraha Educational and Consultancy Services, Dr. Chandra Venkateswaran and her husband *Śrī* G. P. Venkateswaran, for their broad-minded and spontaneous offer of technical assistance for perfecting and laying out the manuscript. In their DTP designer *Śrī* J. Jayakumar I found another amazing God-sent helping hand.

Dr. Jyoti Nevatia, an old-time family friend, had put into my hands two useful volumes on the life of the *Yogācārya Śrī* B. K. S. Iyengar for the benefit of my astrological study. She also supplied me with the birth details and a brief biographical sketch of another Spiritual Master *Śrī* Anandamurthyji (1921-1990 CE). For this co-operation and for having trustingly accepted my astrological and spiritual guidance, I am thankful to her. Likewise, special gratitude goes to a family friend and architect, *Śrī* Deepa Madhavan, who placed in my hands three volumes of the complete works of another Spiritual Master, *Śrī* Ram Chandra, for the benefit of my astrological research. She also made it known to her wide circle of friends that they could trustingly turn to me for astrological guidance.

I am sincerely grateful to Prof. Vasudev Murthy, an author, Management Consultant, and regular Guest Faculty member at the IIM, Bangalore, for his critical assessment of my book. He, likewise, had no hesitation in giving me his birth details for my study and was selfless enough to go through this entire work within the span of a day and come up with valuable critical suggestions, intending only to enhance the readability of the work.

Finally, I am beholden in a special way to a wide circle of well-wishers and friends, some close family members, and many others who had turned to me in the course of the last seven years for astrological guidance in the face of some daunting life crisis. I consider it my good fortune to have been of some use to people, especially when I had gone into *antarmukha* [withdrawal into seclusion for the purpose of spiritual study], so as to respond fully to my astrological calling at that time. Because of their disarming candour and their trusting nature, they were able to air their life problems and dilemmas, which was instrumental in drawing out the right astrological solutions from me. These conversations and consultations were symbiotic and mutually beneficial. As far as I was concerned, it opened up for me an excellent opportunity to gather together and understand a richer variety of astrological patterns – as illustrative examples of the SA and the VA *sūtras* – and in this way, keep my fires of learning kindled. As far as those who sought my guidance were concerned, they too found their satisfaction in having their dilemmas pacified and in securing reliable solutions for their problems through the powerful remedial measures of Hindu astrology.

For me, there was, however, a tinge of sadness at the end of these exchanges, which came from the recognition that Hindus, by and large, were not generally interested in learning more about themselves or in using Hindu astrology as a powerful tool of self-knowing. They were quite satisfied to have their daunting problems resolved through remedial measures, but did not have deeper questions pertaining to the enigmas and paradoxes of human life, also questions to which Hindu astrology offers excellent answers and insights. It is my fond hope, however, that in the near future at least, discerning seekers will aspire to reach for these esoteric spiritual fruits of Hindu astrology as well.

CONTENTS

CHAPTER I

Saṁskāras,†
Beloved Masters, and Jyotiṣācāryas

1. Sources of Blessings – Four Beloved Masters

> *One does not become a disciple by conversion, or by accident. There is usually an ancient link, maintained through many lives and flowering as love and trust, without which, there is no discipleship....You do not become a disciple by choice, it is more a matter of destiny than self-will.* (qtd. in *I Am That* 460)

Frankly speaking, I've found it well-nigh impossible to present my astrological Pilgrimage to *Mokṣa* without touching upon, at least in brief outline, *how I received the blessings for an intense devotional yearning for Mokṣa* on account of my deep involvement with my four beloved Spiritual Masters: *Śrī Śrī Bhagavān* in the first instance, and *Śrī J. Krishnamurti* in the second. *Śrī Śrī Bhagavān* belongs to

†*Saṁskāras* are latent-impressions that are etched strongly in the feeling nature and in the subconsciousness and which manifest in life as *uncontrollable urges and inclinations.* The origin of such impressions invariably goes back to some traumatic or pleasant childhood incident in this life or even to some hidden past-life impressions.

the present generation, while *Śrī J. Krishnamurti* belonged to the previous one.

The Beloved Master Śrī Śrī Bhagavān

Two other selfless Masters also captivated my heart in commensurate measure and both belonged to the previous generation. However, they were consummate *advaitic* Masters: *Śrī Ramaṇa Maharṣi* from Tiruvannamalai in Tamil Nadu, South India; and *Śrī Nisargadatta Maharaj* from Mumbai. Thus, four was certainly the number of Masters that I can count and identify. This is easy, because they came into my life one after the other, each coming being different from the other, and they seem to be fulfilling a certain complex *karmic* pattern.

The deeper significance behind the coming of so many Spiritual Masters need not hold our attention at this stage; we may recognize that by their successive coming, many narrow and insular domestic walls in my philosophical and religious outlook have had to be pulled down. This took me, not dramatically and abruptly but gradually, in stages, *into wider areas of the spiritual life, thereby making it increasingly difficult for me to hold on to zealously guarded philosophical views, which were every now and then being created and held by a narrowly circumscribed 'me and the mine'.*

2. Devotional Yearning – Blessing or Impediment?

This is an appropriate juncture to touch upon the paradoxical nature of my devotional yearning for *Mokṣa.* While giving me the conviction that this has been an indisputable blessing, strangely, it also seems to have become an important impediment, contributing to the very denial of *Mokṣa.* This is not a spiritual dilemma that is unique to me in any way, for all seekers who knowingly or unknowingly are thrown on the path of self-unfoldment and self-fulfilment by the force of their destiny are bound to succumb to this paradoxical dilemma: *while one appears to be rising and approaching the spiritual goal of Mokṣa, alas, one may only be slipping and falling away from that very 'destination' — for want of a better word.*

In fact all my four beloved Masters have been unanimous in their admonition that as *Mokṣa* is not certainly 'a thing attainable' by a seeking self, on account of the self itself being an illusion; it must only be approached indirectly, through the denial and negation of the self rather than through its pampering and subtle aggrandizement, especially in the spiritual spheres of *Dharma* and *Mokṣa.* This pampering and perpetuation of the self is what we know only too well in the spheres of *Artha* and *Kāma,* having become helplessly habituated and addicted to these pleasing processes. By the force of habit, when the self moves into the sphere of *Mokṣa,* it commits that self-same fatal mistake of looking for that aggrandizement, which has been its second nature in the mundane spheres of *Artha* and *Kāma.* This is the one and only dilemma in which all seekers, including the author, are helplessly trapped! It is only our Masters' grace that liberates us from this universal quandary.

3. The Master Śrī Śrī Bhagavān

Returning to the Masters, the coming of my first beloved Master, *Śrī Śrī Bhagavān*, was certainly 'God-given' and a continuation of spiritual association [*saṁskāra*] from past lives, as it all happened rather early in life – during my boyhood when I was still in high school. *This was the only Master with whom I was destined to have a profoundly philosophical and also a very dearly personal relationship.* I did not, of course, come upon my Master on account of my own discerning intelligence; rather, it was beloved mother who discovered his strong spiritual soul at first sight even though he was just about in high school at the time. *Without the least bit of exaggeration, I may say that his coming into my life was like powerful sunbeams instantaneously flooding a dingy house, the moment the windows are thrown open to the world on a chilly wintry morning.*

Each of my inimitable Masters had a very definitive teaching, and underlying that teaching, naturally, a concomitant approach to *Mokṣa* or freedom as well as to the spiritual life. And they certainly pointed to *Īśvara* [God] or *Parabrahma* [Godhead] in unique ways; this served to set apart the teachings of each Master from the others.

The beloved Master Śrī Śrī Bhagavān was, in a strange way, directly responsible for my wandering beyond the precincts of his own philosophical domains, so that my coming face to face with the complementary teachings of my three other Masters became inevitable. For many years, I was under the rather naive impression that four Masters indeed had to remain only four, and an inner compulsion did not even arise in me to search for a grand unification by somehow attempting to string together the four into the unitary wholeness of the one. We humans seem to be programmed by the supreme intelligence of *Īśvara* to always search for the one essence, in a world of bewildering plurality, diversity, and contradiction.

Through his compassion, my philosopher-friend and Spiritual Master *Śrī Śrī Bhagavān* had decades ago initiated me, firstly, into the soul-stirring depths of Hindu philosophy; secondly, into the *God-centred spiritual ethos of the Hindu civilization*; and most importantly and finally, into the waters of self-knowing.

This last terrain was uncharted and very much more difficult than the other two, for it called for *the introversion of consciousness* — a spiritual and *yogic* skill to which I was a perfect stranger at that time. I found this to be slippery ground, and 'seeing', which was the only *sādhana* [spiritual practice] my Master wanted me to do at that time, could never really come to pass until there was the *negation* of all the goals of 'the me and the mine', including the goal of 'seeing' itself. One particularly powerful *sūtra* of *Śrī Śrī Bhagavān,* sent to me in one of his letters, helped me secure the breakthrough insofar as *seeing* was concerned:

To postpone is just another trick of the mind for its continued security;
To postpone is the height of hypocrisy;
To postpone is to be denied of freedom forever.

In these words, *Śrī Śrī Bhagavān* was pointing to our human tendency to postpone *seeing,* that is, looking inwardly at ourselves in the sense meant by my Master *Śrī J. Krishnamurti.* The Chinese philosopher Confucius had said somewhere that he had not come across a single individual in his life who was inward looking and therefore constantly learning! As human beings, we all have the weakness of being unable to look at our own ugliness and at the poverty in our hearts. *Śrī Śrī Bhagavān,* pained by this human condition, was giving an admonition and a wake-up call to me through that *sūtra.*

4. The Master Śrī J. Krishnamurti

As to what *seeing* is all about, the uncompromising *advaitic* Master *Śrī J. Krishnamurti,* who gave it utmost importance, conveys its real significance in the following terms:

> *Acceptance or denial does not alter a fact, nor will reason bring about a necessary impact. What does is seeing the fact. There's no seeing if there is condemnation or justification or identification with the fact. Seeing is only possible when the brain is not actively participating, but observing, abstaining from classification, judgement and evaluation.* (Sri J. Krishnamurti, *Notebook* 74)

The Philosopher-Master Śrī J. Krishnamurti

Finally, when the surrender to *what is* became a palpable reality for me through *negation,* in the sense meant by *Śrī J. Krishnamurti,* I found myself in a new state of equanimity and tranquility in which there was neither excitement at the prospect of success nor any despondency in the face of failure. Though I now realize that surrender to *what is* is rather different from surrender to God, yet, in this unruffled state — as my contentment came from within me rather than from the external world as a result of certain conditions being fulfilled – a certain imperturbability set in and outer circumstances, howsoever unfavourable, could no more take away my contentment. I had also become, in this process, a perfect stranger to boredom. But there have been a few rare occasions when I had lost my contentment momentarily, under extreme duress.

The Master *Śrī J. Krishnamurti* had given the world a *sūtra,* that had become a living personal truth for me:

> *When the heart enters into the mind, the mind has quite a different quality.* (Sri J. Krishnamurti, *Meditations* 8)

Such was the world of *watching what is* into which my Master, the mystic-philosopher *Śrī J. Krishnamurti,* urges us to enter. Unlike my more realistic Master *Śrī Śrī Bhagavān, Śrī J. Krishnamurti* would not tolerate anybody seeking to 'follow him'. Though I have been fully aware of this philosophical tenet of his, I also know that he would not object to someone taking his teachings to be the mirror in which one can well see the clear reflection of one's own ugly self. In fact, for me, it has been only in this latter sense that I have taken *Śrī J. Krishnamurti* to be one of my beloved Masters. *Thus, my subjective sensibility to my Masters is such that they are all very much my Masters, alive in my consciousness and my awareness, and this is all that matters to me! In fact, as we go along, we shall see that we are able to adduce nothing short of a monumental support for this highly subjective stand of ours.*

There is always that gratitude to Master *Śrī Śrī Bhagavān* for having implanted these three *spiritual saṁskāras* [spiritual influences or etched impressions] in my consciousness nearly four decades ago. In case you are wondering what I have been doing during the vast intervening stretch of time after the first initiation had been given to me by my Master, I might tell you that my householder's and *karmayogi's* life has been running all along, in 'slow motion', as it were. While insofar as material success and 'getting ahead' in life is concerned, this may be deemed a handicap of the worst kind, from the point of view of the spiritual life, it might not be such a bad thing at all! For after all, isn't this life in 'slow motion' – which is so much more closer to time coming to an absolute standstill – much better than frenzied, high-speed living where the spiritual life is concerned?

The teachings of my first two Masters, though entirely different in their world views and approaches to the spiritual life and *Mokṣa,* had nonetheless made an indelible impression on my heart rather early in life. *The first Master, Śrī Śrī Bhagavān, made a lasting impression through his wisdom, profound understanding of life, his innate sensitivity, and his versatile intelligence. With the Master Śrī J. Krishnamurti, the heart, senses, and intelligence all came into a beautiful new life, triggered by relentless self-observation. Surrender to 'what is' resulted in a palpable calmness, even though this rarely, if ever, turned into the ebullience of uncontainable joy. I could never meet the advaitic Masters Śrī Nisargadatta Maharaj and Śrī Ramaṇa Maharṣi while they were still embodied, but this has been compensated for more than adequately, in my opinion, through my having been able to drink the nectar of their teachings to my fullest satisfaction.*

Though beloved mother had throughout the course of her life been devoted to the Master *Śrī J. Krishnamurti* and passed this on to me as a family *saṁskāra,* it was the beloved Master *Śrī Śrī Bhagavān* who had, through his rather stern initiation at a particular stage in my life, made it possible for me to drink the nectar of the teachings of this second Master through a sheer compelling necessity! When *Śrī Śrī Bhagavān* had asked me to apply the teachings of *Śrī J. Krishnamurti* to my daily life, he was still young and had neither commenced his spiritual mission nor had emerged as a Spiritual Master, though at some deeper level, he was certainly dispassionately aware of his mission alright.

5. The Master Śrī Nisargadatta Maharaj

After the commencement of the spiritual mission of my Master *Śrī Śrī Bhagavān* from my then *dvaitin's* position, I was, for the first time, able to swing around and make a transition to a provisional *advaitic* vision of life, into which *darśana* [philosophical world view] I could also imaginatively enter through my feeling nature. *Very significantly, however, I could make this transition without ever having to suffer the least disaffection for my erstwhile dvaitin's position.* I use the term *dvaitin* to signify a devotee of God who is so 'frozen' and entrenched in the duality between self and Deity that it becomes well-nigh impossible for him to even intellectually conceive of the *advaitic* truth that the *Ātmā,* or the deepest aspect of his spiritual being, is the 'illuminator' of the universe. Devotion to the Masters, which was highly personal to begin with, underwent a radical change, and a strong element of impersonal devotion to the formless Self animating all Masters became the dominant factor but without posing any threat to personal devotion, its precursor.

At this juncture, in view of my strong inclination to build bridges and swing from one *darśana* to another, it may not be out of place to remember the magnanimity of Spiritual Masters in the Hindu tradition. The freedom granted to a disciple by a Master, insofar as the former's enquiry is concerned, is seen here in the verdict of the beloved Master *Śrī Nisargadatta Maharaj.*

> *The disciple is given full freedom of thought and enquiry and encouraged to question to his heart's content. He must be absolutely certain of the standing and the competence of his Guru, otherwise, his faith will not be absolute, nor his action complete.* (qtd. in *I Am That* 461)

When my spiritual pilgrimage had commenced through my coming into *satsaṅg* with the Master *Srī Srī Bhagavān,* and thereafter, through my coming intimately into contact with the teachings of that heterodox Master *Śrī J. Krishnamurti,* I came upon a *personal devotional approach* to these Masters that was brimming over with an overwhelming feeling of gratitude and adoration. At that time, I had, in my thought and feeling, as any other disciple would do, ascribed an 'identity' to these two Masters which was, to begin with, their respective auspicious physical forms but with which I also associated their respective *upadeśas* and teachings. Such a devotional anchorage indeed stood the test of time, and for a number of years, turned out to be sufficient for providing a constant feeling of contentment and inner gratitude.

The Advaitic Master Śrī Nisargadatta Maharaj

However, with my subsequent coming into the *satsaṅg* of that uncompromising *advaitic* Master *Śrī Nisargadatta Maharaj* many years later, my personal devotional approach to my Masters underwent a radical change with a *strong impersonal element* colouring the devotional approach to my Masters.

All four Masters now had a new identity in my thought and feeling, which superceded their erstwhile identities as 'auspicious physical forms' only. If these auspicious physical forms still continued to move me, it was now not so much due to the devotion they kindled in me nor even due to the impact of the supremely intelligent and loving human personalities of the Masters on me.

Rather, I now saw the Masters as that self-same Self that is equally present in the noble and the Divine as in the lowly and the wretched of the earth – why even in all inanimate objects, inclusive of ethereal space. This radical shift in my devotional anchorage from beloved human Masters with human personalities to the Self left me, in one sense, dead to all the 'excitement' in the spiritual world, and in another sense, bestowed upon me a more robust understanding accompanied by an unperturbed state but, alas, with no corresponding diminishing of my devotional ardour, which was now directed to the Self as the spiritual essence of these Masters rather than to the human Masters *per se*.

I saw the Masters now only as chosen manifestations of the Self and my contentment continued even when physical and emotional proximity to the Masters wasn't possible. If one were to go by the literal meaning of our language, it would appear that one is helplessly trapped in the cage of a human personality, subject to the illusion of duality – the division between the you and the me. However, if we are not deceived by the apparent duality that is inbuilt into our language, then it is simple enough to know that the existence of an infinite number of physical living forms does not necessarily imply the existence of an infinite number of separate selves.

In the light of this insight that all our languages sustain and strengthen our natural delusion of duality, each Master's auspicious physical form now began to appear as an equally lustrous manifestation of that eternal Self, the same Self that clothes itself in countless other physical forms as it continues its infinite and incomprehensible Divine gambolling [*līlā*]. The physical forms of the Masters now begin to radiate a new auspiciousness, which has an impersonal quality, since the Self in its infinite intelligence has chosen these special physical forms to reveal to humanity this ineffable secret and mystery about Itself.

6. Śrīmūrti Upāsana

The history of religions and religious movements has many noteworthy examples of seekers, who in some rushing and tearing hurry, abandon one *darśana* [philosophical world view] for another for the ostensible reason that the second *darśana* is 'more enlightening and soul satisfying'. In my case, I was spared the philosophically and morally agonizing dilemma of having to choose one *darśana* and reject the other. I was able to see each *darśana* as having an intrinsic merit and legitimacy of its own, as it was created by illumined Hindu Sages and Saints for certain types of seekers in accordance with the priceless Hindu insight of *adhikāri-bedha-nyāya*. According to this Hindu principle [*nyāya*], the spiritual path for each initiated aspirant [*adhikāri*] must necessarily be unique and customized in recognition of each seeker's intellectual, emotional, and spiritual capacities.

Thus, though the three Masters who came into my life after *Śrī Śrī Bhagavān's* initiation were all *advaitic* Masters, who did not at any stage recommend *Śrīmūrti upāsana* [worshipping a formful aspect of God in the form of a picture of an *Avatār*, Master, or other Deity], *even as a possible provisional means to the advaitic Realization*, my devotion to my *advaitic* Masters was such that it never ever came in the way of my continuing *Śrīmūrti upāsana*! This is not so much because I have been so dim-witted as not to have had any insight into *advaita*, but only because for me, blessings came both through *Bhaktiyoga* [devotional approach to God and Masters] as well as through *Jñānayoga* [grasping the nature of Godhead and God through insight and understanding].

Thus, without adhering exclusively to any one-sided fanatical position — a pitfall to which seekers in the spiritual life are invariably prone — and without any contradictory swings in perception born of doubt and confusion, I was able to maintain my equipoise on the high road of the golden mean. I accepted the duality between devotee and Deity embodied in *Śrīmūrti upāsana* as the most natural and legitimate prelude to the fullness of the *advaitic Realization* that lay beyond.

The immense quantum leap to Mokṣa over the chasm of duality that Śrī Ramaṇa Maharṣi, Śrī Nisargadatta Maharaj, and Śrī J. Krishnamurti held to be within the reach of man has been for me, a still unfulfilled yearning. In this sense, I have certainly not been blessed like the noteworthy disciples of *Śrī Ramaṇa Maharṣi*: *Śrī Annamalai Swami*, *Śrī Papaji*, and *Śrī Muruganar*, or the many young *Jīvanmuktas* and *Jīvanmukta-bhaktās* of my Master *Śrī Śrī Bhagavān*. Mine has been a pilgrimage that has been advancing ever so slowly and imperceptibly, as a strong and highly malefic Saturn in my Ascendant has had the effect of slowing down my life with the proverbial delays and denials, so well known to Hindu astrologers.

7. The Advaitic Master Śrī Ramaṇa Maharṣi

My whole-hearted acceptance of the *advaitic darśana* came about in a serious way for the first time through my discovery of *Śrī Nisargadatta Maharaj's* teaching, as set forth in his spiritual dialogues *I Am That*. Subsequent to this, I was also drawn seriously to *Śrī Ramaṇa Maharṣi*, his austerity, and his *advaitic* teachings, which completely captivated my heart in the course of my astrological Pilgrimage into his life and *Mokṣa*.

The Advaitic Master Śrī Ramaṇa Maharṣi

The beloved Master *Śrī Śrī Bhagavān* had sent me to *Śrī Ramanasramam* in 1990 and had asked me to reside there for three days. But at that time, I was still lacking the maturity and subtlety to assimilate the *advaitic* teaching of the *Maharṣi* only because — I am ashamed to say — my heart was not vacant enough to be moved by the *Maharṣi* at that stage. I did not, of course, ask my Master why he had asked me to visit *Śrī Ramanasramam.* Now I see that it was a prelude to a genuine spiritual discovery of the true greatness of the *Maharṣi,* which I am venturing to present in this astrological Pilgrimage.

Way back when I was in school, I also remember an excursion to some historic places in Tamil Nadu, including the *āśramam* of *Śrī Ramaṇa Maharṣi* in Tiruvannamalai. *Śrī Śrī Bhagavān,* who had been my philosopher-friend even in those early days and who was also present with me on that particular occasion, did indeed try to draw my attention and convey something significant about the

Maharṣi, but as I must not have been spiritually perceptive at all, it was nothing more than water off a duck's back at that time. I simply lacked the philosophical development at that early stage in my life to absorb my philosopher-friend's wise words about the *Maharṣi.*

On another occasion, probably in 1992, my Master showed me a moving film on the life of *Śrī Ramaṇa Maharṣi.* As I watched silently, I broke down with uncontrollable sobs when I saw the spectacle of the renunciation of the boy *Ramaṇa,* which took the form of *Ramaṇa* throwing off his sacred thread and taking a plunge into a pond. At that time, my Master, who was sitting in a chair beside me while I was seated on the floor next to him, put out his hand on my head so as to soothe this sudden devotional upsurge.

Never did it occur to me during these three preliminary exposures to the Maharṣi's life and Mokṣa that a day would come when I would be so deeply moved that every time I dwelt on the Maharṣi's countenance and his strange life, tears would trickle down in testimony to my devotional adoration of the Maharṣi as one of my beloved Masters. For these and other reasons, I say without the least hesitation that the Master Śrī Śrī Bhagavān has himself been verily the architect behind the coming of the other three Masters into my life as well.

8. Effects of the Hindu Medicine

My inimitable Masters *Śrī Śrī Bhagavān* and *Śrī J. Krishnamurti,* though poles apart in their philosophical outlook, both showed me *the path of learning and understanding* but not so much the path of knowledge, which both held to be only an uncalled-for burden. On account of my having drunk the *Hindu medicine* administered by both Masters to my fullest satisfaction, to the point of inebriation even, the horses of my learning and understanding, now on the gallop, made it nearly impossible for me to be an 'obedient' disciple in the traditional sense.

As the disobedience came from the inebriation rather than from some self-centred egoism, it was an easy task for me to come to terms with the reality of the inebriation in the grip of which I found myself! My other deep consolation and contentment came from the fact that notwithstanding my disobedience, my love for both these Masters did not show the slightest waning in sympathetic adjustment with my disobedience. On the contrary, it enhanced my devotional adoration towards both Masters. *It has been my good fortune to receive, not once, but time and again, almost as a daily blessing, a state of enslavement to my Masters in my heart through an impersonal devotional adoration of all aspects of their lives. But even this blessing has not soothed the ripples of discontent, for the self's prayer for Mokṣa has sadly gone unheeded till now!*

9. The Disciple's Integrity and Subjectivity

As though to assuage my compunction with regard to my disobedience, the pertinent utterances of *Śrī Nisargadatta Maharaj* caught my attention, thereby sanctifying my integrity and upholding my right to untrammelled freedom, which my benevolent Master *Śrī Śrī Bhagavān* had already granted me without a single string attached! The blessings of this freedom given to me by my Master *Śrī Śrī Bhagavān* for being true to myself and for slaking my incessant thirst for learning at cool mountain springs, strangely tallied with the picture of a great Spiritual Master painted by *Śrī Nisargadatta Maharaj* in the following passage:

> *The true teacher, however, will not imprison his disciple in a prescribed set of ideas, feelings, and actions; on the contrary, he will show him patiently the need to be free from all ideas, and set patterns of behaviour to be vigilant and earnest and go with life wherever it takes him, not to enjoy or suffer,* ***but to understand and learn*** (emphasis mine). (qtd. in *I Am That* 478)

To both beloved parents (but more so to mother) and to the four beloved Masters, I am indebted to such an extent that I know not in what manner I may best discharge my debt of gratitude for all the blessings I have received, either through a direct profound association as with Śrī Śrī Bhagavān or through a profound emotional and spiritual involvement with the teachings as in the case of the other three Masters. In this sense, my present astrological and spiritual Pilgrimage to *Mokṣa* may lack 'objectivity' on account of my inability to even temporarily put aside the tethers of devotional bondage to my four Masters. But then, my approach to life has always had a strong subjective orientation in small as well as in big things, and when, some ten years ago, I chanced to find a resonance in *Vidyāraṇya Swāmī's Vedānta Pañcadaśī,* my subjective feelings, which have always guided me, crystallized into an *advaitic insight into the primacy of the Self over all other things in life:*

> *Others are loved for the sake of the Self;*
> *but the Self is loved for none other.*
> *Therefore the love for the Self is the highest.*
> *Hence the Self is of the nature of the highest bliss.* (*sūtra* I. 9)

Thus, while I could thoroughly accept the *advaitic vision* as the final goal of life, *Mokṣa,* with an unquestionable conviction, a 'harmless duality' nevertheless continued to stare me in the face though never ever in an irksome or unpleasant manner. My present astrological Pilgrimage to *Mokṣa* may be considered to be part of my *sādhana* in *Jñānayoga* in order to arrive at a grand unification and a comprehensive unitary understanding, through the powerful methods of Hindu astrology, of the lives, destinies, teachings, and the *Mokṣa* of many Masters, *Avatārs,* and Saints.

10. The Power of Satsaṅg with the Masters

Ādi Śaṅkarācārya has sung in *Bhaja Govindam* how it is association [*satsaṅg*] with Spiritual Masters that is often the means to *Mokṣa* or *Jīvanmukti*:

Satsaṅgatve nissaṅgatvam
nissaṅgatve nirmohatvam |

nirmohatve niścalitatvam
niścalitatve Jīvanmuktiḥ || (*The Hymns of Sankara*, 51)

In the context of my life, I read the following meaning into the noble utterances of *Ādi Śaṅkara*:

Through the means of association with the Masters and/or their teachings, there arises detachment; through this detachment, one secures freedom from delusion; from such cessation of delusion, there arises the unruffled state of being established in the Truth; such an unruffled establishment in the Truth is Jīvanmukti, or Liberation in life.

Briefly, this explains how I too acquired from my four Spiritual Masters, the *ruci* [taste] as well as the *saṁkalpa* and the intense devotional yearning for *Mokṣa*. This might help readers to look back into their own lives so as to recapitulate the *ruci* as well as the *saṁkalpa* for *Mokṣa*, which might have come their way at some time or other, but which might have also suffered an eclipse at a later stage on account of some unexpected greater involvement in the world suddenly coming their way and veiling that intense devotional yearning for *Mokṣa*.

Right from the time my astrological work commenced intensely some nine years ago, my Master *Śrī Śrī Bhagavān* had been magnanimous enough to make available to me some horoscopes of spiritual beings, and last year, he gave me the opportunity to directly converse with some twelve young spiritual seekers from his mission, whose peak enlightenment experiences I could thereby astrologically study. For all the *Mumukṣus*, it was *Śrī Śrī Amma Bhagavān* who was their *Mokṣapradāta* [bestower of *Mokṣa*].

11. Vedācārya Pandit Vamadeva Shastri

On the astrological side, the present work is based on the astrological systems developed by two contemporary *Jyotiṣācāryas* [sanctified teachers of Hindu astrology or its more ancient version of *Vedic* astrology], who have each shaped my astrological thinking and clarity in their respective domains. Firstly, Pandit Vamadeva Shastri, a renowned *Vedācārya,* created a version of *Vedic* astrology (VA) in the spiritual spheres that served to kindle my deep interest in this discipline.

There were, however, many areas in VA that were confusing on account of the conspicuous lack of consensus among various *Vedic* astrologers and the lack of self-consistency as well as reliable predictive accuracy. Contradictions arose when the astrological *sūtras* came into conflict with real life events and situations that they were expected to accurately describe and predict but were unable to (*Systems Approach* 55). Otherwise, the many spiritual insights of Pandit Vamadeva Shastri's VA provided an initial satisfaction for my soul, which had become thirsty for the waters of this astrological knowledge.

12. Professor V. K. Choudhry

As I continued to struggle with the areas of uncertainty in VA, I stumbled upon what I still consider to be nothing short of 'gold' in the astrological terrain: I am referring to the monumental ground-breaking work in the form of the Systems Approach to Hindu astrology (SA) developed by Professor V. K. Choudhry, one of the most creative and original living *Vedic* astrologers of our times. The uneasiness and the well-concealed frustrations that characterized my state prior to coming upon the SA completely vanished, and there was the light of clarity through the use and application of the powerful, completely self-consistent analytical methods of the SA.

However, this newer system of Hindu astrology (SA), in the first instance addressed the problems pertaining to the

The Vedic Astrologer Prof. V. K. Choudhry

material spheres of *Artha* [achievement of professional goals and the acquisition of wealth defined in the most generalized sense] and *Kāma* [marriage, family life, pleasure seeking, enjoyment, desire fulfilment, will, and aspiration], only because in the eyes of the founder, fulfilment in *Artha* and *Kāma* was a necessary prelude to the serious commencement of the spiritual life in the spheres of *Dharma* and *Mokṣa*. It is held in the SA that the first spiritual goal is the attainment of inner peace and contentment, which will then serve as a natural stepping stone for entry into the higher spiritual realms of *Dharma* and *Mokṣa*. We may mention in passing that Prof. Choudhry has repeatedly emphasized the importance of astrologers observing Divine conduct in their lives.

By blending the analytical and predictive tools of the SA with some of the spiritual insights of Pandit Vamadeva Shastri's VA in the spheres of *Dharma* [spiritual learning at a teacher's home in ancient Hindu society, now replaced by modern secular education in schools] and *Mokṣa,* I have endeavoured to study astrology rather comprehensively in the spheres of *Dharma* and *Mokṣa.*

I am, therefore, indebted to both the *Jyotiṣācāryas,* Pandit Vamadeva Shastri and Prof. V. K. Choudhry, though in the case of Pandit Vamadeva Shastri, the inspiration was necessarily indirect, coming from his extensive writings; whereas I had the liberal blessings of my Spiritual Master *Śrī Śrī Bhagavān* for learning and imbibing the SA directly from Prof. V. K. Choudhry, through rapid email dialogues, and I know not how to convey the joy and fulfilment that was mine in the learning of the powerful, yet beautifully simple Systems Approach.

After I completed the full text of the Pilgrimage, I passed the manuscript on to Prof. V. K. Choudhry, seeking the light of his astrological knowledge and wisdom. I have incorporated his valuable insights, some of which, in fact, are probably the fruits of his recent research. My heartfelt gratitude goes to him in this regard – both for his kindness as well as his magnanimity of mind.

CHAPTER II

Hindu Mokṣa

1. Artha and Kāma vis-à-vis Dharma and Mokṣa

Before we venture to learn something about the esoteric notion of *Mokṣa,* it might be good to begin by taking a bird's eye view of all the *Puruṣārthas,* namely, *Dharma, Artha, Kāma,* and *Mokṣa.* These represent the four goals and aspirations of human life in a traditional Hindu society.

Understanding the ramifications of these four goals of human life in ancient Hindu society will give us a definite advantage in that it will awaken us to the importance of having to constantly bear in mind the sphere of life — whether *Dharma, Artha, Kāma,* or *Mokṣa* — in which the individual in question is actually moving at the time his specific astrological question is being taken up for resolution.

We shall see that these four goals and pursuits, taken together, will give us a highly satisfying and all-encompassing picture of human life. In God's beautiful creation, as man is a miraculous synthesis of body, mind, and spirit, it was recognized by ancient Hindus that if society had to have stability as well as ample scope for creativity, then the fulfilment of the appetites of body, mind, and spirit had to be provided for. In meeting these requirements, they took on the challenge of satisfying the appetites of body and mind first, and once this was over and done with, they turned to the subtler challenge of fulfilling the appetites of the spirit.

The former appetites constituted the spheres of life called *Artha* and *Kāma*, whereas the appetites of the spirit were dealt with in the spiritually more advanced spheres of *Dharma* and *Mokṣa*. The ancient Hindus achieved this by blending the 'worldly' aspect of our human nature, which was brought to fulfilment and appeasement in the period of youth and middle age (*Artha* and *Kāma* spheres), with the spiritual aspect of our human nature, which was brought to flower in the afternoon and evening of life (*Dharma* and *Mokṣa* spheres). *For the very reason that they accommodated the worldly as a prelude to the spiritual, ancient Hindu society had built into itself, ab initio, what may appropriately be called 'the completeness and fullness' of human life.*

Put differently, *Artha* and *Kāma* provided for the fulfilment of humanity's physical, emotional, artistic, intellectual, and social appetites. They took into account the important fact that humans were social beings who needed to relate to people, and that the seeking of skill, honour, achievement, vocation, status, wealth, property, and prestige on the one hand [*Artha*]; and spouse, family, pleasure and enjoyment, children, and home life [*Kāma*] on the other, was but an inevitable aspect of being human, and that unless these appetites on the physical, emotional, intellectual, and social planes were fulfilled, there was not much meaning and purpose in the pursuit of a spiritual life in which there was not going to be room for any of these mundane cravings and satisfactions.

The following figure illustrates the progression of goals in a traditional Hindu society. We must start with the upper right quadrant and move in a clockwise direction to follow the progression of these goals. The first quarter of life (the school going years) was devoted to spiritual learning or *Dharma*. This was to be a spiritual foundation for the whole of the adult life to follow but was to bear the highest fruit of *Mokṣa* only in the last quarter of life, which was entirely devoted to the fulfilment of the spiritual life [*Mokṣa*]. Note that the spiritual goal of *Dharma* was the first of the goals of life, whereas the highest spiritual goal of *Mokṣa* was the last of the goals of life.

The Roman numerals in the four quadrants of the following two figures refer to the 'houses' in Hindu astrology to which these spheres correspond.

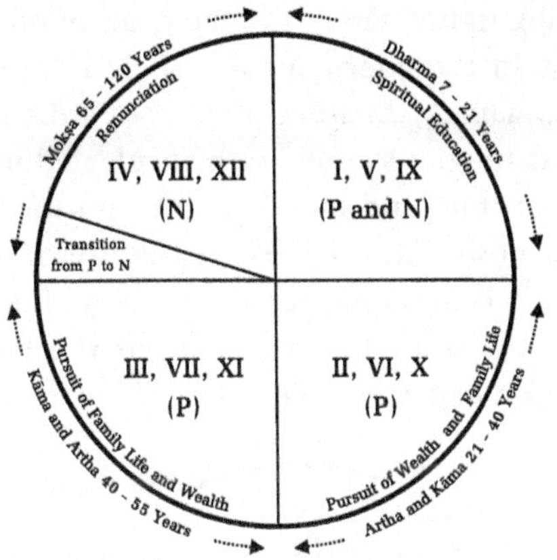

Goals of Life in a Traditional Hindu Society

The second and the third quarters of life were devoted to *Pravṛtti* [involvement] in the worldly spheres of *Artha* and *Kāma*. *Artha* meant the acquisition of wealth and achievements in life, whereas *Kāma* meant the graceful surrender to the temptations of life and the aesthetic enjoyment of the same, which marriage and family life provided for. Significantly, *Dharma* was to be the guiding light even as the individual traversed through these worldly spheres. *Artha* and *Kāma* are necessarily intertwined and constituted the second and third goals of life.

Artha and *Kāma* were intended to bring about a full-blown fulfilment to all desires; at the end of this journey, the individual was spiritually self-composed and mature enough to withdraw from worldly responsibilities and enjoyments through renunciation [*Nivṛtti*]. To facilitate this renunciation and to make the transition to a profound spiritual life of solitude and bliss smooth, ancient Hindus provided for an intermediary third stage of life called *Vanaprastha,* or withdrawal into the seclusion of a forest hermitage. This intermediary stage was intended to make the passage to the profound spiritual goal of *Mokṣa* devoid of any sense of shock on account of withdrawal from the world and its enjoyments.

The following figure pertains to the goals of life in a modern secular society. In a modern secular society by contrast, the first goal of life, namely, *Dharma,* undergoes a dissociation from its spiritual and religious roots with secular education taking its place. The spiritual and moral foundation for the whole of the adult life is now lost; even the possibility of *Mokṣa* in the last stage of life becomes only remote if not an impossibility, as this *Mokṣa* cannot come to pass without the foundation of *Dharma* in the first quarter of life.

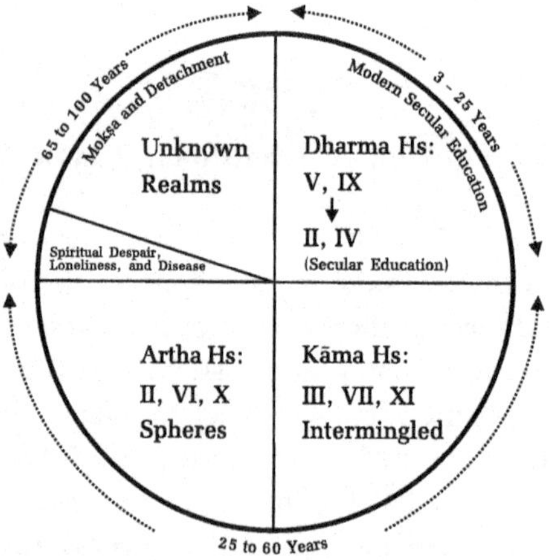

Goals of Life in a Modern Secular Society

The essential interconnectedness of *Artha and Kāma* is as valid in a modern secular society as in a traditional Hindu one. Significantly, on account of the fundamental shift that has occurred in the nature of *Dharma,* the goals of *Artha and Kāma* must now necessarily be pursued without the moral and the spiritual foundation that *Dharma* had provided in a traditional Hindu society.

Worst of all, the aspiration to seek *Mokṣa* does not even manifest, and old age, now bereft of spiritual wisdom and insights, becomes burdened with despondency and despair. Under these conditions, the last goal of life, namely, *Mokṣa,* becomes *terra incognito* for us moderns – unless we seek this through our individual initiative in spite of our modern secular society remaining completely indifferent to our spiritual appetites.

Once we have grasped the meanings of these four goals in the original context of the ancient society, it will then become possible for us to see what the transformed versions of these four goals are in our own contemporary Hindu society, which, at this hour, has unfortunately already succumbed to the pressure of westernizing itself at the expense of losing its Hindu heritage. And this misfortune has struck more forcefully in an important section of the creative minority in Hindu society, namely, the English-educated Hindu intelligentsia.

Narrowing our focus to *Mokṣa* now, we see that throughout human history, whether it was in the very ancient *Vedic* society or in the later civilizations of the world, *Mokṣa* had always remained an esoteric affair as the highest blessing in spiritual life that only a handful of fortunate individuals could receive. For Hindus, *Mokṣa* has always held an irresistible fascination as the fourth and the last goal of human life – the *summum bonum* of life itself. And as moderns who are quite out of touch with the spiritual ethos of our ancients, we might well wonder what the nature of such an esoteric *Mokṣa* could possibly be. We may begin with a panoramic picture of *Mokṣa* in the following *sūtra* of the Master *Śrī Śrī Bhagavān:*

Enlightenment
is Liberation from work,
is Liberation from society,
is Liberation from conditioning,
is Liberation from knowledge,
is Liberation from the mind,
is Liberation from the self,
is Liberation of the the senses,
is Liberation of life.

From this all-encompassing panoramic picture, we may concentrate upon one particular aspect of *Mokṣa,* namely, that centred around the 'self'. Thus, while many different perceptions of *Mokṣa* may be admissible in principle, for our present purposes at least, we may take it to be not only a permanent 'loss' of the very source of all mischief and misery in human life, namely, the *jīvātmā* [the personal self] but also, more importantly, the concomitant 'gain' of a constant awareness and oneness with Godhead. To speak of gain is also wrong, since there is no individual entity left who could be the proud recipient of such a gain after the blessed loss of the personal self has come to pass. This loss of the personal self and the concomitant gain of an awareness and oneness with Godhead is what we will be obliged to concentrate upon even in discussing the life of *Śrī Ramaṇa Maharṣi.*

The British historian Arnold J. Toynbee has articulated clearly the possible impact a single Self-Realized individual can have on the world as a whole:

> *The spiritual level of a society cannot be higher than the average level of the participants; the collective level can be raised only on the initiative of the individuals, and when an individual does rise above the level of his social environment, this is a fruit of a previous victory over himself in his spiritual life.* (*A Study of History* 341)

We may thus recognize it to be the spiritual heritage of humanity that these fortunate individuals have it within their spiritual power to raise the level of the collective consciousness of humanity by their mere presence on the planet. They do not have to 'do something' strenuously as individuals, either physically or mentally, in order to bring to humanity this immense blessing. And even if some of them do set about doing something, much more than their 'doing', it is their mere 'being' or sheer *lokakalyāṇa saṁkalpa* [a determined aspiration for world welfare] that must be recognized to be of far greater beneficence for the spiritual evolution of the species as a whole.

For our part, what is called for is just to be attentive in their presence, if this is possible for us, or at least to tune into their picture in moments of dire helplessness, and if even this is difficult for our temperament, then only to contemplate their teachings. On account of the historical rarity of *Mokṣa,* the question arises as to its exact repercussions for the fortunate individual in question, now that we have an idea of how *Mokṣa* impacts upon society as a whole.

The 'life' of our personal self, or individuality, lies in our 'ownership' of our body and mind, which arises through an imagined association that is the ultimate root of all of our sufferings. *Mokṣa* is the irreversible extinction of this imagined association, and with it, the 'life' of our personal self also comes to an end, thereby ridding us of all our psychological burdens with a finality as though through a decisive master stroke. That this is exactly what happened to the boy *Ramaṇa* is testified to by the *Maharṣi* himself:

> *I have discovered a new thing! This hill, the lodestone of lives, arrests the movements of anyone who so much as thinks of it, draws him face to face with it, and fixes him motionless like itself, to feed upon his soul thus ripened. What (a wonder) is this! Oh souls! Beware of It and live! Such a destroyer of lives is this magnificent Arunachala, which shines within the Heart!* (qtd. in Sri Ramanasramam 100)

In practical terms then, *Mokṣa* is a permanent Liberation from the whole gamut of sufferings that we humans are heir to, sufferings that arise through an imagined association – with the concomitant feeling of the 'me and the mine' – with the body, the mind, and with all sorts of things in the mundane world. Such an imagined association, though considered to be *māyā* [primordial delusion] by the illumined Hindu Sages and Saints, has nevertheless continued to be the most natural thing for us humans, at least, so long as we are still in 'bondage' and fully engrossed in the enthralling 'dream' of our individual and separative existence.

In this state of *māyā* or bondage to the body, mind, or various things of the world, our inner and outer life revolves essentially around a conceptual personal self [*jīvātmā*] that is caught in the conflict of duality between itself and the other. This personal self, while appearing to be the happy enjoyer of a never-ending chain of pleasures in life, is alas, also the unhappy victim of all our never-ending conflicts, hurts, and disappointments as well.

2. The Loss of the Personal Self – A Blessing in Disguise

> *The moment Thou didst welcome me, didst enter into me and grant me Thy divine life,* ***I lost my individuality*** *Oh Arunachala* (emphasis mine)! (Sri Ramana Maharshi, qtd. in Sri Ramanasramam 93)

The *Maharṣi's* use of the word 'loss' here need not unduly perturb us, notwithstanding it bringing to mind the loss of a limb or an eye, the loss of a leg in an accident, or even the loss of a dear one, all of which are evocative of a tragedy or misfortune. For, as it turns out, such unfortunate losses are entirely different from the loss of the personal self. In the latter case, the loss, rather than creating a misfortune is actually an immeasurable blessing in disguise, for it rids us of the enormous psychological burden of having to constantly carry around the personal self that is the very source of all mischief and misery in life.

The mystic philosopher *Śrī J. Krishnamurti,* on account of his having been able to swing in and out of *Mokṣa,* has been able to provide for us some extraordinary insights and glimpses into selfless states of being, which the other Masters have not always been able to furnish for us. Here, then, is one of his typical insights on the importance of losing the self, something almost synonymous with *Mokṣa* or Liberation:

> *Where the self ends, with all its secret and open intrigues, its compulsive urges and demands, its joys and sorrows, there begins a movement of life, that is beyond time and its bondage.*
> (*Notebook* 118)

3. The Intangibility of the Self is the Real Obstacle to Understanding Mokṣa

Were the personal self a tangible 'object', such as a tree, a star, or a man walking on the road, we would have been on much surer ground insofar as our understanding of *Mokṣa* goes. Since we ourselves are this self or the 'subject', talking about the self as though it were an object has the singular disadvantage of having as our object the self, which can never be objectified and can therefore never be an object of study at all – since it can never be anything other than the observing intelligence and the illuminating light. This rules out the possibility of getting to know the self through our conventional sensory perceptions and 'objective' kind of knowing.

The only way to gain some deeper knowledge of this self, which we know only too well to be the creator of untold havoc in every relationship, is through the introversion of the light of our consciousness, which will then enable us to see this self at work as it wreaks every kind of havoc to perpetuate its own imaginary existence. It is the real engine of all our self-centred activity and is ever prone to breakdown and depression! Its capacity to project illusions and goals is never diminished, even with age, and thus, the day never comes in our human lives when the self takes respite from its ceaseless activity of perpetuating itself. Unless we turn the light of our consciousness inward and begin to watch this self at work, there is really no way for us to gain a deeper appreciation of the immense significance of the loss of the personal self, and that this loss is the most fortunate thing that could ever happen to any one of us in the course of our earthly sojourn.

Mokṣa, thus, is awakening to the Realization that this dearly cherished conceptual personal self is, alas, only an illusion, which never really existed! Only the *Jīvanmuktas,* for whom the personal self has ceased through such a Realization, know that our personal self, which is utterly dear to us in spite of its intangibility, is only a temporary cloak or a *veṣa* [mask] on the

Ātmā [the true Self], which is the Source, the Godhead, and the Light of the world.

The above qualitative understanding of *Mokṣa* will, in the course of Chapters III and IV, be translated into quantitative astrological principles [*sūtras*], and the loss of the personal self will be formulated as an astrological *Mokṣayoga* before we venture to have any insights into the *Maharṣi's* Self-Realization.

4. For Whom is this Astrological Pilgrimage Intended?

All the 'rest of us' who are not *Jīvanmuktas* — the tribe to which the author also belongs and whose 'time' has not yet come — must, in the meantime, assimilate the very humbling lesson that there lurks for all of us the grim possibility that our so-called time may never come at all, and it is this which now calls for an urgent and unconditional fresh surrender to *what is* — which at least for the time being has to be taken as the verdict of a fate that is not so fortunate.

Who, then, are the rest of us on whom the fortune of *Mokṣa* has not yet so much as begun to smile? We are the *Brahma-jijñāsus* and the *Mumukṣus,* two distinct kinds of aspirants for *Mokṣa.* The *Brahma-jijñāsus* are, no doubt, genuine seekers, but they are still in the grip of that *māyaic* thirst for this Realization through the process of enquiry and knowing. So long as the grace is inadequate for us, our deluded search must continue in vain, for the search itself can come to an absolute halt only when the Realization dawns that the seeker as the 'I' is also the 'goal'. We could say that *Brahma-jijñāsus* are on the path of understanding and insight, namely, *Jñānayoga.* Our characteristic merit is our profound interest and curiosity, and it is this which lands us on the path of enquiry and understanding.

As *Mumukṣus,* on the other hand, we are those seekers who just have an intense devotional longing for *Mokṣa* without the attendant yearning 'to know', which is the characteristic hallmark of *Brahma-jijñāsus.* You could thus say that as *Mumukṣus,* we are on the path of *Bhakti* or devotion to God.

Thus, in these seemingly forlorn circumstances, as the black cloud of ignorance continues to blind us and hold us in its tight embrace of *māyā,* as *Brahma-jijñāsus* and *Mumukṣus* we may at least, turning to that still-unfulfilled affair in our hearts, seek to take another gnostic and devotional plunge into these astrological waters with a view to possibly pacifying our ever-so-slight vacillations in the face of the present daunting *what is*! In other words, my astrological Pilgrimage is best suited for the kindred souls of my tribe, composed of *Brahma-jijñāsus* and *Mumukṣus.*

Only after the machinery of that imagined association has been permanently dismantled or switched off through a stroke of Divine grace can we hope to know how very apt the words 'imagined association' are. From the point of view of the *Jīvanmuktas,* all thinking, which to civilized people like us is so very dear, is only a dreaming and a journeying in time into the worlds of unreality — utterly unconnected with the Absolute Reality of Godhead.

It is bound to come as a rude shock for us to know that — as all thinking is but the departure of a flight that is ever taking off from the present moment of the Now into the worlds of unreality, either in the past or the future — the door to Absolute Reality cannot possibly be located anywhere else but in the Now, the eternal present. In this sense, the proverbial intangibility of *Mokṣa* arises paradoxically more from its unimaginable nearness to us, why even from an unsuspected absolute identity with us as our very dearest 'I' or Self than from its being far away, beyond the reach of our dim faculties.

5. The Place of this Astrological Pilgrimage

The present Hindu Pilgrimage into the life and *Mokṣa* of *Śrī Ramaṇa Maharṣi* is only an astrological one, for we must remember that this is not the only kind of pilgrimage one can possibly make into the life of this great Sage. Each pilgrimage has its special merits and blessings and may only suit seekers of a particular temperament in accordance with that important *sūtra* of *Sanātana Dharma,* namely, *adhikāri-bhedha-nyāya.* Thus, one can conceive of a mystical pilgrimage to the *Maharṣi's Mokṣa* that would be dear and within the reach of all those for whom mystical journeys occur rather spontaneously.

Alternatively, one can conceive of a philosophical, historical, or even a biographical pilgrimage, depending on one's temperamental disposition. If *Śrī Ramaṇa Maharṣi* were still embodied in our midst, one could also have conceived of a neurological pilgrimage undertaken by neurologists fascinated by the *Maharṣi's* life and teachings.

We may be liberal enough to grant that each such pilgrimage would serve to bring into relief some salient aspects of *Mokṣa,* thereby, possibly increasing our intense devotional longing for the same as well as our correct understanding of what it actually is. For this reason, all such efforts might be quite legitimate and worthwhile and might have the cumulative effect of serving to bring the esoteric nature of *Mokṣa* down from those intangible mystic heights to within the exoteric reach of humanity as a whole.

At any given time in the world, there have always been great Spiritual Masters, Sages, and *Avatārs,* whose main concern has been to awaken a spiritually lukewarm humanity to the enormity of this truth of *Mokṣa.* Our own time also bears sufficient testimony to this timeless pattern. Some readers may wonder whether the present undertaking (this astrological Pilgrimage) is called for at all, when the blessings of *Mokṣa,* have begun to descend rapidly upon so many seekers through the benevolent grace of several illustrious contemporary Masters and *Avatārs.*

As we may well conjecture, the time is approaching for humanity to grasp *Mokṣa* from as many angles as possible, so that at least in our times, our consolidated spiritual heritage of *Mokṣa* is not lost and forgotten, as must have happened repeatedly in the past. It is in this sense that the present introductory work must be viewed as new pertinent astrological light on *Mokṣa* that would be complementary to both the actual blessings of *Mokṣa* as well as to the associated teachings of many Spiritual Masters and *Avatārs.*

Our astrological Pilgrimage, by clarifying a number of nebulous aspects of *Mokṣa,* will hopefully demystify it in this process and, thus, make it more endearing, even to rationalists and sceptics and to people who have not yet set foot into the spiritual realms of human existence in the capacity of spiritual seekers. The Pilgrimage's main attraction, of course, will be its analytical and astrological intelligibility – once we familiarise ourselves with the fundamentals of Hindu astrology – in bringing into focus what kind of sacred phenomenon of consciousness *Mokṣa* actually is.

6. This Pilgrimage and the Spiritual Sacredness of Mokṣa

While technology-based pilgrimages to *Mokṣa,* like that of the neurologist, might run the grave risk of draining away the sacred spiritual essence of the phenomenon through their measurement of its bio-chemical and electrical variables, our astrological Pilgrimage, by contrast, will do *Mokṣa* full justice through its recognition of the role of Divine grace and Godhead as an integral part of and the very essence of the phenomenon of *Mokṣa.* The retention in this Pilgrimage of the sacred spiritual nature of *Mokṣa* need not come as a surprise to us at all as *Vedic* astrology has always been an integral part of the *Vedic* knowledge systems (Vamadeva Shastri), which had been built entirely upon spiritual foundations and a spiritual world view (Rajaram and Frawley).

Thus, in this present work, it is my additional intention to bring home the spiritual sacredness of *Mokṣa* – insofar as

I have been able to grasp the same — at a time when more and more seekers in all parts of the world are turning to this highest blessing in life, hoping to find therein a lasting imperturbability and peace, which all our surfeit of wealth and comforts have been unable to secure for us and which our relentless pursuit of every conceivable kind of sensory gratification has, alas, not been able to vouchsafe for us.

In this prevailing spiritual climate, the fires ignited in my younger years by two beloved Spiritual Masters, spontaneously undergoing a renewed kindling have impelled me from within to embark upon an astrological Pilgrimage to the historically most illustrious site of *Mokṣa,* namely, the life and consciousness of *Śrī Ramaṇa Maharṣi.* By using the powerful insights, wisdom, and predictive power of Hindu astrology, I endeavour to bring the nature and process of *Mokṣa* into far greater relief, thereby hoping to create an intense devotional yearning for *Mokṣa* on the one hand and a Hindu astrological understanding of the same on the other. Without an attunement to its spiritual sacredness, the profound significance of *Mokṣa* might well run the grave risk of being altogether lost upon us.

7. Fundamentals of Hindu Astrology – Not an Insurmountable Barrier

Hindu astrology itself need not be considered as an esoteric discipline that is intelligible only to astrological savants. *In fact, my attempt has not only been to create an intense devotional yearning for Mokṣa but a ruci [taste] for Hindu astrology as well.* I endeavour to do this in a gentle way, without creating the feeling that Hindu astrology is necessarily out of bounds for the intelligent laity just because they have till now been strangers to this *Vedic* discipline.

My study of the *Mokṣa* of *Śrī Ramaṇa Maharṣi* forms part of my larger forthcoming work on Hindu astrology in the spiritual spheres of *Dharma* and *Mokṣa.* In isolating this part of the text from its larger context, I have naturally suffered the handicap of having to present an extract of the whole in a somewhat isolated and dismembered fashion, and it is in order to make good this incompleteness that an introduction to the principles of Hindu astrology has also been added in the form of a separate chapter, namely, Chapter III. Hopefully, after this addition, this astrological Pilgrimage will also become reasonably more self-contained.

CHAPTER III

Hindu Astrology as a God-Centred Vidyā

1. Jyotiṣa – A Very Brief History

Jyotiṣa is a *Saṁskṛta* term that in the ancient *Vedic* and Hindu societies had stood not only for *Vedic* or Hindu astrology but also for its 'inseparable' other-half, *Vedic* or Hindu astronomy. However, on account of the ravages of time – especially with the coming of the British Raj and the subsequent new avatar of western civilization in the form of the relinquishing of God and the concomitant *apotheosis* of science and technology – a somewhat unfortunate bifurcation between *Vedic* or Hindu astronomy and *Vedic* or Hindu astrology came to pass.

Hindu astronomy, on account of its new dependence on the very desirable technological tools of the West, shifted its allegiance away from the *Vedic* ethos, while Hindu astrology, which had no such advantage to derive from the new technological avatar of western civilization, retained its allegiance to the *Vedic* tradition with its unmitigated spiritual outlook.

Thus, today, while Hindu astronomy is more in the nature of an ancient relic and has passed on into its new technological and secular avatar of Indian astronomy, Hindu astrology, by contrast, still continues to be very much the Hindu *vidyā* that it always was: a God-centred system of learning, devoted to a deeper philosophical understanding of human life, *karma,* and destiny. In my larger work, I go into greater depth as to how what was originally a God-centred system of integral knowledge in ancient times – namely, *Jyotiṣa* – gradually suffered a bifurcation ever so slowly and imperceptibly such that in the end, both branches began to give the impression of being two independent disciplines of learning. However, the continued inevitable dependence of Hindu astrology upon astronomical data through the use of the ephemeris (a table of day-to-day planetary positions for a whole year) created confusion, with no one knowing with consummate clarity any more how exactly Hindu astrology differed from Hindu astronomy.

And we might add that in the absence of a clear insight and understanding with regard to the nature of these two branches of *Jyotiṣa,* Hindu astrology came increasingly under the attack of rationalists, who became the champions of the day in an emerging technological civilization. For, there weren't enough erudite votaries of Hindu learning who could take on headlong these ill-founded criticisms and repulse the attacks of spiritually blind rationalists.

2. Hindu Astrology is a Profound Philosophical Study of the 'Movement of Life'

While Hindu astrology employs planetary positions to understand the dynamics of the movement of life, it has nothing to do with planetary motions *per se,* and certainly, it would be completely erroneous to hold that 'the planets rule our lives' when God alone has dominion over our lives.

While *Vedic* and Hindu astronomy studied the motions of the celestial bodies, *Vedic* and Hindu astrology had nothing to do with the motions of the physical planets *per se.* From the point of view of *Vedic* and Hindu astrology then, its field of study is rather the mysterious 'movement of life' in the lives of individuals. As *Vedic* and Hindu societies had a through-and-through spiritual outlook, this was also naturally the hallmark of their astrology, which became one of the intellectual and spiritual pursuits in those ancient societies.

According to those highly perceptive founding fathers, the *Ṛṣis* [Sages], all movement throughout nature only reflected 'the rhythms or the moods of God'.

Thus, for them, both the orderly movement of planets as observed from this earth station as well as the rhythm of the mysterious movement of life on planet earth itself were governed only by the self-same 'moods of God'. One movement was found to be predictable, namely, the movement of the planets, whereas the movement of life, in the life of an individual seemed to be mysterious and unpredictable.

Hindu astrology is a God-centred system of learning [*Jyotirvidyā*] in which the foundational principle is that every life event for any individual has to have a one-to-one mapping with planetary positions on the natural zodiac. By calibrating the various life events of an individual with the changing planetary positions on the zodiac, one begins to see the significance of the planetary positions within the context of a human life. Both movements are the same in the highest sense in that they are reflective of the changing moods or rhythms of God. This is the most important principle of ancient astrology, whether it belonged to China, Mesopotamia, Arabia, Egypt, or the *Vedic* civilization.

3. Three Fruits of Hindu Astrology

Predictions of coming life events; averting a bad fate through remedial measures; insights and wisdom into human life — these may be considered to be the three fruits of Hindu astrology.

Astronomy studies the motions of the planets and other celestial objects moving on the zodiacal belt; astrology, with its passion for philosophical profundity and the enigmas and paradoxes in human life, studies the structure of human destiny and sees it arising from the structure of time itself. We are usually under the strong impression that the best fruits of Hindu astrology are its predictions: when disease might strike, when losses might come to us, when we might go abroad, when a marriage might be made or broken, when we might be honoured, and when we might possibly die, suffer some humiliation, or lose in a litigation.

However, predictions are not the only desirable fruits of Hindu astrology. Even more valuable than predictions are the philosophical fruits such as insights into life and wisdom, for the astrologer can determine, in a given life, when hard times might come, when the time is fertile for a certain kind of activity, and when a certain action might meet with success or result only in failure. On the basis of such insights and judgements, astrologers can tell us whether it is prudent to act at a certain time: whether it will be propitious to commence the construction of a house, whether some big suffering is in store for us, etc. Thus, Hindu astrology has always been well known for predictive knowledge undergoing a metamorphosis into insights, wisdom, and a deeper understanding of life. But these insights and wisdom are not all that there is to Hindu astrology.

4. Astrological Remedial Measures and their Power

There are the very potent remedial measures in Hindu astrology, which are, in most of the cases, capable to a large extent of alleviating miseries. Thus, this Hindu *vidyā* does not make a doomsday prediction and leave you in the lurch, completely vulnerable to the onslaughts of a 'bad' fate. No! On the other hand, it teaches you how to raise the 'low energies' of the planets in your natal horoscope through special kinds of worship of Hindu Deities corresponding to the *Navagrahas*, through special empowerment of planetary energies [*kavach*], or even through daily charities [*parihāras*]. In many cases, Hindu astrology suggests some other methods to overcome, well in advance of its occurrence, a bad affliction in the charts, and in this way, teaches the individual how to get more out of life by intensifying his/her intelligent efforts in accordance with the detailed prescriptions of the remedial measures given to us by the *Vedic Ṛṣis*.

Thus, we may say that Hindu astrology not only gives predictions and warns us about coming events, it also helps us to greatly soften the blows of fate and to overcome *karmic* obstacles in life through intelligent effort – centred round the Hindu Deities – either on the physical plane or on the higher, devotional and astral planes. A doctor prescribes medicines which are expected to change the ill health of the body, while a Hindu astrologer would ask us to expend intelligent efforts on a daily basis. These might include a small but heartfelt charity or devotional worship of a certain Deity that stands for the energy of one of the weak *Navagrahas* in our horoscope.

5. Validity of the Geocentric System for the Study of Planetary Movements

One of the criticisms of rationalists has been that *Vedic* astrology uses a geocentric system for tracking the planets, and they argue that since it has been firmly established by Copernicus and Kepler that it is the planets that go around the Sun, astrology necessarily suffers from an aberration in its very foundations! What, however, the rationalists do not seem to understand is that astrology has never concerned itself with planetary motions *per se*, but rather only with the 'movement of life' on this earth plane.

As it is this movement of life that is the field of astrological study, it is but natural to use a system of co-ordinates for which the earth station is taken to be the centre. Thus, the geocentric system is contextually the most appropriate for Hindu astrology. To use a heliocentric system would be as absurd as it would be to use an ellipsoidal system of co-ordinates for a problem that has perfect spherical symmetry. Mathematicians and astronomers will be able to grasp the appropriateness of this analogy.

6. Special Vocabulary and 'Observables' of Hindu Astrology

In broad terms, Hindu astrology seeks to understand the laws of time governing the complex patterns of the ebb and flow of fortunes in the affairs of humans. It sees these waves of good times and bad as held in a certain potential and unmanifest form in the womb of time, suddenly fructifying and bursting into reality at just that moment when they actually descend upon us as the life events of our personal destiny. However, this entire business of the ebb and flow of fortunes has to be understood only in terms of the natural planetary rhythms observable by us, which we must now understand to be the rhythms and the moods of God.

There are three naturally occurring observable motions of the earth that give us all the rhythms of time. These rhythms might pertain to small periods of time, such as the day and night cycle of 24 hours, the annual cycle of orbital motion of one year; or the immense cycle of time, such as the precessional cycle of about 24,000 years.

Before we actually introduce the special vocabulary, concepts, and observables of Hindu astrology, it might be well to bear in mind that astrology is fundamentally a one-to-one mapping between the fortunate and unfortunate life events on the one hand, and the positions of the moving planets on the zodiacal belt, on the other.

Broadly speaking, we must become sensitive to four sets of astrological variables and observables. First, there are twelve zodiacal signs, which provide the field or background against which to observe the planetary movements. In what follows, Sections 7-12 below deal with these zodiacal signs. The set of nine planets—the most important dynamic variables or observables—constitute the second set of variables. Sections 13, 19, and 24 are devoted to this second set.

The twelve houses, which encompass all the spheres of human life, constitute the third important set of astrological variables, and this is dealt with in Sections 14 and 16. The nested major and minor cycles of time constitute the fourth and last set of astrological observables. Sections 22 and 23 deal with this fourth set. Astrological skill largely consists of the ability to simultaneously see all the above sets of astrological variables, so as to arrive at a comprehensive and insightful picture into a life crisis or the destiny of an individual. This is further elaborated upon in Section 25.

7. The Celestial Sphere, the Ecliptic, and the Zodiacal Belt

The first rhythm of the earth's motion is already very familiar to us; this is its annual orbital motion around the Sun. Upon looking up into the heavens on a clear night when the Moon is not too bright, we see what appears to be the immense hemispherical dome of the sky (celestial sphere) studded with a multitude of 'fixed' star groups and patterns, and if we watch for several hours at a stretch, we shall find these fixed patterns of the constellations rising in the East and then slowly rolling on towards the West on the celestial sphere on account of the earth spinning on its polar axis from West to East.

In addition, when we observe the motion of the Sun from the earth station, it is the Sun that appears to orbit the earth in a circle. This apparent circular path of the Sun formed on the celestial sphere is called the *ecliptic*. If we take an angular width of about nine degrees on either side of this *ecliptic*, we obtain a circular band or belt on the celestial sphere, which may be called the *zodiacal belt*.

The Sun and all the other planets of the solar system are seen to move across this zodiacal belt as the earth makes its annual orbital motion around the Sun. The patterns of the fixed constellations [*rāśis*] that we see on the zodiacal belt provide the convenient milestones and the background over which these planetary motions are seen to occur from our earth station. The motion of the Moon is, of course, the easiest to observe as it traverses the zodiacal belt, completing one lunar month (full circular orbit on the zodiacal belt) in roughly 27 days.

The second rhythm of the earth's motion comes from its spin. The earth spins around its polar axis in an anti-clockwise direction, that is, from West to East, and this gives us the feeling during daylight hours that the Sun rises in the East and sets in the West; at night, this gives us the feeling that the various fixed *rāśis* [zodiacal signs or constellations] 'roll' on the dome of the celestial sphere, again from East to West.

This would mean that once in 24 hours, which is the time taken by the earth to spin once fully around its axis, the sweeping panorama of the zodiacal belt completes one full rotation of 360 degrees. In other words, it takes the spinning earth just four minutes to cover one degree of the circular zodiacal belt. Alternatively, for a fixed point on the earth, the zodiacal belt appears to turn around the earth at the rate of four minutes per degree. To repeat, the diurnal spinning motion of the earth gives us the feeling that at night the *rāśis* of the zodiacal belt 'rise' on the horizon; then the entire zodiacal belt is seen to roll on the celestial sphere, moving towards the West. Likewise, every night and through the weeks and months, we may observe the movement of the planets on the zodiacal belt across the 'fixed' zodiacal signs and constellations.

8. Precessional Motion of the Earth and the Shifting of the Vernal Equinox

The third rhythmic motion of the earth is called precession. It is the very slow sweeping around of the earth's axis of spin; the periodicity of this is the enormously long time-span of roughly 24,000 years. We need not go more deeply into this third motion at just this point, except to take note that the precessional motion of the earth's axis is responsible for the very slow shifting of the *vernal equinox* on the zodiac in an anti-clockwise direction. We know that as the Sun moves on its path of the ecliptic through the year, the duration of day and night keeps on changing, and after the winter months, during which the nights are longer, comes the first day of Spring (currently March 21), wherein the duration of the day equals the duration of the night. This is the day reckoned as the *vernal equinox*. The *vernal equinox* precesses at the rate of 54 seconds of arc per year, or takes 24,000 years to complete one revolution over the zodiacal belt.

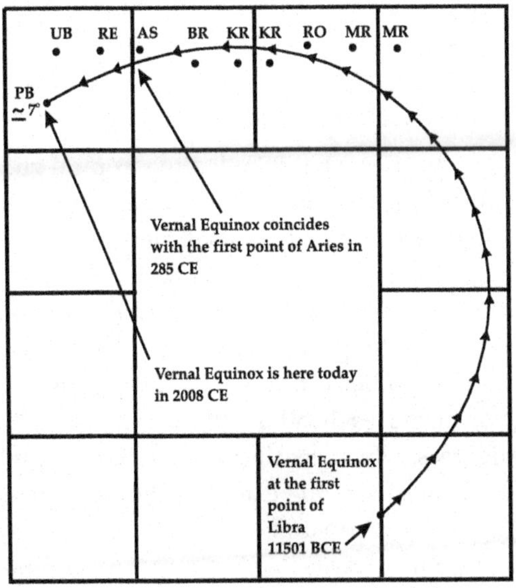

Shift of the Vernal Equinox with the Ages or Yugas

The above figure illustrates this slow movement of the *vernal equinox* on the zodiacal belt with the passage of the ages or *yugas* and brings home to us those *yugas* of Hindu society in the remote past (*Dwāpara* and *Treta*) when *Mokṣa* was the *summum bonum* of life.

The closing of the *Ṛg Vedic* period corresponds to 3800-3700 BCE, which is also the period to which Lord *Rāma* is assigned in *Śrī Yukteśwar Giri's* chronology of the *yugas*. The *Purāṇic* chronology of the *yugas* assigns the beginning of *Kaliyuga* to 3102 BCE, synchronous with the passing away of Lord *Kṛṣṇa*. The *vernal equinox* was in *Mṛgaśiras* [MR] during 4500-3500 BCE. It was in *Rohiṇī* [RO] during 3500-2500 BCE. This was also the period of the *Mahābhārata* war of 3100 BCE. At the present time in 2008, the *vernal equinox* is approximately at 7° in the *nakṣatra Purva Bhadrapada* [PB] in the sign Pisces. RE, AS, BR, KR stand for the *nakṣatras Revati, Ashwini, Bharani, Krittika* respectively (*Vedic Aryans* 174-205).

9. The Tropical Zodiac, Sidereal Zodiac, and Ayanāṁśa

Western astrology uses what is called the tropical zodiac, whose starting point or 'first degree of Aries' coincides with the *vernal equinox*. As the *vernal equinox* is itself not a fixed point on the zodiac but is shifting in an anti-clockwise direction on account of the precession of the earth's axis (at the rate of 54 seconds of arc per year), with the progression of time, the tropical zodiac and the sidereal zodiac (followed in Hindu astrology) keep slipping away from each other; the mismatch at this time is around 23 degrees, which is called the *ayanāṁśa*. It follows from this that the *ayanāṁśa* is the extent of the displacement [*aṁśa*] of that 'milestone' in the Sun's journey [*vernal equinox* – *ayana*] from the first point of Aries.

On account of the slow shifting of the equinoxes with the passage of time, the *ayanāṁśa* cannot remain a constant figure but must necessarily also change from one year to another, and more pronouncedly, from one century to another. As the exact beginning of the natural zodiacal sign Aries [*Meṣa rāśi*] is a matter of convention and has not been globally and universally agreed upon, there is often a slight discrepancy between one choice for the *ayanāṁśa* as against another. The government of India has decided upon the Lahiri *ayanāṁśa,* which currently is 23 degrees and 58 minutes (in May 2008). This choice of *ayanāṁśa* would correspond to the *vernal equinox* falling on the first degree of Aries in 285 CE. As *Vedic* astronomers were well aware of the precession of the earth and the consequent equinoctial shifting, the sidereal zodiac of the Hindus is faithful to the actual observable positions of the planets; whereas the tropical zodiac does not reflect the actual observable positions of the planets on account of there being a mismatch between the starting points of the two zodiacs to the extent of the *ayanāṁśa.*

On the whole, what is important for us to realize is that in terms of these diurnal and annual cyclical rhythms of time in which the earth is involved, the coming and the going of fortunes in human affairs is studied in Hindu astrology.

10. The Most Effective Point (MEP) of the Ascendant

That point of the zodiacal belt that coincides with the position of the horizon just at the time of birth, for a given place of birth, is called the Most Effective Point (henceforth MEP) of the Ascendant (henceforth Asdt). This point, which is highly sensitive, serves to mark the uniqueness of the individual who has come into manifestation on the earth plane at that precise moment of birth. The zodiac, being a circular strip, is conveniently divided into twelve equal *rāśis* [constellations] or parts called the zodiacal signs. Thus, the MEP corresponding to a given human birth must always fall within one of these twelve zodiacal signs. Each sign has an angular width of just 30 degrees. The Ascendant [*lagna*] — that which has 'ascended' over the horizon at the time of birth — which signifies the first house, and the underlying zodiacal sign serve to characterize that particular individual.

The ancient Hindu Sages divided each *rāśi* into two and a quarter *nakṣatras* [asterisms]. Each *nakṣatra* was either a single star or a small group of stars within the given zodiacal sign. The word *nakṣatra* itself has the etymological meaning of 'the guardian of the night', and we may well imagine how the progression of time itself was measured by the careful observation of the rising and the setting of these *nakṣatras.* The *nakṣatras* on the zodiacal belt can be observed only at night. From this it follows that if we are able to watch one half of the zodiacal belt through the course of a given night, we will be able to watch the complementary other half of the zodiacal belt only six months later, when the earth goes over to the diametrically opposite position in its circular orbit around the Sun.

From the earth station every night, we are able to observe the rising and the setting of some of the 27 *nakṣatras* on the zodiacal belt. Likewise, even the movement of all the *Navagrahas* [nine planets, including the mathematical positions of *Rāhu* and *Ketu,* which are the north and the south nodes of the Moon] is always seen against the background of these *nakṣatras,* which serve to define and identify the twelve zodiacal signs. We may either divide the zodiacal belt into twelve strips, each being 30 degrees wide, in which case, these strips are called *rāśis* [constellations or signs]; alternatively, we may divide the zodiac into 27 fine-grained smaller strips characterized as the *nakṣatras.*

11. Zodiacal Signs and Nakṣatras are Pregnant with Cosmic Unmanifest Potentialities

Each of the twelve zodiacal *rāśis* or the 27 zodiacal *nakṣatras* is pregnant with a series of cosmic unmanifest potentialities. Usually, one or more of these potentialities springs into manifestation whenever 'activated' through the transit of various planets, over the MEP of a particular house or other natal planetary positions, when these happen to occupy that particular zodiacal *rāśi* or *nakṣatra.* Such transits fructify at certain specific times in the lives of individuals.

Thus, each of the twelve zodiacal *rāśis,* or each of the 27 *nakṣatras,* holds not just one potentiality but very many. We must think of the series of these potentialities as arranged on an ascending energy scale, with one potentiality differing from another only because it has a characteristically higher or lower energy value. For convenience, we may think of them as analogous to the successive products of fractional distillation, which come into manifestation only at higher and higher temperatures (higher and higher energies).

'Strengths or energies' of the planets are not assigned in Hindu astronomy but only in Hindu astrology, whose purpose is entirely different from that of Hindu astronomy. If this distinction between astronomy and astrology is not clearly grasped on account of the bias given to us by modern physical sciences, we may well fly into a rage when we hear of planets having strengths and weaknesses as they wander over the various *rāśis* and *nakṣatras* of the zodiacal belt.

12. The Twelve Zodiacal Rāśis

Rāśi	Zodiacal Sign	*Rāśi* Beginning	*Rāśi* Ending
Meṣa	Aries	0°	30°
Vṛṣabha	Taurus	30°	60°
Mithuna	Gemini	60°	90°
Kaṭaka	Cancer	90°	120°
Siṁha	Leo	120°	150°
Kanyā	Virgo	150°	180°
Tulā	Libra	180°	210°
Vṛścika	Scorpio	210°	240°
Dhanus	Sagittarius	240°	270°
Makara	Capricorn	270°	300°
Kumbha	Aquarius	300°	330°
Mīna	Pisces	330°	360°

As we will be concentrating more upon the zodiacal *rāśis* [signs] rather than on the zodiacal *nakṣatras,* we may make a brief acquaintance with their names and at least with some of their primordial characteristics (significations).

It is important to realize that in Hindu astrology, the *Navagrahas* [nine planets, including *Rāhu* and *Ketu*] have more fundamental importance than the *rāśis,* as they alone are the *dynamical variables,* reflecting the benefic as well as the malefic influences of time; whereas the zodiacal signs stand for the twelve different cosmic climates of time and the ground or the fields upon which the movement of life comes to pass. We will come to see that the *Navagrahas* represent 'the movement of life'.

The luminaries, the Sun (Su) and the Moon (Mo), rule over just one sign each in the zodiac, the fiery sign Leo and the watery sign Cancer, respectively. All the other planets, namely, Mars (Ma), Venus (Ve), Mercury (Me), Jupiter (Ju), and Saturn (Sa), are such that each planet is the lord of two different signs. And the two signs falling under the lordship of a given planet are not on the same footing. One of the signs has what is called a *Mūla Trikoṇa* (MT), while the other sign is a non-MT sign.

MT *Rāśi*	Zodical Sign	Lord of the MT *Rāśi*
Meṣa	Aries	Ma
Kaṭaka	Cancer	Mo
Siṁha	Leo	Su
Kanyā	Virgo	Me
Tula	Libra	Ve
Dhanus	Sagittarius	Ju
Kumbha	Aquarius	Sa

MT Signs and their Lords

Rāśi	Zodical Sign	*Rāśi* Lord
Vṛścika	Scorpio	Ma
Vṛṣabha	Taurus	Ve
Mithuna	Gemini	Me
Mīna	Pisces	Ju
Makara	Capricorn	Sa

Non-MT Rāśis

Individuals are understood by Hindu astrologers on the basis of their strong planets, which rule their charts and consequently also their lives, rather than on the basis of their *rāśis*. Thus, in the horoscope of *Śrī Ramaṇa Maharṣi,* as Mars and Saturn are the strong planets, and his Asdt MEP falls in the zodiacal sign Virgo, we may hope, in the life of the *Maharṣi,* to see not only the primordial characteristics (significations) of the Virgo Asdt but also the significations of Mars and Saturn manifesting in his spiritual-psycho-physical personality.

As we shall learn in Sections 14 and 16, the houses are the various outer spheres of life in Hindu astrology. The twelve zodiacal signs in their totality hold what we may consider to be cosmic unmanifest potentialities necessary for all the diverse spheres of life; these cosmic unmanifest potentialities, which, on account of being triggered by certain planetary transits, then manifest as various life events in the twelve spheres of our outer life (houses).

Thus, depending upon the zodiacal sign in which the Asdt MEP falls for a given individual, the primordial characteristics of that zodiacal sign get impressed upon the psycho-physical personality and temperament. For this reason, those with a Virgo Asdt use their heads more than their feelings in their general approach to life, whereas those with a Cancer Asdt invariably meet life from their dominant 'feeling' nature. Likewise, Leo Asdts, who have intelligence and a sense of self as their hallmarks, have an innate tendency to be at the centre of attention. We shall, however, not go further into these primordial characteristics of the various zodiacal signs but shall invoke them whenever the need arises in a certain context.

13. The Navagrahas Signify the Presence of Īśvara in our Lives

As Hindu astrology is a God-centred *vidyā* with its roots in the *Vedas,* which are spiritual through-and-through in content, God is central to the whole framework of Hindu astrology. Unlike their meaning in Hindu astronomy, the *Navagrahas* in Hindu astrology are understood to be the nine aspects of *Īśvara* [God]. While Hindu *Dharma* speaks of *Īśvara* only in holistic and indivisible terms, Hindu astrology goes much deeper and gives us detailed insights and wisdom into the way *Īśvara's* blessings manifest in the various spheres of our life. The sanctity and existence of the *Navagraha sannidhis* in Hindu temples is ample testimony to the fact that in Hindu astrology, the *Navagrahas* are not just physical planets but also the various aspects of *Īśvara.*

As *Īśvara* assuredly has a benevolent aspect as also a malevolent one, the totality of life, which is *Īśvara's* complete manifestation, has both aspects. In Hindu astrology too, the functional benefic planets (FBs) bring the grace of *Īśvara* into our life, while the functional malefic planets (FMs) represent the wrath of *Īśvara,* manifesting as sufferings, obstacles, disappointments, enmity, failures, losses, debts, ill health, every kind of deprivation and failure, and even death and *Mokṣa.* Thus, the *Navagrahas* represent the presence, in our life, of the various aspects of *Īśvara,* both benefic as well as malefic. In Section 19, we shall go more deeply into the nature of the FBs and FMs in the field of our life.

Of course, the way the presence of *Īśvara* (grace as well as wrath) changes in our life exactly follows the change in the positions of the nine planets, but barring this important correspondence, the planets are not merely celestial physical objects in Hindu astrology at all; rather, they are the symbolic representations of the presence of *Īśvara* in various spheres of our life. This is a very subtle point and is usually lost sight of.

14. The Houses in Hindu Astrology

While the twelve *rāśis* of the zodiac are pregnant with the cosmic unmanifest potentialities, which are the primordial characteristics (significations) of those twelve signs, the houses (Hs) are the various departments of outer life in the sphere of manifestation. And just as the twelve signs encompass the full circle of the zodiacal belt, so too the twelve Hs, which bear a natural analogy to the underlying twelve signs, encompass the full circle of the zodiacal belt. Taking the zodiacal sign underlying the Asdt MEP as the first, the houses' are given a serial numbering. Thus, if the Asdt MEP falls in the Aquarius sign, then the first house is in the sign Aquarius, the second in the sign Pisces, and so on, till the twelfth house falls in the sign Capricorn. On the other hand, the natural ordering of the signs goes like this: The first sign is always Aries, the second is Taurus, the third is Gemini. . . . till finally we come to Pisces, the 12th sign.

15. Kālapuruṣa – The God of Hindu Astrology

Kāla means time, and *Puruṣa* means, in this context, the Supreme Spirit. Thus, *Kālapuruṣa* means the God of Time. On account of the God-centred nature of Hindu astrology, the God of Hindu astrology, namely, the unmanifest *Śiva* as *Kālapuruṣa,* is imagined to be positioned in a recumbent posture, with his head falling in the first sign Aries and his feet falling in the last sign Pisces. Such a mapping of *Kālapuruṣa's* body onto the natural zodiac immediately creates some significations of the signs insofar as the various parts of the human body are concerned.

Thus, the first sign, Aries [*Meṣa*], signifies the head; the second sign, Taurus [*Vṛṣabha*], the neck and throat. . . . the fifth sign, Leo [*Siṁha*], signifies the digestive system. . . . the tenth sign, Capricorn [*Makara*], the knees. . . . and the twelfth sign, Pisces, signifies the feet and ankles of *Kālapuruṣa* and thereby also the feet and ankles of the human body.

To return to the Hs in Hindu astrology, we must learn what their various significations are, for only then do we know to which house or department of life in astrology a given life event actually belongs.

16. Significations of the Houses

Significations are the fruits that spring into manifestation from the houses in the form of life events and circumstances. Thus, the significations of a given house constitute a characteristic set of life events that pertain only to the sphere of that particular house. These are the possible 'meanings' of that particular house in Hindu astrology.

In Hindu astrology, one finds all varieties of significations figuring side by side, without any proper ordering and classification. We must use the spheres of *Artha, Kāma, Dharma,* and *Mokṣa* and the scale of planetary energies in order to create a more cogent and systematic enumeration of the significations of each house. We must also understand, in broad terms, how the three *Śaktis* of the Divine Mother drive the twelve houses. Once we grasp the nature of the three *Śaktis* and their diverse manifestations through the *Artha, Kāma, Dharma, Mokṣa,* angular, trinal, and Sun-like houses as well as the foundational role of *Ātmā* in Hindu astrology, we will be well prepared to delve directly into the significations of the houses.

Icchā, Kriyā, Jñāna Śaktis

The Divine Mother stands for *Śakti* [the blessing or energy of *Īśvara* in manifestation]. This *Śakti* operates in three different ways, and it is not always understood that while there are indeed clear-cut differences between the three kinds of *Śaktis*, all are, nevertheless, fundamentally the self-same power or energy of *Īśvara*. In physics we study how energy is energy, whether it is heat energy, light energy, electrical energy, or nuclear energy. It is much the same even here, except that we must always remember that heat is heat, light is light, and electricity is only electricity.

The *Śakti* that manifests as our will in life or as our aspiration, intention, and desire is called *Icchā Śakti*; this is the energy or the power of *Īśvara* that drives the *Kāma* Hs, the IIIH, VIIH, and XIH. When these houses are strong in a horoscope, the opportunity for spiritual flowering might be reduced unless the profound interest given by the IIIH falls in the spheres of *Dharma* or *Mokṣa*. Strong *Kāma* houses generally bestow a strong will, aspiration, and intent upon the individual; it is through the pursuit of these willful urges, aspirations, and inspirations that the individual finds fulfilment in life. *Icchā Śakti* provides the starting energy and the vitality in the individual for all achievement, whether in the worldly sphere of *Artha* or even in the spiritual spheres of *Dharma* and *Mokṣa*.

The IIH, VIH, and XH are *Artha* Hs; they bestow the urge for achievement and dynamic action on the stage of life. The XH is the summit of the *Artha* Hs and when strong, indicates that there is enough grace of the Divine Mother for skill, recognition, and achievement in the sphere of one's vocation. The Divine Mother's energy, which drives these *Artha* Hs, is called *Kriyā Śakti*; this is the *Śakti* that is so conducive for the 'unspiritual' *rājasic* process of becoming. It must, however, be noted that by no means are we deprecating the *Artha* and *Kāma* houses; in fact, without strong *Kāma* and *Artha* houses, grace would be in short supply for manifesting spiritual works in the world. The reason is that in such a case the engines of will and aspiration would be far too weak, thereby shutting down the human drama of will, action, and achievement.

Likewise, the angular houses, the IH, IVH, VIIH, and XH, must also be deemed to be the houses of action and becoming. They are called *Lakṣmī sthānas,* meaning houses that are very favourable for the *Śakti* of the Divine Mother to come into manifestation in the outer world. The IVH is, however, exceptional in that although it is an angular house, it is primarily a house of being [*sattvaguṇa*], as it is a spiritual house of the *Ātmā* after *Jīvanmukti* and a house of *asmitā* prior to it. In contrast to the angular houses, which are houses of becoming, the *Dharma* houses, sometimes called *Viṣṇu sthānas,* are houses of being, since they are undoubtedly spiritual and *sāttvic* houses. In Hindu spiritual terminology then, 'becoming' would signify a dominant role for *rajoguṇa;* 'being' would signify a dominant role for the spiritual *sattvaguṇa.*

Apart from *Icchā* and *Kriyā Śaktis,* there is the purely *sāttvic* and spiritual *Jñāna Śakti,* which drives the *Dharma* and even the *Mokṣa* houses, especially when an individual has crossed over to the spheres of *Dharma* or *Mokṣa.* The trines are the *Dharma* houses, namely, the VH, IXH, and IH, whereas the *Mokṣa* houses are the IVH, VIIIH, and XIIH. From among the houses, the IVH, VH, and IXH are *sāttvic* and spiritual houses, whereas from among the planets, the Su, Mo, and Ju are *sāttvic* and spiritual. In the ensuing Chapter (Section 11), while delving into the horoscope of the *Maharṣi,* we will revisit the *Śaktis* of the Divine Mother with a view to gaining a deeper understanding of the Divine Mother's *saṁkalpa* for the *Maharṣi's* Self-Realization [*Mokṣa*].

The Sun-like Houses in the Systems Approach

It is very significant that in the SA, the IIH, IIIH, and IXH have been singled out and identified as 'Sun-like' houses, since they are endowed with great Sun-like power for achievement on the stage of the world. VA, of course, does not accord any such special power to these Sun-like houses, but rather places greater emphasis only on the two houses of profession, namely, the IIH and XH, which are identified as the house of professional status, and the house of professional skill, merit, and achievement.

The Hub of the Twelve Houses

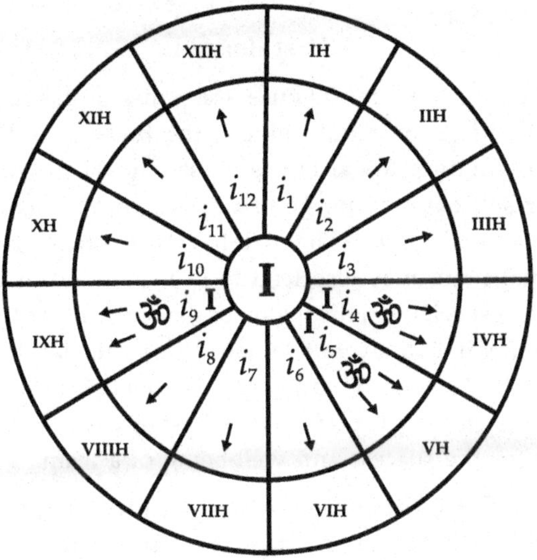

The 'I', Aham, or Sat-Chit-Ānanda as the Hub of the Twelve Houses

The figure above enables us to bridge the gulf between our Hindu spiritual perceptions and our knowledge of human life and destiny, as understood in Hindu astrology. That the *Ātmā* [Self or I] is the essence of humans is not always recognized and celebrated in astrology. In this figure, however, the blissful *Ātmā* is seen to be the common ground on which all the twelve houses stand. If a certain house is strong or strong planets are placed therein, the individual derives happiness or *Ānanda,* which is the essence of the *Ātmā,* by engaging in the activities of that house. In each of the twelve houses of astrology, the *Ātmā* masquerades as an appropriate *anātmā,* which is nothing but the *Ātmā* disguised in a highly conditioned form. The *sāttvic* spiritual houses, the IVH, VH, and IXH are exceptional in that under certain favourable conditions, the underlying blissful *Ātmā* becomes available in all its pristine purity, either as the Self in the IVH or as God in the V and IX houses. In all other houses, the *Ātmā* is generally disguised as the *jīvātmā.*

First House

This is the most important house, the house of the personal self [*jīvātmā*] and its physical vehicle, the body. It indicates the overall orientation towards life. A strong IH provides much scope for self-expression, good reputation and achievement, whereas a weak and afflicted IH would put us at a strong disadvantage and may also lead to ill health and vulnerability to diseases, especially in the region of the head, as the IH signifies not just the whole body, but the head in particular. In a certain sense, the lord of the IH is like the captain of the team of the *Navagrahas;* a strong captain rather than a weak one is always desirable for the success and well-being of a team.

A weak and afflicted IH, however, as in *Śrī Ramaṇa Maharṣi's* case, would be a blessing in disguise insofar as the spiritual life is concerned. The reason for this is that the annihilation of the personal self, which is what *Mokṣa* tantamounts to, can then be more easily accomplished. However, an afflicted IH makes the body highly vulnerable to ill health in many forms as well as creates many hardships in life. *In the ancient Hindu and Vedic societies, since the personal self was anchored to God, and Dharma through a prudently-chosen auspicious conditioning, the IH was taken to be a Dharma house.* The Sun is the significator of the IH in both VA as well as in the SA.

Second House

This is a 'worldly' house, for a strong IIH gives us good *Artha* or wealth of some kind, though not necessarily in monetary form but in some form that comes to us through the dint of our own efforts. It is also the house of *Vāk,* family cohesion, and status or position in society. A strong IIH makes us strong in the world, while a weak IIH can become helpful for the spiritual life in the spheres of *Dharma* and *Mokṣa. Śrī Ramaṇa Maharṣi's* IIH was weak in his natal chart. That is to say, in 'the mood of God at the time of his birth' the IIH carried less grace, and this became a favourable factor in his breaking the bondage with family and choosing a renunciant's life. In both VA as well as the SA, Jupiter signifies the earning capacity of the IIH, while Mercury signifies childhood, speech, and education — the other significations of the IIH.

Third House

This house lies in the sphere of *Kāma,* that is, the enjoyment of life in the form of profound interest and curiosity in competitive activities, businesses, hobbies, or even in the arts and sciences. It is also a house of courage and holds the potential for teamwork as a means to achievements connected to the profession and mission in life. A strong IIIH indicates good entrepreneurial drive, motivation, ambition, inspiration, and self-expression.

In *yogaśāstra,* the IIIH is identified as the *prāṇamayakośa* [*kośa*: sheath, suggesting coverings upon the infinite *Ātmā* or absolute spirit] or the *prāṇic* body, and shows how strong and vital the *prāṇic* body is. The IH, of course, stands for the 'food body' or the *annamayakośa,* namely, the physical body. *Śrī Aurobindo* has pointed out that individuals with strong *prāṇaśakti* find it difficult to surrender to God, for they have so much vitality, energy, and drive that it becomes easy for them to achieve things themselves rather than by turning to *Īśvara* for Divine grace in moments of helplessness. In both the SA as well as VA, Mars is the significator of the IIIH.

Fourth House

This is considered to be a *Mokṣa* house in VA. It is so because *Mokṣa* comes from extinguishing the light of *asmitā* [I-am-ness], which is one of the significations of the IVH. We apply these principles in Section 30 of Chapter IV, which deals with the necessary and sufficient conditions for *Mokṣa.* When the IVH is strong, it accordingly shows good power of understanding and a capacity to be emotionally happy and contented. In *yoga,* what is identified as *manomayakośa* is the IVH of Hindu astrology, and its significator is the Moon.

In the chart of someone who has been blessed with *Mokṣa,* the IVH would signify the infinite *Ātmā,* or the Universal Spirit; whereas in the chart of an unenlightened individual, the IVH would represent the very core and the source of the personal self in its *sāttvic* aspect, the light of I-am-ness. *If the IVH is strong and also ruled by a sāttvic planet such as the Mo, the Su, or Ju, then the individual in question has a great sense of well-being and also a great sense of contentment and inner tranquility. This, from the point of view of VA, is the 'witness consciousness of I AM', represented by the Hindu Deity Ganeṣa. But even in the blessed state of inner tranquillity arising from the 'witness consciousness of I AM', there is indeed a sense of being only as a separate self. This feeling of being a separate entity goes only when one has been blessed with Mokṣa, which is really the dissolution of the personal self as well as the 'witness consciousness I AM'. This subtle distinction between the 'witness consciousness of I AM' and the asmitā of I-am-ness is further elaborated in Chapter IV.*

If, on the other hand, the IVH is weak and afflicted, the individual in question is likely to be emotionally insecure and unstable, and this would mean that the personal self is weak and troubled. If some *Mokṣa*-giving lord comes and settles close to the MEP of the IVH, this could serve as a strong necessary condition for *Mokṣa* itself. Prof. V. K. Choudhry holds the IVH to be the house of *Ātmavicāra.* In VA as well as in the SA, the Moon is the significator of the IVH and the mother, while Ve is the significator of vehicles, comforts, and luxuries. In the spheres of *Artha* and *Kāma,* the IVH is also, a house of marriage, house and home, happiness, vehicles, and properties. In the sphere of *Dharma,* it is a house of education.

We may present here a very subtle *sūtra* of VA and the SA: Each house has, in fact, many significations, spread out in all the four spheres of life – *Artha, Kāma, Dharma,* and *Mokṣa* – even though its dominant signification may usually be taken to lie only in one of the four spheres of life. For this reason, in examining the horoscope of an individual, one must always ascertain the sphere of life in which that individual is placed at just that time before one ventures to make sensible pronouncements about the fruits that may be expected in such-and-such period of life, for such-and-such house, etc.

Fifth House

In VA, this is considered a *Dharma* house. In ancient Hindu society, children used to be sent to a *gurukulāśrama* around the tender age of seven and were expected to be prepared for life through a comprehensive system of intensive spiritual learning [*Dharma*]. If the VH was strong, if there were good planets in the VH, or if the planet Jupiter – the significator of the VH – was strong, then it was found that the child learnt things quickly and well, and thus the VH came to be associated with subtle learning, especially spiritual learning.

The VH is also the house of creative intelligence and sensitivity in relationships. In terms of the light of I-am-ness, the IVH shows how 'bright and intense' this light is. The VH, by contrast, shows how swiftly and with how much angular sweep and velocity this light of I-am-ness may be turned around and directed in any desired direction of choice. Thus, the VH becomes, on account of this swivelling flexibility, the house of creative imagination and creative intelligence, as it affords us the capacity to 'rotate and focus' the light of our intelligence on any object of choice, in any direction of choice!

Thus, it is the house of *seeing,* as seeing requires swiftness and the capacity to turn the light of I-am-ness in the most flexible manner possible – even upon the workings of the personal self itself. The *advaitic* Master *Śrī J. Krishnamurti* has based a greater part of his teaching on *seeing*. As the planet of swift perception, Me is in the Master *Śrī J. Krishnamurti's* VH as well as in the VH of *Śrī Śrī Bhagavān*; it is not surprising that even the Master *Śrī Śrī Bhagavān* had prescribed for me, many years ago, just this *seeing* as the correct Hindu medicine for spiritual poverty and spiritual sickness. In *yogaśāstra*, what Hindu astrologers identify as the VH is called the *vijñānamayakośa*, or the sheath of insights, wisdom, and higher intelligence, which can lead to learning and illumination.

That each house has many significations in each of the four *Puruṣārthas* of life can be seen more clearly in the case of the VH, which we consider a little further for the purpose of illustration. The VH, while being the house of *Iṣṭadevatā* [beloved Deity] and the house of *mantrajñāna* and advising capacity in the spiritual sphere of *Dharma*, is also a *Kāma* House, with significations towards romantic dalliances, pleasure seeking, speculative ventures, gambling, and other such enjoyable recreational activities.

It is the house of love in expression and also intelligence at play, whether this be in the sphere of romance or on the path of *Bhaktiyoga*.

The various significations are distinguished from each other depending only upon the energy or the strength of the house and the strong planets that characterize the horoscope. If the strong VH lord, for example, has entered into the professional XH in the natal chart, then we may expect the profession to have an intellectual dimension or the dimension of creative advising capacity. In the SA as well as in VA, Jupiter is the significator of the VH.

Sixth House

This is an *Artha* house, specifically connected to achievement of goals. The other *Artha* houses are the IIH and XH, both of which are also identified as the professional houses. In seeking achievement, especially in the field of one's vocation, there are always many challenges posed by the forces of enmity, jealousy, ill health and disease, misunderstandings, as well as other losses through accidents, theft, and litigation. This unhappy and 'dark' area of human life is identified in Hindu astrology as the sphere of the VIH. It is one of the *duhstānas* or malefic houses.

If the VIH is strong in a natal chart, then we may be sure that one will overcome these above-mentioned challenges. There then emerges the possibility of making one's mark in the area of public recognition, skilful achievement, and honour, provided the XH is also strong. A strong VIH gives financial solvency and good health and makes it easy for us to overcome the obstacles mentioned above [SA *sūtra*]. While these are the significations of the VIH in the spheres of *Artha* and *Kāma*, there are also many other significations once the individual has moved from mundane life into the spiritual spheres of *Dharma* and *Mokṣa*.

The VIH is the house of service and *Karmayoga* as also the house of *yoga* generally. In addition, it is held in the SA that a strong VIH gives us the urge to seek a profound understanding in unconventional and new fields. In Prof. V. K. Choudhry's words, "*The VIH is the house of delving deep into Ātmavicāra or finding logical meanings and expressions of various facets of life.*" In this sense, the VIH is rather similar to the IIIH of profound enquiry, understanding, and curiosity. As the VIH is the house of arguments, challenges, oppositions, and questioning on account of its rather wilful nature, the profound enquiry and investigative approach bestowed by it has the taint of being prone to some damage because of the angle and the direction from which this profound enquiry comes into existence. On account of this nature of the VIH, the individual in question finds it difficult to simply accept things as given and will try to arrive at an analysis that might be considered debatable in established circles. It is for this reason that the VIH does not confer recognition like the benefic houses do, and hence, the labours endowed by the VIH will be in the nature of service or

Karmayoga. A strong VIH gives us the *karmayogic* capacity to undertake challenging and painstaking missions in life.

In VA, Mars signifies the aspects of enmity, litigation, and injury connected with the VIH; Saturn signifies the disease aspect of the VIH. In the SA, on the other hand, Mercury is taken as the significator of the VIH.

Seventh House

In VA, this is the house of marital relationships, overseas residence and travels, and long-standing partnerships in the professions and in business. It is a *Kāma* house. Thus, a strong VIIH blesses an individual with a good marital relationship, and this then consumes an individual's attention to such an extent that the spiritual life is obliged to take a back seat — if other spiritual influences in the chart are not strong. On the other hand, an afflicted VIIH along with a very weak and/or afflicted Venus, which is the significator of the VIIH — as in the case of *Śrī Ramaṇa Maharṣi* — will definitely preclude marital relationships as well as marital pleasures.

Eighth House

The VIIIH is one of the two important houses of *Mokṣa,* the other being the XIIH. Its real meaning is that the lord of the VIIIH, the *Mokṣakāraka,* has the potential of extinguishing the light of I-am-ness, which is the essence of the IVH of individual consciousness. When the lord of the VIIIH is strong in a natal chart, as was the case with *Śrī Ramaṇa Maharṣi,* we must read this to mean that at the time of birth, the mood of God was highly favourable for the blessings of *Mokṣa* at some stage or the other in life, since the highest signification and the highest energy of the VIIIH must correspond only to the highest goal of life, *Mokṣa.*

As is the case with any house in Hindu astrology, there are always lower and higher significations. Thus, there are also significations for the VIIIH in the spheres of *Artha* and *Kāma* apart from its well-known signification in the sphere of *Mokṣa*. It is recognized in VA that the VIIIH is mysterious and profound, and thus there will be significations of the VIIIH that will come into manifestation in a spiritual life, either as *Kuṇḍalinī* awakening or as mystical journeys into other planes of consciousness, even as *Mokṣa* itself. The manifestations depend on the strength of the *Mokṣa* lord in the natal chart.

In the sphere of *Artha,* the VIIIH can bestow what are called easy gains such as inheritance, a windfall, or unearned wealth. When its influence prevails on the profession, it might place us in situations where we will have to deal with collective wealth such as that managed by financial institutions, banks, and insurance companies, or even be involved in research. It is also a *duhsthāna* like the VIH, except that its maleficity is much more difficult to deal with. While a weak VIH can create ill health and trouble through litigations, planets placed in the VIIIH can lead to accidents, recurring illnesses that are intractable, bankruptcy, or even dishonour and disgrace.

Worst of all, in the sphere of *Kāma* or pleasure seeking, the VIIIH might get us involved in underworld activities centred around addictions, perversions, and crime. It can also create very unusual death-like experiences, either in the mystical life or in life-threatening adventurous activities. On the whole, the VIIIH is a heterodox house, and in the case of the *Maharṣi,* it bestowed not only *Mokṣa* when he was just sixteen but also a classic experience of the 'death of the body' many years after his *Mokṣa*. In Chapter IV, we discuss this 'death experience' of the *Maharṣi,* which was so very different from the *Mokṣa* process. Saturn is the significator of the VIIIH in both VA as well as in the SA.

Ninth House

In VA, this is the house of *Īśvara, Guru* [Master], philosophy, faith, grace, fortune, and the higher spiritual life of *Dharma* [virtue]. It is the highest of the *Dharma* houses or houses of learning, the others being the IH and VH.

In ancient Hindu society, the bedrock of the entire society was *Dharma,* which for the Hindus meant a joyful adherence to a comprehensive system of natural justice that governed not only human relationships but the relationship with and dependence on the whole of the natural world. As law and jurisprudence in our own times have been but derived from the ancient *Dharmaśāstras,* the IXH has also come to cover, in our modern times, law and jurisprudence as well as higher learning in these vocations.

Thus, the IXH encompasses not only spiritual learning, wisdom, philosophical wonder, sensitivity and attunement to *Īśvara,* and a higher sense of natural justice and fortune, but in modern society, legal and judicial spheres as well as higher education and learning. People with a strong IXH are generally law-abiding, virtuous, and noble-minded with high ideals and faith. They are also fortunate in many respects in life, as the IXH is also the house of fortune or God's grace. On the other hand, people with a weak or afflicted IXH and an afflicted Su in the natal chart can be unfortunate. This misfortune can manifest as the premature death of the father, since the IXH, whenever it has an MTS [*Mūla Trikoṇa* sign], automatically becomes the house of the father, as he is the one who protects us and fulfills all our needs till we begin to stand on our own feet. These significations of the IXH with regard to the father is more true in a conservative Hindu society than in a modern one, for in the latter case, an emphasis on greater individuality and independence has diminished the significance of the beneficence that might come from one's parents.

In the spheres of *Artha* and *Kāma,* the IXH, in modern times, has also come to stand for higher education abroad, overseas travels, as well as residences overseas, for the simple reason that fortune in modern times has come to be tied up with overseas travels and revenues therefrom. This, then, is an example of how the astrological *sūtras,* as house significations, keep changing with the structure and values of society within whose confines astrological knowledge is being sought.

A strong IXH will help us to achieve our goals more easily, both through grace as well as through virtuous efforts. A strong IXH also brings easy gains, but in an auspicious way, as the result of good fortune and *pūrvapuṇya* [spiritual merits from past lives]. It is only in the SA that the IXH is associated with *pūrvapuṇya,* whereas in VA, it is the VH (rather than the IXH) that is associated with *pūrvapuṇya.* In the SA, the VH is considered to be a house of spiritually meritorious deeds in the present birth, whereas VA considers the IXH to be the house signifying spiritually meritorious deeds in the present birth. Ju is the significator of the IXH. This would mean that if the horoscope has no MTS in the IXH, but there is a strong Ju, irrespective of the lordship of Ju, many of the significations of the IXH will manifest in the life of the concerned individual. In the SA, the Sun is also taken as a significator of the IXH.

Tenth House

The XH is called *karmabhāva,* as it is the house of action *per se.* A strong XH is one of the important factors that make for good character and a virtuous nature, as reflected in action. If the spiritual houses, such as the IVH, VH, or the IXH get involved in the XH, then the individual in question acts in spiritual ways and is motivated by spiritual inspiration. A strong XH gives us the urge to make our presence felt before the public gaze and also makes it easy for us to make an impact upon the world. However, in this process, as already explained in the context of the energies of the Divine Mother, we are likely to become too extroverted by plunging headlong into the unspiritual process of becoming. The significators of the XH in VA are the Sun, Mercury, and Jupiter. In the SA, the Sun and Mercury alone are the significators, while Mars is also admitted into the sphere of the XH as the significator of executive authority in view of its aggressive and commanding nature.

Eleventh House

This is the highest of the *Kāma* houses. It is the house of the fulfilment of goals and aspirations, often in great abundance. It signifies friends, income and gains, luxuries and gifts in profusion – especially gains coming through an association with friends, well-wishers, benefactors, sponsors, fans, and followers. If this house is strong, then the aspirations and life purpose of the individual are more easily fulfilled. As it is the highest of the *Kāma* houses, a strong XIH bestows the individual with comprehensive and continuously expanding goals, by achieving which the individual can more easily make a mark on the world stage. In traditional Hindu society, which was very dominantly family-centred, caste-centred, and hierarchic, the XIH signified elder brothers, for in that society, it was only the elder brothers who could lend the proverbial helping hand by virtue of the greater power and privileges that they enjoyed in that hierarchic social order. Jupiter is the significator of the XIH in both VA as well as in the SA.

Twelfth House

In VA, the XIIH is considered a *Mokṣa* house as *Vedic* society had spiritual flowering and *Mokṣa* as its highest goal. If, however, the individual in question is still travelling in the mundane spheres of *Artha* and *Kāma*, the XIIH has quite different significations – it then comes through as a *Kāma* house, a house of pleasure, wandering, sleep, rest, relaxation, holidaying, shopping, charities, donations, and spending or losing money; more generally, it becomes the house of losses and expenditures. Likewise, it can also create hospitalization, imprisonment, and confinement in some far-off place such as a secluded *āśrama* far-removed from civilization, a remote 'Siberia', or foreign country.

In the spiritual spheres of *Dharma* and *Mokṣa,* the XIIH can bless an individual with meditative states, deep *samādhi,* or trance-like states; when the XIIH lord is very strong, this house can also bless us with its highest signification of *Mokṣa.* In this sense, it is similar to the other *Mokṣa* house, the VIIIH. The *Mokṣa* bestowed by the VIIIH may be routed through 'death' or death-like experiences or mystic journeys and may also have an aspect of profundity and mysteriousness, which are hallmarks of the VIIIH of *Mokṣa.* When *Mokṣa* is granted by the XIIH lord, one might simply be separated from one's consciousness and mind without these accompanying mysterious and exciting hallmarks of the VIIIH. In the spheres of *Artha* and *Kāma,* the significator of the XIIH is Venus in the SA, while in the spheres of *Dharma* and *Mokṣa,* the significator for the XIIH in both VA and the SA is the *Nirvāṇakāraka Ketu.*

17. The Rāśi Chart and the Divisional Charts

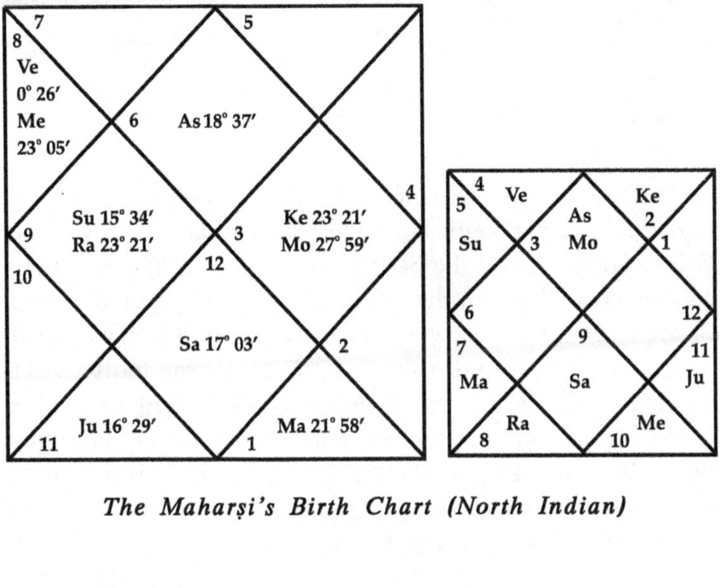

The Maharṣi's Birth Chart (North Indian)

Sa 17° 03′	Ma 21° 58′		Ke 23° 21′ Mo 27° 59′
Ju 16° 29′			
Su 15° 34′ Ra 23° 21′	Ve 0° 26′ Me 23° 05′		As 18° 37′

		Ke	As Mo
Ju	D-9 Chart used for: 1. Strengths of planets 2. Spiritual [IXH] potentials 3. General fortune in life		Ve
Me			Su
Sa	Ra	Ma	

The Maharṣi's Birth Chart (South Indian)

Note: The *Maharṣi's* horoscope in the South Indian (above) and North Indian (previous) format:

DOB = December 30, 1879; Rectified TOB = 12:19 a.m.; TZ = - 05:21 hours LMT; POB = Tiruchuzhi, Tamil Nadu, India (78°E 17′, 9°N 25′); Lahiri *ayanāṁśa* = 22° 10′

The divisional charts D-5, D-10, D-20, and D-24 of the *Maharṣi* appear in the South Indian format towards the end of this section.

In the *rāśi* chart [the natal chart, referred to as the horoscope] of the South Indian format, we can see an array of twelve boxes around the periphery of a square figure, with an empty square space in the centre of the square figure. The real meaning of the horoscope must be taken to be an insight or vision into time [*hora*] insofar as the life of the individual is concerned. The first point of *Meṣa rāśi* [Aries sign] commences at the top-left end, not exactly at the NW corner of the square figure, but after skipping the NW corner box and moving to the right, at the very beginning of the natural zodiac. The second sign is *Vṛṣabha* [Taurus], and counting in this way in the clockwise direction, we arrive at the twelfth sign Pisces, which is in the NW extremity of the square figure. The names of the twelve signs are not written down in the twelve boxes, as astrologers remember and understand where each sign is in the natural zodiac. Note that the zodiacal circle has been arranged in the form of this square figure only for convenience.

The Asdt that marks the IH is always marked 'As'. All houses are counted in the clockwise direction starting with the Asdt as the IH. The immediate house after the Asdt house in the clockwise direction is thus the IIH, while the previous house is the XIIH, etc. Realize that each house stands on the ground of a particular zodiacal sign with its characteristic primordial significations. The life drama occurring in that particular house transpires in the cosmic climate and ground provided by the particular zodiacal sign. This is true of each of the twelve houses. Thus, the zodiacal signs, which are pregnant with the cosmic unmanifest potentialities, definitely colour and shape the life drama transpiring in each house, depending on the nature of the Asdt and the strength of the planets at the time of birth.

Notice the positions of the *Navagrahas*, or the nine planets, distributed in the various houses in the *rāśi* chart. Sometimes a suffix 'R' is attached to some planets, showing that the planet has retrograde motion when viewed from the earth station. The North node and the South node of the Moon, *Rāhu* and *Ketu*, always move in the anti-clockwise direction, which is the direction opposite to that in which the planets usually move.

There are about sixteen (at least twelve) divisional charts, which carry additional detailed information about the strengths of the planets not already contained in the main *rāśi* chart. Each divisional chart corresponding to a given house throws more light on the strengths of the planets within the context of that particular house. Each house of the *rāśi* chart, we must remember, also has a divisional chart. To examine a house thoroughly after we have examined the strength of the lord of that particular house in the *rāśi* chart, we must move on to the *navāṁśa* chart, and thereafter, even to the corresponding divisional chart. Once we have surveyed these three charts, we must enter into the crucial astrologically skillful act of *simultaneously seeing* the three charts with our eyes riveted on the lord, the significator of that particular house, and the *lagnas* of the two divisional charts in question. Only then will we have a comprehensive and reliable picture of the potential that a particular house holds for us.

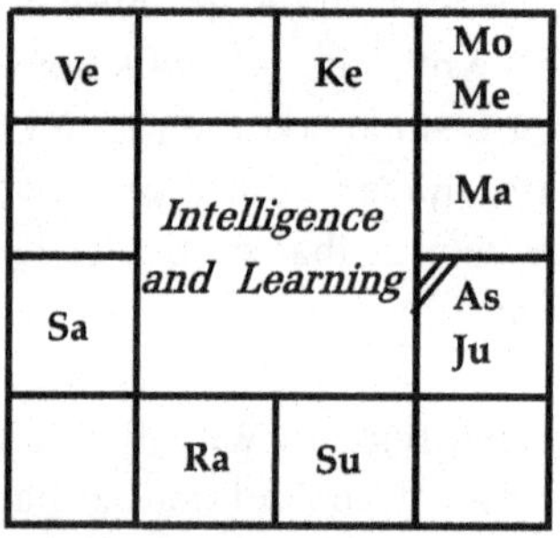

Fig. 1

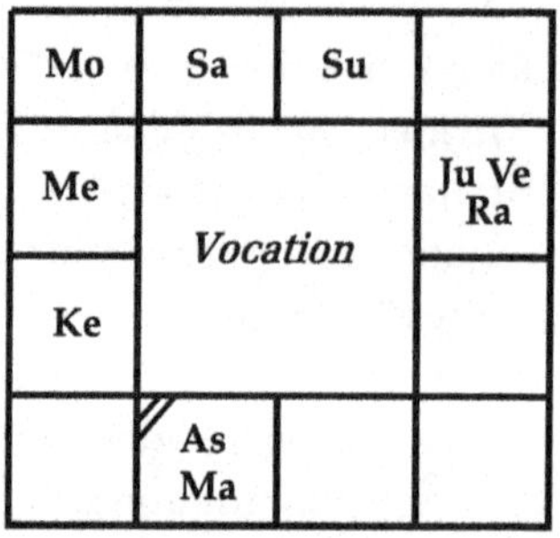

Fig. 2

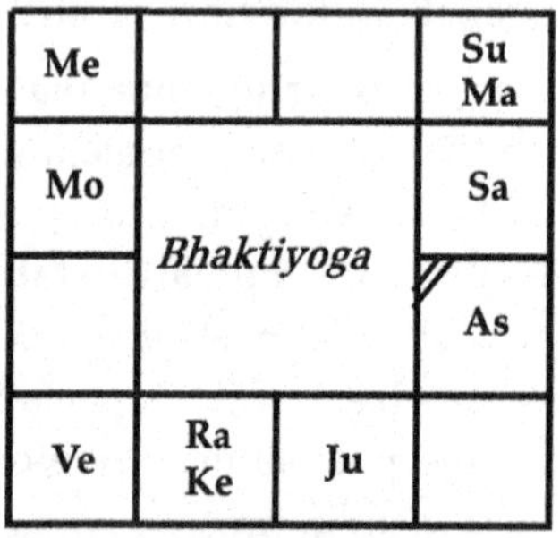

Fig. 3

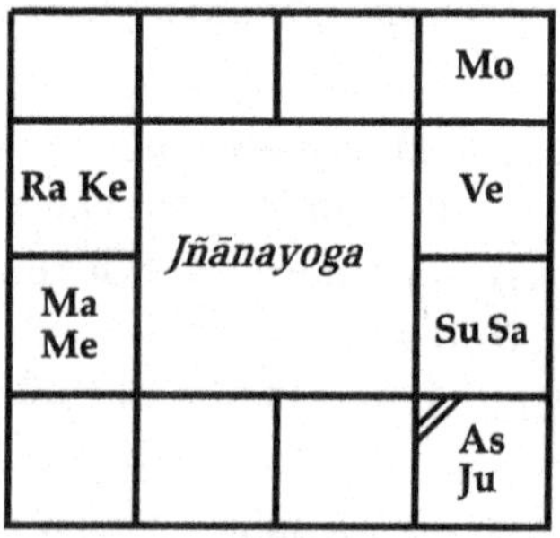

Fig. 4

Four Divisional Charts

1. Pançāṁśa (D-5) 2. Daśāṁśa (D-10)
3. Viṁśāṁśa (D-20) 4. Caturviṁśāṁśa (D-24)

The question arises as to how we should interpret the *rāśi* chart. If we remember the *Vedic* and the God-centred origins of Hindu astrology, we will naturally arrive at the spiritual interpretation given in Section 18. An interpretation of this nature is extremely important, for it gives intelligible meaning to an abstract astrological *yantra* [geometrical design], and the intelligible meaning, in turn, inspires us to continue onward with our astrological Pilgrimage.

18. The 'Mood of God at the Time and Place of Birth'

By the term horoscope, we mean the main *rāśi* chart, which gives the positions of the *Navagrahas* at the time of birth, as well as the smaller *navāṁśa* divisional chart, which is the most important of all the sixteen divisional charts. If we wish to have a richer amount of information from the horoscope, we would have to include not only the *navāṁśa* divisional chart, but all the other divisional charts as well. For a first approximation, however, the main *rāśi* chart and the *navāṁśa* divisional chart taken together are good enough as a faithful representation of the 'mood of God at the time and place of birth'.

As we have emphasized earlier, the planets do not govern our lives. Rather, the horoscope reveals the mood of God at the time and place of birth. In Section 13 of this chapter, we saw how the *Navagrahas*, the nine planets of Hindu astrology, are not merely physical planets at all, but have the higher spiritual significance of denoting 'the presence of *Īśvara* [God] in our life' in both His benefic as well as malefic aspects. This is a very important insight and will enable us to forge ahead into the unknown and mysterious depths of Hindu astrology.

Alternatively, the mood of God is what the *advaitic* Master *Śrī J. Krishnamurti* refers to as the *what is*. This is the reality we experience at each moment of our life, both the pleasant as well as the unpleasant, within our consciousness and without, in the outer life circumstances in which we find ourselves. Surrender to *what is* tantamounts to accepting the mood of God at each moment of our life with equanimity, and this naturally would preclude any desire on our part to change the present reality into something much more pleasing to the *jīvātmā* or the personal self.

There is a distinct branch of Hindu astrology called Horary astrology [*praśnaśāstra, praśna* standing for the question], in which the seeker comes to the astrologer with a certain burning question that has been afire in his consciousness and has entered into his heart. When he places this question before the astrologer, the latter, for his part, immediately draws the horoscope corresponding to that moment of time and ascertains what the mood of God at that juncture is – whether favourable or unfavourable for the fulfilment of the *jīvātmā's* desire.

Even what astrologers call transit charts and transit significant events (TSEs) portray the mood of God at the particular moment of time when the transit event is being studied. Thus, the mood of God reflected in the TSE corresponding to the *Maharṣi's Mahānirvāṇa* would indicate that the liberated *Ātmā,* or the Self, was about to drop the physical vehicle, which was necessary for coming into manifestation. Likewise, the TSE corresponding to the *Mokṣa* of the boy *Ramaṇa* at age sixteen clearly shows the high favourability in the mood of God for the descent of the blessings of *Mokṣa.* As the mood of God is the ultimate verdict and there is absolutely no force beyond it, those who can skillfully decipher this mood shall know whether God's grace – at the particular instant when the question is being taken up – is favourable for the *jīvātmā's* quest or not.

The most important lesson is seen in the inescapability of duality in the mood of God at the time and place of our birth. In fact, we may go so far as to say that much of spiritual growth consists in learning to accept and surrendering to the duality that is inherent in the mood of God at each instant of time. We know only too well that life is full of this duality; often the good and the bad, the high and the low, the right and wrong, the Divine and demonic, the sacred and profane exist side by side, thereby posing for us all the enigmatic paradoxes of life. In this context, an *advaitic* aphorism pronounced many years ago by the Master *Śrī Śrī Bhagavān* comes to mind. The aphorism urges us to turn our backs on the mundane world with an enlightened spiritual indifference and cautions us about the danger of creating *karmic* bondages, even to the so-called good and noble things in life:

Nothing is good, Nothing is bad;
Nothing is high, Nothing is low;
Nothing is right, Nothing is wrong.

In one of his own compositions, *Śrī Ramaṇa Maharṣi* has contemplated on *Aruṇācala Śiva* as the very source of this duality in life. The *advaitic* vision transcending duality is once again all too evident:

> *Oh Arunachala! As soon as Thou didst claim me, my body and soul were Thine. What else can I desire?* ***Thou art both merit and demerit, Oh my life! I cannot think of these apart from Thee.*** *Do as Thou wilt then, my beloved, but grant me only ever increasing love for Thy feet* (emphasis mine)*!* (qtd. in Sri Ramanasramam 96)

19. The Functional Benefics as Devas; Functional Malefics as Asuras

The *Vedic* Sages, who must definitely have been aware of this duality in the mood of God, must have felt the need, for this very reason, to polarize the wholeness of God into a benevolent Divine aspect and a malevolent demonic one. Thus, in Hindu astrology, for any given Asdt, the *Navagrahas*, which represent in their totality the wholeness and the completeness of God, are divided into functional benefic planets (FBs) and the functional malefic planets (FMs). The FBs serve to bring Divine grace into life and, therefore, represent the benevolent Divine aspect of God [*devas*]. The FMs, which represent the malevolent aspects of God [*asuras*], create all sorts of obstacles and sufferings in life and thus stand for the denial of God's grace or His wrath. These two groups, the FBs and the FMs, stand accordingly for *devic* and *asuric* forces respectively, and through their mutual warring conflict, portray the perplexing duality of life.

In one sense, life is a tug of war between these *devas* and the *asuras*, and spiritual life or spiritual flowering is then the challenge of integration of these *devic* and *asuric* forces, thereby transcending their duality. The function of the *devas* in this regard is to create and sustain life structures whereas the *asuras* attempt to tear down and destroy the creative work of the *devas*. By life structures we should understand an enduring and happy home life, a good marriage, healthy and happy children, prosperity, success in one's vocational work, good health, acquisition of assets and properties, creation of good and noble works, and even success in spiritual pursuits.

We must not be under the naive impression that the *devas* are good and desirable while the *asuras* are bad and undesirable. This would be too approximate and simplistic a perception, devoid of the comprehensiveness and the all-embracing nature of God.

For example, longevity in a horoscope is indicated by the strength of Sa, the *ayuṣkāraka* [significator of longevity], as well as the strength of the lord of the VIIIH. It is well known that the VIIIH denotes obstructions of all kinds; yet when the VIIIH is strong in a horoscope, there is enough blessing in the mood of God for greater longevity, and easy gains as well. Thus, the grace of God is abundant even when the FM lords or the *asuric* lords are strong in the chart. Likewise, a strong XIIH lord and a strong VIIIH lord hold the potential for *Mokṣa* in the mood of God at the time and place of birth.

20. Life Drama Decided by the Nature of Strong Planets

What we have to observe in the mood of God at the time and place of birth are the strong houses and whether these are the *Kāma, Artha, Dharma,* or *Mokṣa* houses. If the *Dharma* or *Mokṣa* lords are strong in the mood of God, then we may be reassured that the life drama will transpire dominantly in the *Dharma* or *Mokṣa* spheres of life. On the other hand, if only the *Artha* or

Kāma lords are strong, then we have to conclude that the life drama will transpire dominantly in the *Artha* and the *Kāma* spheres of life. It is in this way that the repercussions of the mood of God at the time and place of birth must be deciphered.

21. The Mansion of Life and its Various Chambers

The *rāśi* chart may be likened to a large mansion representing the totality of our life, whereas each of the sixteen divisional charts – beginning with the most important divisional chart, the *navāṁśa* or D-9 – must be understood as a detailed picture of each of the houses in the *rāśi* chart. Thus, these divisional charts may be thought of as the many chambers that exist within the mansion of our life.

As the horoscope represents the mood of God at the time and place of birth, and as this mood carries His grace as also His wrath (denial of grace), we may imagine this mood of God in the form of a large cloud, composed of intermingled luminous and dark patches, that has actually permeated and occupied the mansion of our life (represented by the *rāśi* chart). This model will give us more insights into the subtle aspects of the divisional charts. The luminous parts correspond to God's grace, while the dark patches correspond to the denial of His grace (wrath). Depending on the part of the cloud – whether luminous or dark – that enters into a particular chamber, the affairs of the house to which this chamber corresponds either flourish or suffer denial and deprivation. Thus, taking the *daśāṁśa* divisional chart (D-10) as an example, if the luminous portion of the cloud signifying the benevolent mood of God enters the chamber corresponding to this divisional chart, there is sufficient grace for success and achievements in the professional sphere. In this way, the indications of the *rāśi* chart have to be blended with those of any divisional chart in order to ascertain the final outcome of the mood of God for any given house.

The mood of God can also be more benevolent than malevolent *on the whole,* in which case the individual is more blessed and fortunate, with fewer sufferings in life. If, on the other hand, the mood of God is more malevolent than benevolent as far as success in materialistic life is concerned, then there may be great sufferings in life. In this case, it often happens that the mood of God removes the individual from the spheres of *Artha* and *Kāma* and places him or her in the spiritual spheres of *Dharma* or *Mokṣa.* This was, in fact, the case with *Śrī Ramaṇa Maharṣi.*

A successful life in the spheres of *Artha* and *Kāma* usually proceeds from a mood of God at the time and place of birth that has strong FBs. On the other hand, a spiritual life in *Dharma* or *Mokṣa* is indicated at the time of birth by a mood of God having strong *Dharma* or *Mokṣa* lords and afflictions to houses and planets pertaining to the *Artha* and *Kāma* spheres. Thus, if we know how to decipher the mood of God prevailing at the time and place of birth, we have a rough idea of the route that destiny might take in life. For the *Maharṣi,* two FMs, Sa and Ma, were very strong in the mood of God at the time of his birth. In addition, Ma was a *Mokṣakāraka,* as it ruled the VIIIH of *Mokṣa.* Both these FMs also created strong afflictions in the *Maharṣi's* chart.

22. Subjective Time and Astrological Clock Time

In the modern sciences as well as in our mundane work-a-day life, time, as the most fundamental and foremost 'independent' variable in our descriptions of nature, has legitimately been accorded an objective character. The definition of time intervals calls for the selection of events that we as human beings may observe. If we select reasonably 'impersonal' events that transpire in our so-called sensory 'external' world and that are accepted by convention to have an 'objective' character, then the definition of time that follows from such events also has a correspondingly objective character. Thus, there is only one globally synchronized objective clock time that is universally agreed upon by all nations and governments. Accordingly, individuals throughout the world follow only this one universal clock time. Of course, this objective character of time is fully consistent with there being different time zones in different countries and continents of the earth.

Such an objective definition and measurement of time is appropriate and even inevitable when we have to deal with 'objective reality' in our physical world. Here, by objective reality we should mean the circumstance of different human observers performing the same experimental observations and measurements of selected events in different parts of the world at 'different' times but always arriving at the self-same invariant and inviolable laws of nature. The perfect agreement between these different human observers insofar as their observations of these selected events in the natural world are concerned is what gives time its objective character. But let it be noted that this objective character only pertains to observations in the external objective reality of the natural world.

When we observe our individual life events on the other hand, we enter inevitably into an entirely different world, and in this subjective realm, there is no question at all of experiencing any objective reality that is common to all human observers. *In fact, this personal reality of the individual human being, which changes from moment to moment, is not even accessible to observation by other human observers.* Thus, in the sphere of our subjective world, we cannot adopt the same definition and notion of objective time that has become familiar to us through its long usage in the objective world.

As we have to live in two entirely different worlds simultaneously — in the objective world as well as in the subjective world — in which each human experiences an intimate personal reality that is entirely subjective — even though objective clock time is the same for one and all — we have the challenge of having to keep track of and time the sequential chain of individual human life events, which necessarily follow only a subjective clock time and which therefore have to vary from one individual to another.

A system of time, if it is to be useful in the study of astrology, has to meet this important requirement of being able to assign an entirely different 'value of time' and 'season of time' to different human individuals, but corresponding to the self-same given moment indicated by objective clock time. For this reason, subjective time, which must be defined by the subjective life events of an individual, has to be necessarily different in its experiential content from the objective clock time that is given to us by the modern sciences.

This distinction between objective and subjective time will become evident from the following simple consideration: When an individual A has a bereavement in the family on a certain day at a 'certain time', its impact on the individual A has to be necessarily so profound and deep that the individual A experiences this subjective life event with a feeling of great loss and consequent sorrow. If s/he has a neighbour B who was fortunate enough to receive some important recognition for professional work, let us say at the 'same time' that the bereavement occurred in the life of A, then obviously 'at the very moment' that was sorrowful and full of emotional pain for A, B should have been in high spirits, and s/he would have been full of happiness, with a sense of well-being.

Thus, even though the objective clock time was the same for both individuals A and B, when significant subjective life events occurred in their respective personal lives, that moment was experienced entirely differently by the two individuals; one became sorrowful at the very same moment when the other was happy. Thus, the subjective time associated with the flow of subjective events in each life is necessarily different in experiential quality, meaning, and impact for each individual. *Astrological time is of this subjective nature.*

To keep things simple in this illustration, we may suppose that these life events occurred at exactly the same place and at the same time in the lives of the individuals A and B. We need no better illustration than this to reach the following conclusion: If the field of individual human experience and individual human life is our domain of study, then we certainly need a system of time that has built into it, *ab initio,* the subjective nature of time, which we have brought to light through the above illustration.

The objective world of science is impersonal, while the subjective world of astrology is personal to the core. Readers familiar with Einstein's theory of relativity can have some satisfaction, and their feeling of uneasiness with regard to subjective time may diminish to some extent, when they consider that even in relativistic dynamics – an important realm of modern science – time has already undergone a subjective reorientation. Thus, when we move from the discipline of classical dynamics – one of the fundamental branches of the older Newtonian physics, in which time plays a crucial objective role in view of all motion occurring only 'in time' – to Einstein's relativistic dynamics, we find time losing its objective character and well on the way to taking on a subjective nature. Clock time in relativistic dynamics is not the same for all observers and begins to vary from one observer to another whenever one of them is moving with a uniform relativistic speed with respect to the other.

Although in this sense, time has certainly become more personalized and subjective, and even observer dependent in comparison to classical dynamics, yet it is only when we move into the highly subjective disciplines of *Vedic* and Hindu astrology that we find it absolutely mandatory, from fundamental considerations, to make time perfectly and totally subjective in nature, and not merely subjective under certain special conditions such as that of relativistic speeds in Einstein's relativistic dynamics.

23. The Cyclical Structure of Time – Viṁśottarī Daśā System

We have already encountered the most fundamental and monumental principle of Hindu astrology: the God-centred nature of *Jyotirvidya*. This principle produced the additional insight that the horoscope of an individual is nothing but the 'mood of God at the time and place of birth' — when the earthly sojourn began.

We now present the second fundamental principle of Hindu astrology, which deals with the meaning and structure of time — how this 'clock' time, the *Viṁśottarī daśā* system, accounts for the subjective nature of time in human life and experience. It will be shown to meet the conditions that not only our experiences from one moment to another in our own life are different but also that the experiences of two different human beings, even at the same place and same time, are generally found to be entirely different.

The 'clock' of this subjective astrological time for each individual is the *Viṁśottarī daśā* system of time. *Maharṣi Parāśara* in his classical work on Hindu astrology, *Bṛhat Parāśara Horā śāstra,* lays down, to our great amazement, more than thirty different systems of time that may be used for special life situations, all of which fully accommodate our demand that time be subjective in the context of Hindu astrology. These subjective systems of time coming from Hindu astrology have a beautiful cyclical structure, just as all other time periods in human life — the day and night cycle, the lunar monthly cycle, and the solar annual cycle. The *Viṁśottarī daśā-bhukti* system used by Prof. V. K. Choudhry and Pandit Vamadeva Shastri happens to be one of the most universally used systems from among the thirty or so systems of time available to Hindu astrologers. *Viṁśottarī* means a full cycle of 120 years, as this was considered to be the normal span of human life in more virtuous *yugas* [ages] in the remote past. *Daśā* means a major cycle.

To *Maharṣi Parāśara,* one of the founding fathers of this ancient system of astrology, the *Viṁśottarī daśā* system of time must have come as a revelation. Accordingly, no proof can be given that this is the appropriate system of time that gives full expression to the fact that time in Hindu astrology, being highly subjective, has to necessarily differ from one individual to another. The *Navagrahas,* the basic variables in portraying the mood of God at the time and place of birth, also occur here, giving time a *Navagraha* structure.

Daśās	*Duration in Years*
Ketu	7
Venus	20
Sun	6
Moon	10
Mars	7
Rāhu	18
Jupiter	16
Saturn	19
Mercury	17
Viṁśottarī daśā	120

The Viṁśottarī Daśās for the Navagrahas

In this *Viṁśottarī daśā* system of time, each of the above *daśās* is further sub-divided into nine disproportionate parts corresponding to the nine *Navagrahas.* Thus, for example, the Ke-Ke *daśā-bhukti,* which signifies the Ke sub-period [*bhukti,* or minor season of life] in the Ke main period [*daśā*], has a duration of 4 months and 27 days [7 x (7/120) = 49/120 years]. If we repeat this calculation for a given *daśā* and *bhukti,* we obtain the duration of that particular *daśā-bhukti.*

Śrī Ramaṇa Maharṣi was born in the Ju-Ve *daśā-bhukti* on 30 December 1879. The astrological subjective clock time by which the physical body of the *Maharṣi* aged is given by the flow of the following *daśā-bhukti* cycles in his life. Here we must note that 'time' must not have made any sense to the *Maharṣi* at all, as he was established in the timeless state while still wearing a human body, which was nevertheless subject to the ravages of time.

Daśā-bhukti	*Beginning*	*Ending*
Sa-Sa	31 May 1886	3 June 1889
Sa-Su	21 May 1896	3 May 1897
Me-*Daśā*	31 May 1905	31 May 1922
Ke-*Daśā*	31 May 1922	31 May 1929
Ve-*Daśā*	31 May 1929	31 May 1949
Su-Su	31 May 1949	17 Sept 1949
Su-Ma	19 Mar 1950	25 July 1950

The Pertinent Daśā-bhuktis

Note: Day of *Mokṣa*: July 16, 1896, in the Sa-Su sub-period; day of *Mahānirvāṇa*: April 14, 1950, in the Su-Ma sub-period.

Thus, the structure of time in VA is defined in terms of the major [*daśā*] and minor [*bhukti*] periods corresponding to the *Navagrahas*. Just as the *Navagrahas* in VA have been seen to encompass the totality of life as the various aspects of God, likewise even the 'space of time', which must also be only an aspect of the fullness of God as *Kālapuruṣa*, is assigned a *Navagraha* structure involving nine major periods or cycles, each of which is again unequally divided into nine sub-cycles or minor cycles corresponding to the *Navagrahas*.

As a consequence, the structure of time in the life of an individual can consist of anything from three to six, or even seven major cycles, with the chain of nine minor cycles within each of the major cycles. All this was the original 'movement of revelation' that must have come to *Maharṣi Parāśara*, whom we may take to be one of the illustrious founding fathers of Hindu astrology.

24. The General Significations of the Navagrahas

The general significations of the *Navagrahas* is a distinct area in Hindu astrology in which it is so obvious that astrology is entirely different from astronomy. Each of the nine *Navagrahas* represents a large number of 'life variables', which we call significations. The house significations have already been covered in a previous section pertaining to the houses, namely, Section 16. As planets rule the houses, the significations of houses automatically become the significations of planets as well, insofar as the lordship of planets over houses is concerned.

However, apart from these house significations, planets also have general significations that have nothing to do with their lordship over a particular house and that simply stand for their general characteristics. As there were four distinct goals in ancient Hindu society in which *Jyotirvidyā* developed, the planetary significations too must be understood as belonging to one or other of these four goals of life [*Puruṣārthas*].

As we have made clear earlier on, the general significations of each planet depend on how energetic that particular planet is in both the natal chart and the transit chart (see Section 18). We also saw how only the strong planets bestow God's grace in abundance, whereas weak planets might not only *delay* the onset of God's grace, there might even be a complete *denial* of this grace if the concerned planet is both weak and afflicted in the natal chart.

Thus, certainly, stronger planets bestow more desirable and bigger bounties. For this reason, remedial measures in Hindu astrology are always concerned with the challenge of raising the 'low energies' of planets in the natal chart. In general, higher significations manifest in life when planetary energies are higher, and lower significations manifest when planetary energies are lower. Thus, taking into account all these aspects, we may say many factors in confluence decide which ones among the many planetary significations actually come into manifestation.

We now consider the general significations of the *Navagrahas* so as to convey a sense of how they are responsible for shaping human personalities. If we reflect on the handful of people we have had the opportunity of knowing very well in life, we should, with the help of these general significations, be able to tell which planetary energy was dominantly driving their personality.

In enumerating the general significations of the *Navagrahas,* we are by no means attempting to provide an exhaustive list but will be more than satisfied if we create a broad general understanding of what each planet stands for in the shaping of human natures and temperaments.

General Significations of the Sun (Su)

The Su is the king in the royal cabinet of the *Navagrahas* and is a *sāttvic* and spiritual planet, denoting the *Jñāna Śakti* of the Divine Mother. The Su is the significator of the VH of creative intelligence as well as the XH of profession and authority. In addition, it is also the significator of the IH of the head and the self, as the Su is the *Ātmakāraka* or the true Self. Thus, its significations are: intelligence, Self-Realization, independence, character, honesty, integrity, will power, courage, sense of self, and people in positions of authority or our relationship with them. The Su also signifies the father, husband, and male progeny. Among the professions, it rules medicine, positions of administrative authority, and even government careers. In medical astrology, the Su rules the heart and digestion.

General Significations of the Moon (Mo)

The Mo is the queen in the royal cabinet of the *Navagrahas* and is a mutable and *sāttvic* planet, denoting the *Jñāna Śakti* of the Divine Mother, especially when it rules the IVH, VH, or IXH.

The Mo, being the planet of the Divine Mother, signifies the mother in the first instance and the wife in the second, as the Mo is the secondary significator of the wife (SA *sūtra*). It also signifies emotional expression and emotional intelligence, capacity for empathy, care and concern, understanding, flexibility in the feeling nature, memory power, kindness, compassion, capacity for sensitivity and love in relationships, easy gains in life, and capacity for public relationships. A strong Mo is an asset in relating to life and for popularity with the masses. In the SA, the Mo is the significator of the XIIH. A strong Mo bestows a strong immune system. It signifies the nursing and hospitality professions as also hoteliering, catering, moneylending, and professions centred on manufacturing foods that are sweet or derived from milk.

General Significations of Jupiter (Ju)

Ju is the *Bṛhaspati,* the teacher of the gods in the royal cabinet. It is a *sāttvic* and spiritual planet, denoting the *Jñāna Śakti* of the Divine Mother. Ju is the foremost planet of Divine grace in Hindu astrology. This importance of Ju is amply reflected in its being the significator for so many houses. In VA it is the significator of the IIH, VH, IXH, XH, and XIH. *No other planet in Hindu astrology has such an expansive role.* Ju signifies faith, Divine inspiration, sensitivity to God, *Guru,* grace, *Dharma,* spiritual teaching, intelligence and wisdom, knowledge of the *sāśtras,* love of philosophy, virtue, generosity, an innate tendency to share with others, aspirations of a noble nature, inclination to build philosophies and institutions of higher learning, and most important of all, love of higher knowledge – learning the same and teaching it to the world.

In the spheres of *Artha* and *Kāma,* Ju signifies wealth, fortune, and treasuries. In the professions, it governs advisory roles in finance, management, banks, law, jurisprudence, higher education, astrology, and vocations that are spiritual in nature. In VA, it is the *Bṛhaspati* or highest kind of teacher and can indicate a certain orthodox approach to one's religious life through the observance of ceremonies, rituals, etc. Importantly, it is the planet of abundance, and a strong Ju not afflicted in the natal chart represents considerable Divine grace in the mood of God at the time and place of birth. In terms of body organs, it rules the liver, pancreas, and the arteries.

General Significations of Saturn (Sa)

Sa is the 'servant' in the royal cabinet of the *Navagrahas* and is a *tāmasic* planet, therefore favourable for a spiritual life in the *Nivṛtti mārga* [path of renunciation or withdrawal from the world]. Because of its *tāmasic* nature, Sa carries the *Icchā Śakti* of the Divine Mother. This role of Sa gives us an insight into its intrinsic nature, which is one of wanting to serve and being helpful to others in a spirit of selflessness. A strong Sa definitely bestows not only the spirit of service mentioned above but also detachment and renunciation, which are the highest spiritual excellences on the *Nivṛtti mārga.*

A strong Sa also confers the capacity for succeeding in great missions and difficult undertakings. It bestows responsibility, a love for detailed and concentrated work, and a capacity for leadership over commoners and routine workers, who in a civil society are the counterparts of the servants in a royal cabinet. People with a strong Sa are usually fortunate with their servants.

Sa also indicates the thinker in contemplation; a strong Sa blesses one with seriousness, capacity for being responsible, duty-consciousness, austerity, discipline, and a capacity for introversion and self-examination. A malefic and afflicting Sa can create perversions and take one into the darker spheres of life. A strong Sa endowed *Śrī Ramaṇa Maharṣi* with all the spiritual virtues on the *Nivṛtti mārga,* including the virtue of celibacy.

General Significations of Mars (Ma)

Ma is the commander-in-chief of the royal cabinet of the *Navagrahas* and is therefore necessarily a *rājasic* planet, carrying the *Kriyā Śakti* as well as the *Icchā Śakti* of the Divine Mother. It thus stands for courage, a strong will, impatience, aggression in action, rationality, a tendency to be cruel, pride, arrogance, insensitivity, passion for action, lack of consideration for others, a passion for technology, love of adventurous sports, martial ventures (not through virtuous charisma but through ruthless domination), and the virtue of generosity. It is the planet of seeking and restlessness. Because of their exuberance of energy, vitality, and lack of introspection, those with a strong Ma are well known for their rash actions and head-long seeking.

While a strong Ju is known to create shortcuts in life, a strong Ma often calls for stupendous expenditure of energy in the process of achieving goals.

As it is the planet of warfare and aggression, a strong Ma always bestows vitality and a powerful entrepreneurial drive, so essential for success in the outside world. The professions arising from Ma are those of a surgeon, chemist, metallurgist, technologist, mathematician, lawyer, policeman, or scientist. In *Śrī Ramaṇa Maharṣi's* case, a strong Ma as lord of the VIIIH endowed the boy *Ramaṇa* with excellent sporting abilities and also blessed him with the highest signification of the VIIIH, which is *Mokṣa*. It was also responsible for giving him the experience of death on Tortoise Rock in 1912. After the *Maharṣi's Mokṣa*, the *rājasic* energy of Ma was not manifesting in his physical body anymore, as he was patently physically inactive. We must therefore conclude that the energy of Ma was internally transmuted into the fiery *Ātmajñāna* [fire of Self-Realization], which became his natural state of being.

General Significations of Venus (Ve)

Ve is a *rājasic* planet in the royal cabinet, and side by side with Ju has the role of teacher — but only for the *asuras*. It carries the

Icchā Śakti of the Divine Mother by virtue of its being the significator of the VIIH. Traditionally in VA, it is the significator of marriage and wife as well as comforts, luxuries, jewellery, vehicles, riches, prosperity, and other such wealth. Unlike Ju, which is a *sāttvic* and spiritual planet, Ve's significations are more tied up with the VIIH of pleasure and relationships with women. In this sense, Ve signifies a leaning towards comforts and luxuries as well as towards sensual pleasures.

On the benefic side, Ve is tied up with life-saving drugs and is the prime significator of creativity and artistic expressions such as in the fine arts, dance, drama, music, poetry, etc. It is also the significator of food and cooking. Aesthetic refinements, cultural sensitivity, appreciation of all arts, and all forms of enjoyment need a good Ve, which is also the planet of social propriety and social sensitivity. Beauty, youth, love of flowers, tenderness, precious stones and gems are the other significations of Ve. Because Ve is traditionally a teacher insofar as the professions are concerned, it signifies management of wealth, teaching, modelling, hoteliering, and vocations in art and architecture, cinema and theatre, advertizing, fashion, and luxury items. Insofar as the spiritual life is concerned, a strong Ve that is well placed can bestow great devotion and *Ānanda* [Divine bliss].

General Significations of Mercury (Me)

Me is the young prince in the royal cabinet of the *Navagrahas* and is a mutable and *rājasic* planet, carrying the *Kriyā Śakti* of the Divine Mother. A strong Me indicates a good analytical capacity and also confers a witty and humourous nature. It is the significator of education, memory, speech, and childhood. It signifies communication, trade and commerce, information and its transmission, and is a mutable planet like the Mo. A strong Me is an asset for lawyers, accountants, auditors, businessmen, astrologers, media people, teachers, mathematicians, authors, and research scholars. In terms of the body parts,

Me signifies the nervous system, skin, neck, throat, lungs, and the faculty of speech.

General Significations of Rāhu (Ra) and Ketu (Ke)

Ra and Ke, the north and south nodes of the Mo, are understood to be *karmic* significators in VA (*Astrology of the Seers* 80). In the SA, their distinct malefic significations pertaining to the spheres of *Dharma, Artha* and *Kāma* have been clearly identified by Prof. V. K. Choudhry (*Systems Approach* 76-85). In astronomy, they have been identified as important mathematical points on the Mo's orbit where it intersects the *ecliptic,* and their significance is confined to their role in causing eclipses.

Ra signifies the work we have to do in this life in accordance with *karmic* laws. Ke signifies the '*karmic* inheritances' or *saṁskāras* that have been carried forward from 'past lives' and which, in turn, manifest as the propelling energy that drives our houses and planets (Vamadeva's VA *sūtra*). What Ra impels us to do in life depends very much upon what our *saṁskāras* are, that is, the forces and influences from past lives. These *saṁskāras,* carried by Ke, might be of the auspicious kind (benefic *karma*) or of the inauspicious kind (malefic *karma*).

Generally, if these nodes are strong and unafflicting (by the criteria of the SA), and are well placed, then the interpretation is that benefic *karma* has been brought forward from past lives. If, on the other hand, the nodes are placed in the malefic houses, the VIH, VIIIH or XIIH and are afflicting or are themselves afflicted, then the interpretation is that they carry negative and malefic *karma,* which must then necessarily manifest as negative *karmic* obstacles and misfortunes. On the whole, the decipherment of the *karmic* significations held in the nodes is generally difficult on an *a priori* basis; much, however, can be learnt from actual case studies on an *a posteriori* basis.

Ra bestows energy for action as well as imagination and originality. When not spiritually yoked to the *saṁskāra* bank contained in Ke or to Ke's sobering and restraining influences, it can push us too far ahead into the material world of desires, cravings, and their satisfactions. There is an inevitable clouding of our perceptions, fear, or even depression, if the Ra's materialistic urges are not balanced and tempered by Ke's compensating influences of inhibition, doubt, withdrawal and introspection. Ke's strong influence takes us on the spiritual path but may be too constrictive for worldly success. Ra's strong influences, on the other hand, might make us prone to deception, manipulation, selfishness, fear, and greed (SA *sūtra*).

Ke, when strong, inclines us towards renunciation, self-knowledge, self-abnegation, and the pursuit of spiritual illumination. In the spheres of *Artha* and *Kāma*, Ke's impact lands us in sudden setbacks and reversals, whether this be in the professional sphere or in marital life (SA *sūtra*). Ke's aspect on Me sharpens the mind and blesses it with a spiritual perception, whereas Ke's mutual *yoga* with Ju makes for a *karmayogi* or for a vocation inspired by service.

Notice this contrast: Ra's close affliction of Ve creates a conflagration of our sensual cravings, while Ke's affliction of Ve creates excessive inhibition and a tendency to put our Venusian cravings on a fast. On the whole, the nodes – where they impact on houses or afflict the planets – represent the duality of life and make us vulnerable to losing our balance through succumbing to such extreme *karmic* forces. We may tilt either towards Ra or towards Ke, and in this way, become imbalanced by swinging to the extremes of extroversion or introversion respectively. By seeking a steady and disciplined spiritual growth, the dual influences of the nodes may be well balanced, and this in turn leads us to a middle path, which is neither too extroverted (Ra) nor too introverted (Ke).

25. Simultaneously Seeing – Four Systems of Astrological Variables

Till now, we have considered the following four sub-systems of Hindu astrology:

(i) Zodiacal signs, representing in their totality the *Kālapuruṣa,* or the unmanifest Godhead of Hindu astrology from head to foot (Sections 11, 12, 15).

(ii) The twelve houses, encompassing the totality of life as the manifestation of the three energies of the Divine Mother (Sections 14, 16).

(iii) The *Navagrahas,* representing the presence of the nine aspects of *Īśvara,* benevolent as well as malevolent (Sections 13, 19, 20, and 24).

(iv) Subjective clock time [*Viṁśottarī daśā* system], with the *Navagraha* cyclical structure assigned to each individual so as to facilitate a profound philosophical understanding of time in human affairs (Sections 22, 23).

In essence, these are the four major tools of Hindu astrology, which may be considered as sub-systems of the comprehensive system of astrology. Whether the astrologer is looking at the horoscope, which pertains to birth time, or at some other transit chart pertaining to some other time, s/he has to employ the astrological skill of simultaneouly seeing all the dynamic variables in the four sub-systems all at once and arrive at a verdict as to what the mood of God has to offer corresponding to that chosen time.

Now that we have acquainted ourselves with these sophisticated tools and methods of the Hindu Sages, we may, in the following chapter, take a direct plunge into the life and *Mokṣa* of *Śrī Ramaṇa Maharṣi.* Therein, we shall sober ourselves with a Hindu astrological understanding of *Mokṣa* in the life of this great Sage, through a devotional yearning for the same.

CHAPTER IV

A Hindu Astrological Pilgrimage into the Life and Mokṣa of Śrī Ramaṇa Maharṣi

In this latter half of the Pilgrimage, we seek to understand the profound nature and structure of the *Maharṣi's Mokṣa* or Liberation from the point of view of the powerful predictive tools, insights, and wisdom of Hindu astrology.

1. The Maharṣi's Place in Sanātana Dharma

The *Maharṣi's* place in the annals of *Sanātana Dharma* is best described in the words of one of his earliest biographers, Prof. K. Swaminathan:

> *Ramana Maharshi belongs to the line of seers, beginning with the Upanishadic masters and including Buddha and Sankara, who taught by precept and example jnana marga or the path of knowledge. After Sankara (788-820 CE) the Maharshi is the most outstanding representative of this path.* (3)

We might add to this truth by clarifying that the *Maharṣi,* in contrast to the *Buddha* and *Ādi Śaṅkara,* was no founder of any religion, nor did he even aspire to change the world as great spiritual visionaries and *Avatārs* have sought to do throughout human history. One way to understand his radically different approach to the spiritual well-being of humanity is through our clear recognition that the *Maharṣi,* on account of his *advaitic* Realization, was in no position to see the world as 'imperfect and therefore needing improvement' as compassionate world teachers and *Avatārs* have throughout history. In fact, he found the world to be already immaculate in its perfection. His was the vision of the timeless transcendent God of the Hindu world, *Śiva* Himself.

For the *Maharṣi* to have had a destiny like that of the *Buddha* or *Ādi Śaṅkara* as the founder of an epoch-making spiritual mission and as the active giver of new life to *Sanātana Dharma* even in the *Pravṛtti* [involvement in the world through action and achievement] spheres of life, the Divine Mother's *Śaktis* in his life should have acted entirely differently. There should have been strong benefic planets in *Dharma* houses, and the strong planets conferring *Jñāna Śakti* should have been placed strongly in the angular houses. Such a horoscope would have placed the *Maharṣi* actively on the stage of the world. However, as we shall see more clearly in the following sections, such a *Dharmasaṁsthāpana* [re-establishment of *Dharma* after it has succumbed to an inevitable collapse in the last phase of a great world cycle] was not the *saṁkalpa* of *Aruṇācala Śiva,* whose purpose was entirely different in His coming as *Śrī Ramaṇa Maharṣi.*

2. The Jīvātmā in Hindu Society

Even for readers who are no strangers to Hindu astrology and who, for this very reason, might contemplate beginning directly with Chapter IV, I would like to suggest that it might be helpful for them to take a look at both Chapter I and Sections 1 and 2 of Chapter II before they actually venture further. These sections offer an acquaintance with the *jīvātmā* [the personal self], and as the whole question of *Mokṣa* itself revolves around the dissolution of the personal self, those earlier sections provide the warming up, necessary for this chapter. Moreover, as one cannot speak of *Mokṣa* in the Hindu spiritual tradition without invoking the beloved Masters, this necessitated my dwelling on the sources of my spiritual inspiration — the four beloved Masters — in Chapter I.

In this infinite symphony that *Īśvara,* the supreme controller, is orchestrating, there is really nothing that belongs to us as individuals and that we may consider to be inalienably our own. Thus, all that we call 'mine' is only for a while, and in due course, it passes away, even as our own bodies pass away into the dust. Like 'mine', the sense of a personal self — the 'me' — is equally transitory. This is so as we ourselves, and even life, are only fleeting affairs, and moreover, all things belong only to *Īśvara,* the supreme controller.

Yet, in spite of such an all-round conspiracy against the 'me and the mine' implanted by the supreme controller in every bit of His creation, when we turn our spiritual attention to our daily life, wherever we happen to look, we find only one universal pattern: all of us busily engaged in every kind of frantic effort at sustaining and strengthening the 'me and the mine'! This strengthening is done in both subtle as well as in gross ways. Here, then, is a paradox and contradiction between the will of *Īśvara,* operating in the form of that conspiracy against the very existence of the 'me and the mine' on the one hand, and humans on the other, struggling to uphold and strengthen this 'me and the mine'.

3. God Gaṇeśa and His Curious Vāhana – the Mouse

There is a curious mythic symbol very dear to Hindus, which we may now invoke in order to throw more light on the place of the personal self (me and the mine) in Hindu society. The mouse is a consummate craftsman where survival skills are concerned, having the God-given rhythm of surfacing only at night after the entire household has gone to sleep, getting at its food by using its sharp teeth to cut through any obstacles, and finally hoarding its accumulations!

This is exactly what even the most docile and *sāttvic jīvātmā* [the personal self that has surrendered and attuned itself to God] as the 'me and the mine' does for its own survival! Thus, the Hindu Sages could not have picked a more appropriate mythic symbol for the *vāhana* [vehicle] of our God *Gaṇeśa,* as it is upon the back of this ridiculously puny and self-centred but nevertheless gentle and docile mouse that the auspicious presence of the 'I AM', as the witness, is stationed in *Īśvara's* scheme of creation! The mouse as the *vāhana* of God *Gaṇeśa* represents the personal self that has surrendered to God, but significantly, even this surrendered *jīvātmā* is not entirely free of its self-centredness and its innate tendency to be self-protective in all its survival endeavours!

Lord Gaṇeśa

The Hindu mythic form of the witness consciousness of the I AM (*Gaṇeśa*), the first born of *Śiva,* is seen in the figure above, riding on his *vāhana* [vehicle], the mouse. *Gaṇeśa* corresponds to the auspicious planetary energy of a benefic Jupiter, and therefore, naturally has the Divine power (*Jñāna Śakti*) to overcome all obstacles in life. For this reason, He is considered to be the patron God of Hindu astrology.

Clearly, wisdom is needed to distinguish between the personal self, rooted in the taint of the *asmitā* [I-am-ness] and represented by the mouse, and the Divinity of *Gaṇeśa,* who, as the witness of the I AM, rides upon this swiftly and cunningly moving mouse. We shall return to God *Gaṇeśa* and His mouse after noting what the *Yogasūtras* have to say about the *asmitā.*

Patañjali's Yogasūtras (*sūtra* II. 6) throw important light on how the seat and support of individual selfhood, the *asmitā,* is formed in the first place. As the *Yogasūtras* are among the authoritative *Mokṣaśāstras* of the Hindu world, I invoke them to gain a clearer perspective into the *asmitā* as well as into *Mokṣa.*

> *Asmitā is the identity or blending together, as it were, of the power of consciousness (Puruṣa) with the power of cognition (Buddhi).* (qtd. in Taimni 142)

The commentator Taimni clarifies further:

> *The Saṁskṛta word Asmitā is derived from Asmi which means literally 'I am'. 'I am' represents the pure awareness of Self-existence and is therefore the expression or Bhāva, as it is called, of pure consciousness or the Puruṣa. When the pure consciousness gets involved in matter and owing to the power of Māyā, knowledge of its Real nature is lost, the pure 'I am' changes into 'I am this' where 'this' may be the subtlest vehicle through which it is working, or the grossest vehicle, namely the physical body.* (143)

One of the important lessons for us in this Pilgrimage is the realization that for *Mokṣa* to come to pass, even the auspicious root of the taint of individuality, namely, the witness consciousness of I AM, must finally go; it is this realization that manifests as the Hindu ritual of immersing our beloved God *Gaṇeśa* annually in the waters, whereupon *Gaṇeśa* dissolves and disappears into the world of the *pañcabhūtas* [the five primordial elements: earth, water, fire, air, and ethereal space].

Patañjali's sūtra I. 51 reiterates this same truth:

> *With the cessation [of identifying with] even this last impression ['I am'] all [others] having been restrained, there results the seedless 'nirbīja' cognitive samādhi.* (qtd. in Govindan 61)

The *yogi* Marshall Govindan gives us a particularly appropriate image for understanding the final dissolution of the witness consciousness I AM:

> *Like the proverbial stick, which is used to poke the fire and is at last itself cast into the fire, even the last impression 'I am', used to detach the Self from identification with objects (prakriti) of consciousness, is detached from. What remains is effulgent Self awareness, independent of all. There is no more division between the knower and the known, not even the feeling of 'I have realized God', no more birth nor death.* (61)

Fortunate are those few who have ceased to be the 'mouse' in life but have been blessed enough in having their being, for the most part, in the witness consciousness of the I AM, which is the true aspect of *Gaṇeśa*. They will find that sometimes miracles happen in their lives by their simple and innocent wishing, and such people do not have the pressing urgency to worship their external God with the ulterior motive of seeking the fulfilment of some desire. Instead, they turn to God only out of a genuine devotion from their state of innocence, as they have taken their abode with *Gaṇeśa,* the God of being.

Being thus poised in the state of the witness consciousness of I AM is a preliminary step, which can possibly lead us to the final goal of *Mokṣa,* provided, of course, that other factors also become favourable for us. This point has also repeatedly been emphasized by the *advaitic* Master *Śrī Nisargadatta Maharaj.*

At least in ancient Hindu society, the subtle dynamic tension between the will of *Īśvara,* the supreme controller, and the personal self to choose what it pleases resolved itself naturally, and settled down to a state of dynamic equilibrium, so to speak. In that society, in the spheres of *Artha* [achievement of vocational goals] and *Kāma* [an aesthetic enjoyment of all aspects of life, desire fulfilment, and pleasure seeking], we were allowed to retain our sense of the 'me and the mine' (the mouse 'ruling'); in the higher spiritual spheres of *Dharma* and *Mokṣa,* the Divine will of *Īśvara* was to prevail and take precedence (*Gaṇeśa* 'ruling'), for which we often prepared ourselves through spontaneous devotion and surrender, with our spiritual maturity in these higher spheres even giving us the urge to renounce the me and the mine (the mouse) at the Lotus Feet of God.

In passing, we may note the wisdom of the ancient Hindus in associating only the mouse and not the more aggressive rat with *Gaṇeśa.* Through its innate gentleness, it is the mouse (the self that has mellowed and humbled itself) rather than the more aggressively disposed rat that qualifies to serve *Gaṇeśa* through its surrender. There is another cryptic truth in assigning the mouse to be the *vāhana* of *Gaṇeśa*: so long as the blessings of *Mokṣa* have not descended, *Gaṇeśa* is paradoxically at the mercy of the mouse, for it is within the power of the mouse to hijack *Gaṇeśa* in the process of fulfilling its own desires. Put differently, the witness consciousness is inherently inaccessible, and unstable even when it becomes accessible, on account of individuality still being present.

The material world pertains to the spheres of *Artha* and *Kāma* [achievement and enjoyment], and it is more or less taken for granted that in these spheres life goes on very much along the lines of sustaining and strengthening the me and the mine. In the higher spiritual spheres of *Dharma* and even more so in the highest sphere of *Mokṣa,* the me and the mine do not carry any 'respectability', and *Mokṣa* itself may be best viewed as nothing but the loss of this entire mechanism of the personal self, whose active organs and instruments are the me and the mine.

Again, in the material spheres of *Artha* and *Kāma,* to speak of getting rid of the me and the mine is to injure and insult the personal self, which *veṣa* we have mistakenly taken to be our true identity, when, in fact, our true identity is something entirely auspicious and infinitely greater, as pointed out time and again by the *Maharṣi* in his *upadeśa* [spiritual teaching] to the world.

> *When the mind turns inward seeking 'who am I?' and merges in the Heart, then the 'I' hangs down the head in shame and the One 'I' appears as itself. Though it appears 'I-I', it is not the ego. It is Reality, Perfection, the Substance of the Self.* (qtd. in Sri Ramanasramam 119)

In these worldly spheres, it is therefore taboo to bring up the whole question of losing the self or losing the entire mechanism of the ego. On the other hand, in the higher spiritual spheres and in the highest sphere of *Mokṣa,* the goal itself is to be rid of the activities of the ego. In these higher spheres, this 'loss' is the one thing that all true spiritual seekers hanker after and travel to the ends of the earth in the hope of coming upon!

The strange thing is that the boy *Ramaṇa* did not hanker after *Mokṣa,* the highest spiritual *prasāda* [grace] in human life. It came to him quite uninvited and unexpectedly, when he did not even have any spiritual *sādhana* [austerities and practices] to his credit to deserve this ultimate blessing! Since the 'personal self' has always acted as a divider, separating us from the 'other' and the world, its 'loss' cannot be anything but a final homecoming to the blissful state of oneness with the ocean of the universal consciousness of *Īśvara.*

This work is an astrological understanding of how the boy *Ramaṇa,* through the grace of *Aruṇācala Śiva,* came to lose the mechanism of the personal self, a mechanism that nevertheless has constituted the implicit bedrock of all civilized societies, past and present.

The *Maharṣi* has articulated this truth – of the loss of the personal self – in one of the stanzas (62) of the Marital Garland of Letters:

> *Hast Thou not bartered cunningly Thyself for me (for my individuality is lost)? Oh, Thou art death to me, Oh Arunachala!* (qtd. in Sri Ramanasramam 90)

4. The Systems Approach to Hindu Astrology

A number of new insights into Hindu astrology as well as its basic principles have been provided in Chapter III so that the reader has no reason to feel ill at ease when taking up this chapter. Also, the principles of Hindu astrology have been cast in such a form that they are not only thought provoking but also of inspirational and philosophical value; in this way, they give us the much needed impetus to get on with the Pilgrimage.

The reader should not, of course, imagine that Chapter III alone confers upon us a mastery over all the necessary astrological skills. Such a mastery only comes slowly when the principles are thoroughly understood and applied to hundreds of different situations. Thus, Chapter III only aims at making us comfortable with Hindu astrology. Those who are familiar with philosophy are likely to be more pleased, as wisdom and insights into life are very important fruits of Hindu astrology. If spiritual seekers find this astrological Pilgrimage rewarding in helping them learn about themselves and others, and if readers with astrological knowledge are inspired by the life and Self-Realization of the *Maharṣi* – as understood here in astrological terms – I would be more than satisfied.

As we delve into the horoscope of the *Maharṣi* from the point of view of Prof. V. K. Choudhry's Systems Approach to Hindu astrology (SA) and Pandit Vamadeva Shastri's *Vedic* astrology

(VA) we shall find, to our satisfaction, that the chart begins to reveal all the spiritual mysteries and excellences as well as the details of the *Maharṣi's* life, almost facet by facet. For the present, however, we shall confine our attention only to the many aspects of Self-Realization [*Mokṣa*] of the *Maharṣi,* approaching the same from one or both of these astrological systems depending upon which aspect of *Mokṣa* we actually happen to be looking at.

The Systems Approach was originally developed in an attempt to weed out all the inner contradictions and inconsistencies in Hindu astrology but as specifically applied to the material spheres of *Artha* and *Kāma,* in which spheres much of the modern world finds itself engrossed.

In the present study however, although we essentially use the SA for:

(i) Its simplicity, astrological insights and clarity.
(ii) Its strong emphasis on the importance of the Most Effective Point (MEP) of the Ascendant (Asdt).
(iii) Its analytical clarity into the functional nature of planets, delineating the FBs and FMs.
(iv) Its predictive precision and analytical clarity into transit significant events (TSEs).

The domain of our study is certainly not *Artha* and *Kāma,* but rather, the spiritual spheres of *Dharma* and *Mokṣa.*

It is in the latter spiritual spheres that the astrological insights of *Vedic* astrology become illuminating. This latter System of VA was specifically designed for the spiritual spheres of *Dharma* and *Mokṣa,* and by blending both the SA and the VA judiciously, we attempt to show to what extent a Hindu astrological enquiry might give us profound insights and a deeper understanding into the *Maharṣi's* life in the spheres of *Dharma* and *Mokṣa.*

Śrī Ramaṇa Maharṣi's horoscope has a Virgo Asdt, and it will be good for us to remember that as the signs Virgo, Scorpio, and Pisces are the *duhsthānas* in the natural zodiac, all three of them are expected to be difficult Asdts insofar as success in worldly life is concerned. In particular, a Virgo Asdt, by virtue of having five FMs, offers greater scope for the destruction of life structures to exceed the creation and sustenance of those structures. We familiarized ourselves with these contrary roles of the FMs and the FBs in Section 19 of Chapter III. Turning now to the SA, the *Navagrahas* have the following functional nature for a Virgo Asdt:

(i) Sa, which is the lord of the VIH, is considered to be an FM, (and not neutral as in VA).

(ii) Ju and the Mo ruling the IVH and the XIH respectively are considered to be FBs (and not FMs as in VA).

(iii) The Su ruling the XIIH is again considered to be an FM (and not neutral as in VA).

(iv) However, Ma ruling the VIIIH is considered to be the most malefic planet (MMP) and an FM (as in VA).

(v) Me and Ve ruling the benefic IH and IIH respectively are naturally considered FBs (as in VA).

This is in line with our expectation, that two different systems of Hindu astrology, would generally have entirely different functional natures for the *Navagrahas*.

In the SA, as all the lords of the malefic houses are FMs provided the malefic houses have an MTS, it follows that for the Virgo Asdt, the FMs are five in number: Sa, Ma, Su, Ra, and Ke. In our analysis, we shall adopt the SA scheme for the functional nature of planets but shall also be receptive to certain valuable insights from VA regarding significators of 'impulsive egoism', etc. In VA, it must be noted that the lords of the *Kāma* Hs (IIIH and XIH) in addition to the VI lord, are considered malefic (*Astrology of the Seers* 164). When two such malefic lords form a close *yoga,* they might boost the motivation for outer achievement but have the potential for unleashing a highly malefic force of 'impulsive egoism', as in the illustrative case of Adolf Hitler (*Astrology of the Seers* 274).

5. A Fleeting Glimpse of the Maharṣi

The highest fulfilment of *Mokṣa* came about for a few of the *Maharṣi's* devotees who had undertaken the prescribed *sādhana* [spiritual practice] of *Ātmavicāra* – but only through the *Maharṣi's* grace, even as it was only through the grace of *Aruṇācala Śiva* that he himself secured the blessings of *Mokṣa* consequent to such an expeditious enquiry driven by a great sense of urgency. We see the *Maharṣi* acknowledging the Divine source of his *Mokṣa* quite clearly, in the following passage:

> *The moment Thou didst welcome me, didst enter into me and grant me Thy divine life,* ***I lost my individuality,*** *Oh Arunachala* (emphasis mine)! (qtd. in Sri Ramanasramam 93)

As the essence of the *Maharṣi's* life was his Self-Realization, which lies far far beyond the dominion of intellectual understanding, we should be sceptical of an intellectual enquiry being by itself adequate for the purpose of revealing the Self; for as our study shows, even in the case of the boy *Ramaṇa,* Divine grace from *Aruṇācala Śiva* flowing through the planet Jupiter actually 'conducted him by the hand', so to speak, through the whole process of *Ātmavicāra.* It is therefore not difficult to see that such a circumstance is entirely different from human beings volitionally undertaking such an *Ātmavicāra* without any awareness of the dimension of Divine grace that lies beyond them. Put simply, the time of Divine grace favourable for such a *sādhana* has actually to arrive for the whole process of the *Ātmavicāra* to bountifully fructify.

Thus, a certain scepticism of the efficacy of intellectual enquiry *per se* is very much present as a self-evident, implicit precondition in the *Maharṣi's* encouragement to us to undertake *Ātmavicāra.*

It was also for this very reason that the *Maharṣi* was given to very little verbal communication as a general approach to life. On the other hand, it was only through his silence that he was able to effectively convey the truth of his ineffable Self-Realization to the world at large. The Divine Mother's *Kriyā Śakti* ruling the IIH of speech was weak, and moreover, Me, the vehicle for this *Kriyā Śakti* and the significator of the IIH of speech, was also weak and afflicted; this manifested in the *Maharṣi's* life as his spontaneous *mouna*.

6. The Body is Necessary for Obtaining an X-ray Picture

One of the fruits of Hindu astrology is the decipherment of the mystery of destiny underlying each unique human life. The horoscope, in fact, throws light on who that particular individual could possibly be, what the probable branches of his or her destiny could be, and how *Jñāna Śakti, Kriyā Śakti* and *Icchā Śakti* operate and manifest in his or her life — taking certain definite trajectories through the various spheres of life.

Insofar as the true identity of the individual is concerned, in the sense in which the *Maharṣi* had meant, we may be gratified to know that there is a provision in Hindu astrology that the Su in an individual's chart, as also the lord of the IVH, signifies the *Ātmā* or the *Paramātmā,* which is the original state of Pure Consciousness (Awareness) into which we automatically pass once we have secured the blessings of *Mokṣa.* But this is only a mere potentiality, which the Su and the lord of the IVH as the general significators of the *Ātmā* hold. If this potentiality is activated concomitant to other factors, then the individual becomes fortunate in being able to receive the blessings of *Mokṣa.* If not, as in the vast majority of cases, the potentiality remains without any fructification as nothing more than a bud, perishing at the end of that human life without ever coming to flower.

Hindu astrology, apart from making such a provision for realizing the deepest identity of the Self, also interestingly throws light on the possible structure of inner and outer destiny for individuals — whether the grace of God propels them into the material spheres of *Artha* and *Kāma* or hurls them into the spiritual spheres of *Dharma* and *Mokṣa.* What actually happens thereafter to them on their pilgrimage in these spheres is what is unveiled in the horoscope.

In such a decipherment, we must not be under the grossly mistaken impression that the horoscope in and of itself (i.e., without reference to any life data) is capable of bringing the mystery of each human destiny fully into relief. It is only when aided and supplemented by the vital information of the actual human life that the astrological decipherment can proceed to the full limits of its deductive clarity and maturity; even as only when a body is actually brought and placed in the path of the X-ray beam that an X-ray picture of the human body becomes a feasibility. In this sense, biographical essentials of the individual's life are necessary ingredients for astrological decipherment, at least up to a certain critical threshold. Therefore, the *Maharṣi's* chart, in the light of his biographical details, must help us understand who he was — both in terms of his inner as well as his outer destiny — and what the purpose of his coming into this world was from the point of the view of the cultural and spiritual evolution of the species.

Another significant question for us would be what insights and wisdom Hindu astrology could give us into his life and Self-Realization over and above what a good biography can provide. The answer to this question has, of course, just been fleetingly glimpsed, for if we may compare a richly fleshed out biography to the human body in the above analogy, then the X-ray picture of the body would correspond to the astrological insights and decipherment of the destiny of that human life. Thus, just as the hidden skeletal structure supporting the body is brought into striking relief in the X-ray picture, the deeply chiselled contours and furrows of destiny on the terrain of life can be brought into striking relief through astrological *sutrās,* provided, of course, adequate information about that life is known and utilized in the astrological analysis.

If we wish to make our Pilgrimage more fruitful and interesting, we must not succumb to the temptation of wanting to be secure in our exploration by adhering exclusively to an insular, one-track approach of astrological analysis to the exclusion of every other significant spiritual and historical light. Moreover, a one-track astrological approach would be quite dry, couched as it would be in the entirely abstract and symbolic language of astrology, comprehensible only to astrological savants.

For these reasons, we must first of all embed our analysis in the proper historical and cultural context, for it is against the background of this socio-historical matrix that the astrological light can be so much more illuminating. Having adduced support for our line of approach, we now delve into this socio-historical matrix, from which cradle the *Maharṣi* emerged into the fullness of his spiritual illumination.

7. Socio-Historical Context of the Maharṣi

The *Maharṣi* was a contemporary of both *Mahātmā Gandhi* as well as *Śrī Aurobindo.* We might remind ourselves that the latter was a multi-faceted personality: a *karmayogi, Vedic* Seer, and patriot all at once. We need have no hesitation in according to the *Maharṣi* the highest exalted position of having been an *Avatār,* which even *Mahātmā Gandhi* and *Śrī Aurobindo* were, although in their respective spheres, which were entirely different from that of the *Maharṣi.*

Historically, his was an age when the British Raj was steadily approaching its twilight hour, and the whole land was plunged into the tumult of the freedom struggle in its successive unfolding phases. The attention of a struggling India in those times was turned particularly outward. *Mahātmā Gandhi* was the godly *Avatār* who gave meaning and direction to this national struggle, while *Śrī Aurobindo,* though profoundly committed to the cause of a new emerging India, was nonetheless not in the vanguard of this struggle any longer, as he had already made the very deliberate choice of retreating into the spiritual spheres of *Dharma* and *Mokṣa.*

However, insofar as the *Maharṣi* was concerned, India's freedom was not the mission for which *Aruṇācala Śiva* entered him when he was just about sixteen. He was – by Divine dispensation – to attract the attention of the world towards the attainment of the highest human goal of *Mokṣa,* of which he was verily an embodiment. This was his specific mission, judging by his 'balance sheet' at the end of his life.

He could not swerve one inch from his focal point of being established in the Self, for *Mokṣa,* though yoking him with the Self, by its very nature of *Kaivalya* had also placed him in the highest state of solidarity and oneness with the whole of the human family and the created world. The *Maharṣi's* viewpoint and apparent spiritual indifference to the political turmoil of his times and to the tragedy of a subjugated India can only be understood by *Jīvanmuktas* or *Mumukṣus.* The nearly exact influence of Sa, the *Nivṛtti* planet of austerity, seriousness, aloneness, and renunciation, was behind the *Maharṣi's* inability to be drawn into the world, however exciting and inviting it might have been. To all else, for whom the physical plane is all that there is in human life, the *Maharṣi's* indifference would have remained utterly bewildering.

8. Basic Features of the Horoscope

We shall linger here, just for a brief moment, to take note of a certain remarkable coincidence concerning the *Maharṣi's* place of birth. As we will soon discover, the life of the *Maharṣi,* being in many ways the real story of the unmanifest *Aruṇācala Śiva* Himself – but in the sphere of manifestation – the appropriateness of Tiruchuzhi as his birthplace is of great note.

Tiruchuzhi in Tamil means the 'sacred nothingness', which in the Tamil *Śaiva sampradāya* [*Śaivite* tradition], cannot refer to anything but the state of *Śiva* prior to the commencement of His creation and His dance. As this prior state is what the *advaita vedāntins* call *Parabrahma* and the *śaivites* call *Paramaśiva,* and since it was this blessed destination that *Ramaṇa* was fated to reach through the blessing of *Mokṣa,* a more apt name for his place of birth is difficult to imagine. The presiding Deity in Tiruchuzhi, *Śiva* Himself, was known as *Bhūminātha* [Tirumeninathar, in Tamil].

(i) Date of Birth (DOB) = December 30, 1879

(ii) Given Time of Birth (TOB) = 1:00 a.m.

(iii) Rectified TOB = 12:19 a.m.

(iv) Given Place of Birth (POB) = Tiruchuzhi (78°E 17′; 9°N 25′) (about 38 miles from the southern city of Madurai in Tamil Nadu, India)

(v) Time Zone = - 05:21 Hours LMT

These birth details indicate a Virgo Asdt with the Most Effective Point (MEP) at 18° 37′ in the *Hasta nakṣatra* and with the natal Mo in the *janmanakṣatra Punarvasu.* All known aspects of the *Maharṣi's* life and personality traits had to be taken into account in arriving at this rectified TOB (see birth charts in Section 17, Chapter III and Table of *Daśā-bhuktis* in Section 23).

9. Virgo Ascendant Holds a Potential for Jñānayoga and Advaitic Realization

In Hindu astrology, we know that the zodiacal sign underlying each Ascendant (Asdt) has a number of primordial characteristics, which the detailed configuration of the *Navagrahas* in a given horoscope with that Asdt can bring into manifestation in the life of that individual (Section 11, Chapter III). The Virgo Asdt, in the system of VA, has the primordial characteristic of being favourable for *Jñānayoga* and *advaitic* Realization coming to flower in the life of an individual. Other primordial characteristics of the Virgo Asdt pertinent to our analysis of the *Maharṣi's* chart will also be examined once we gain an understanding of the potential for *Jñānayoga* and *advaitic* Realization.

The ground for such spiritual potentials being present in the Virgo Asdt is the following: The foremost planet of Divine grace, Ju, the *Anugrahakāraka* [giver of grace] and significator of the IXH of God and grace, rules the IVH of the *Ātmā* or God in the SA. Under these conditions, we may expect Ju to function as an *Anugrahakāraka par excellence,* that is, as the bringer of the highest blessings, especially for *Dharma* and *Mokṣa.*

In VA, the IXH is the house of God, whereas the IVH is the house of the Self or the *Ātmā.* When an individual has an experience of God-Realization, s/he perceives the Divine in the 'other', rather than in the 'self'. With Self-Realized Sages on the other hand, Divinity is perceived primarily in the Self and not in the 'other'. An *advaitic* Realization is one that creates the perception that the Self alone exists everywhere as a continuum; in this state, there is no question whatsoever of the 'other' being accommodated, as plurality has no place in such an *advaitic* perception.

The IXH lord, Ju, tantamounts to being 'God', and is the source of Divine grace. In a horoscope with a strong Ju, grace is perceived by the individual as coming from a Divine source unless Ju comes to rule the IVH, in which case alone Divine grace is perceived to come from the 'Self'. Thus, for the Virgo Asdt, as the 'internalization of God' has taken place, the grounds necessary for an *advaitic* Realization are readily available.

Ju ruling the IVH is in itself a rather insufficient condition. When this condition is fulfilled, as in the case of Virgo Asdts, we are left with two options: the individual either might enter into an *Ahaṁ Brahmāsmi* kind of Realization, as in the case of *Śrī Shirdi Sai Baba,* or the individual might recede behind the sphere of manifestation (namely, *Brahman)* and come to rest in the timeless transcendental source of *Parabrahma,* as in the case of *Śrī Ramaṇa Maharṣi.* Both cases may be deemed *advaita Vedantic,* while *Śrī Ramaṇa Maharṣi* must be deemed to have settled in the highest state of *advaitic* Realization — one in which *Śakti* has no more scope for her *līlā* [Divine play] and *māyā*.

Moreover, as the Su is the most 'massive' of the *Navagrahas*, the magnitude of renunciation and self-effacement that the Su is capable of bestowing for a Virgo Asdt by virtue of ruling the XIIH is also proportionately massive. The Su's lordship of the XIIH for such of those Virgo Asdts who have entered the *Nivṛtti mārga* also indicates that their souls have a massive longing for renunciation and spiritual solitude or *antarmukha* through a massive self-abnegation. For these reasons, we may consider the Virgo Asdt to definitely have some decided advantages to suit the *Maharṣi's* spiritual purpose, which certainly falls in the *Nivṛtti mārga*.

10. SA Sūtras on Afflictions as Blessings in Disguise for the Spiritual Life

In the SA, the strengths of the functional benefics (FBs) and the functional malefics (FMs) are assessed first in accordance with the SA criteria of strengths; the 'afflictions' are studied next, as they pave the way for all sorts of misfortunes and sufferings in life. As a general rule in the SA, strong planets give the grace of God more abundantly in the spheres of the houses over which they rule; weak planets *delay* the fructification of expected results; additionally, if the afflictions to weak planets are severe, then the *delay* might well ripen into a permanent *denial* — unless remedial measures are resorted to (Prof. Choudhry).

While in the mundane spheres of *Artha* and *Kāma*, the SA has established that strong planets are essential for a successful life; for a spiritual life in the spheres of *Dharma* and *Mokṣa* 'success' of the individual is not quite the same thing. For, the very climax of spiritual life is in the losing of the self with its well-known activities executed through its instruments of the me and the mine. However, the emphasis placed by the SA on strong planets must be still taken seriously, even in the spiritual spheres of *Dharma* and *Mokṣa*.

We shall now take a closer look at the radical shift in the very definition of success in the spheres of *Artha* and *Kāma* on the one hand and in the spheres of *Dharma* and *Mokṣa* on the other. In the former spheres, success may be equated with the acquisition of wealth and name (*Artha*) and the grace to enjoy a happy married life with progeny (*Kāma*). The SA tells us that strong planets ruling the *Artha* and *Kāma* houses ensure this success, provided that afflictions to the *Artha* and/or *Kāma* houses do not deny grace in these spheres.

However, when we come to the spiritual spheres of *Dharma* and *Mokṣa,* success is defined in an entirely different way. Here, capacity for devotion (*Bhakti*), capacity for philosophical understanding and wisdom in life (*Jñāna*), and the capacity to be detached from the world (*Vairāgya*), as well as the absence of craving for wealth, name, pleasure, and family life are the spiritual virtues that ensure success.

The mood of God at the time and place of birth must thus be such that all the above-mentioned spiritual virtues are granted *ab initio*. Usually, afflicted II and IV houses deny family life and wealth, while an afflicted VIIH denies marital life and conjugal happiness. If the spiritual planets, the Su and Ju, are strong in the mood of God at the time and place of birth, and/or one or more of the *Dharma* and *Mokṣa* houses are strong, and/or the D-9 chart is strong, then we may say that success in the spiritual spheres is vouchsafed by the mood of God at the time and place of birth. It will be good to hold in the mind this new definition of success for the spiritual life.

Thus, eventually, whether the *jīvātmā* [the personal self] is crowned with worldly success or not — in the eyes of the world and in its own eyes — cannot be reckoned to be the question of burning importance in the spiritual spheres of *Dharma* and *Mokṣa* as it is in the spheres of *Artha* and *Kāma*. In fact, in the spiritual spheres, even if there is an abundance of Divine grace for success on the stage of the world, the *jīvātmā* is urged to remain indifferent to these laurels and travel all the way to the final destination of the loss of the self. Such a loss of self alone wipes out every trace of separative individuality and establishes us in the final state of oneness with Absolute Reality, the Self.

In the SA, it is understood that when a planet is badly placed in the *rāśi* chart or debilitated in the *navāṁśa,* it loses energy and thereby becomes weak. If, in addition, a planet enters into a close association, either through conjunction or aspect, with an FM planet, it is said to suffer what is called an 'affliction', which then also creates a weakness of a more grievous kind.

The best way for us to understand an affliction is to use the model of a soldier on the battle field firing away with his machine gun, and with the enemy unfortunately trapped in the firing line. In this model, the firing soldier stands for the FM planet. The enemy who unfortunately wanders into the firing line we will have to liken to the house or planet that gets afflicted by the FM planet in this grievous way.

Strong FM planets are assets even for the spiritual life, as we shall see in the case of *Śrī Ramaṇa Maharṣi.* They do 'harm' only when they afflict houses or other planets, either in the natal chart or during prolonged transit stationary afflictions. Paradoxically, the afflictions, which are not so welcome on account of their being unfavourable for a successful life in *Artha* and *Kāma,* have more credibility and favourability in the spiritual spheres of *Dharma* and *Mokṣa.*

The reason for this sudden reversal of the maleficity of the afflictions comes from the realization that, after all, as it is only in the worst adversities that we learn to surrender to the Divine will, and as these afflictions create just such adversities, which are spiritual blessings in disguise; we may look up to these afflictions in the horoscopes of spiritual beings with a better sense of ease, without any tinge of regret attached to the same, as happens, for example, when we examine a horoscope with afflictions in the worldly spheres of *Artha* and *Kāma.*

Put differently, one side of the affliction will represent adversity and suffering in the spheres of *Artha* and *Kāma,* while the same affliction will also open the doors to a higher spiritual life in the spheres of *Dharma* and *Mokṣa,* provided we humble ourselves and learn to surrender to the Divine will in these trying adversities. Thus, in *Dharma* and *Mokṣa* astrology, even the SA will tell us that these afflictions represent hidden doors to the spiritual life. We may also note, in passing, that in view of afflictions being blessings in disguise, at least insofar as the spiritual life is concerned, it may be more appropriate in the spheres of *Dharma* and *Mokṣa* to deem them as potentially benevolent influences which are actually in the nature of 'blessings in disguise'.

In the light of these fundamental considerations in the spiritual sphere, we may ask the pertinent general question: Under what special conditions does the spiritual life come into existence in the first place, and under what special conditions is the spiritual life also unfortunately denied? It turns out that broadly speaking, three distinct patterns exist, which answer our general question concerning spiritual flowering and blessings for the same.

In the first pattern, afflictions exist in the worldly spheres of *Artha* and *Kāma* and no planet in these spheres is strong. Additionally, no planet in the *Dharma* and *Mokṣa* spheres is strong either.

First Pattern

Denial of entry into the spiritual spheres of Dharma and Mokṣa — If strong spiritual planets and/or strong lords in these spheres are not present in the chart, then the severe afflictions and weaknesses of the planets/Hs in the Artha and Kāma spheres, will only serve to ***drown and trap*** *the individual in a life of struggle, confining the individual thereby entirely to the worldly Artha and Kāma spheres.*

When *Dharma* or *Mokṣa* lords are weak and/or afflicted, afflictions in *Artha* and *Kāma* spheres produce no spiritual awakening and 'no door opens'.

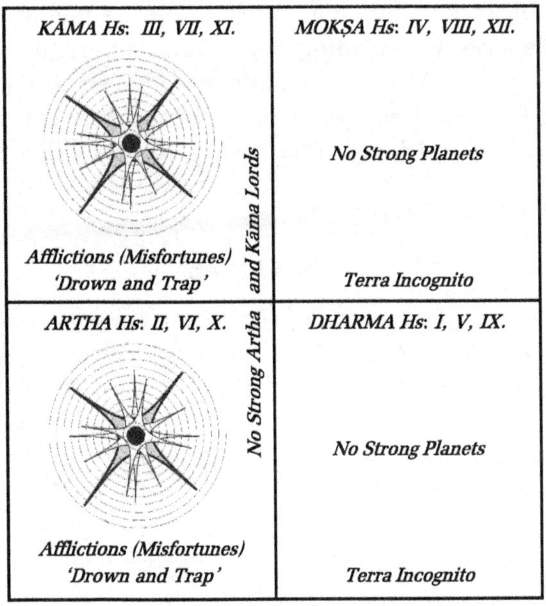

Afflictions Drown and Trap Individuals in Artha and Kāma Spheres

This SA *sūtra* accounts for a certain quite common phenomenon: the absence of spiritual awakening in the lives of individuals in our society, a phenomenon at which we might have wondered on many an occasion but for which we might not have found any satisfactory explanation.

The phenomenon is simply that in spite of people being subjected to horrendous sufferings in their lives in the *Artha* and *Kāma* spheres – such sufferings never seem to become instrumental and sufficient to lift them to the higher spiritual planes of compassion, empathy, awareness, and detachment. The above SA *sūtra* accounts for the absence of spiritual awakening in people's lives, in spite of a strong impetus for spiritual life through the horrendous sufferings that seem to be their lot.

In contrast to this first pattern, which is one of spiritual barrenness notwithstanding horrendous sufferings, a second pattern emerges whenever in addition to the serious afflictions and weaknesses of planets in the *Artha* and *Kāma* spheres, the individual in question also has strong *Dharma* or *Mokṣa* lords in his/her chart.

Second Pattern

Entry into the spiritual spheres facilitated by strong Dharma and/or Mokṣa lords (illustrating the Nivṛtti mārga or withdrawal from the world) — If severe afflictions and weaknesses of the Artha and Kāma lords coexist with strong Dharma and Mokṣa lords, then we have the best illustration of the highest spiritual life, characterized by all the higher significations of the strong Dharma or Mokṣa lords. This is called the Nivṛtti mārga.

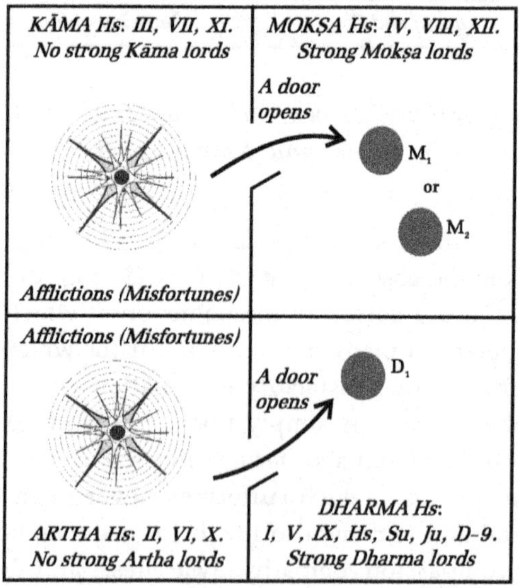

Afflictions Become Blessings in Disguise
(Nivṛtti Mārga)

Strong *Dharma* or *Mokṣa* lords open a door into their spheres creating a *Nivṛtti* pattern whenever *Artha* and *Kāma* lords are weak and badly afflicted.

When these conditions are fulfilled, as in the typical illustrative example of *Śrī Ramaṇa Maharṣi,* the individual, so to speak, rather than being drowned and trapped in the *Artha* and *Kāma* spheres, becomes fortunate enough to be able to make an exit from them because in this pattern, the presence of strong *Dharma* or *Mokṣa* lords serves to open a door into the spiritual spheres. The situation is rather akin to refugees being driven out of their homeland but being fortunate enough in securing the blessing of sanctuary in lands far away from their own. For *Śrī Ramaṇa Maharṣi,* who was 'exiled' from the mundane spheres of *Artha* and *Kāma,* the land of *Mokṣa* offered sanctuary.

Third Pattern

The spiritual life and mundane life are blended together, without any contradiction and without an outright renunciation and withdrawal from mundane life — If strong spiritual potentials in the form of strong Dharma and/or Mokṣa lords, a strong Su and/or Ju, or a strong D-9 chart coexist with strong Artha and/or Kāma lords, then we have a mixture of Nivṛtti and Pravṛtti in that spiritual life. That is, while the individual is spiritual, s/he also has involvement in the world and may also enjoy 'success' in the worldly spheres.

In this pattern too, spiritual awakening or spiritual flowering does come to pass on account of the spiritual potentials in the chart — in the form of a strong Su or Ju, strong *Dharma* and/or *Mokṣa* lords, etc. However, on account of some of the *Artha* and/or *Kāma* lords also being strong, the individual is neither *drowned and trapped* as in the first pattern, nor is s/he *exiled and driven out* from habitation in the *Artha* and/or *Kāma* spheres as in the second pattern. In fact the good strength of some of the *Artha* and/or *Kāma* lords, also keeps a door open for her/him, to return to the mundane *Artha* and/or *Kāma* spheres as often as s/he desires.

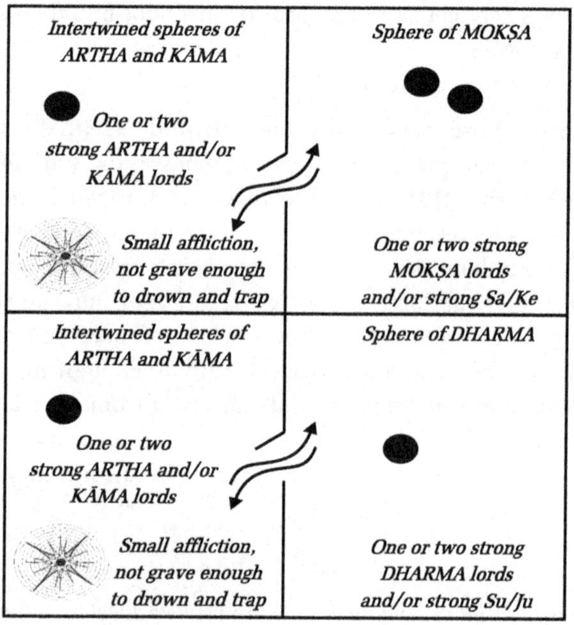

A Mixture of Pravṛtti and Nivṛtti Spiritual Patterns

Consequently, spiritual beings conforming to the third pattern come to enjoy the best of both worlds. They are indeed spiritual, but strangely, this is quite consistent with their amphibious existence on account of the Divine grace they enjoy in the mundane world as well. In fact, all spiritual beings who head spiritual missions and accomplish something of practical value belong to this third pattern. I cite the illustrative example of His Holiness Pope Benedict XVI. In his chart, in addition to a strong *Dharma* lord of the IXH and the exact impact of the spiritual planet Ju on the Asdt, a strong Asdt lord and Ju ruling the XIH of *Kāma* (house of aspiration) have blessed him with Divine grace not only in the spiritual sphere but also in the mundane spheres of *Artha* and *Kāma*.

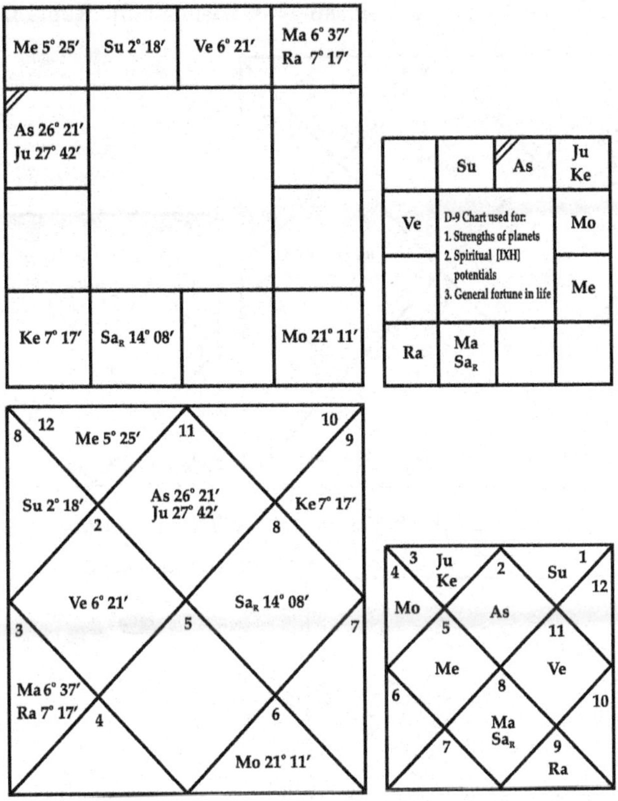

Rāśi and Navāṁśa Charts of His Holiness Pope Benedict XVI

Note: The above pair of horoscopes illustrates the third pattern of spiritual life. The upper charts are in the South Indian format while the lower charts are in the North Indian format.

Now that we have familiarized ourselves with the three broad patterns of spiritual life and have understood all of them as originating in the mood of God at the time and place of birth, we are well equipped to examine the afflictions in the *Maharṣi's* chart, as they represent the hidden doors and blessings in disguise through which the *Maharṣi* was destined to secure the blessing of *Mokṣa* from *Aruṇācala Śiva.*

Hidden Doors and Blessings in Disguise for Ramaṇā

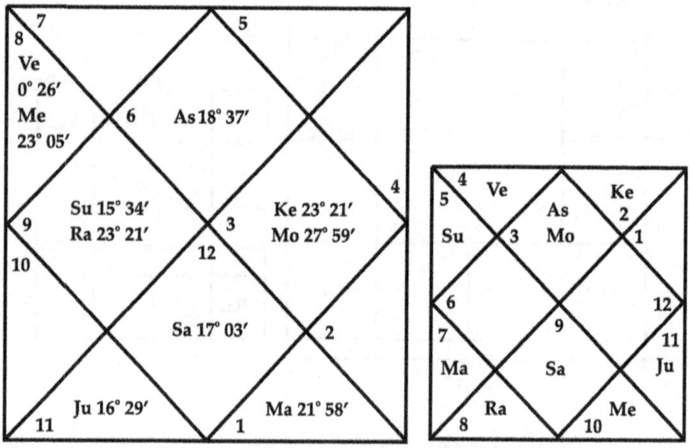

The Maharṣi's Birth Chart (North Indian)

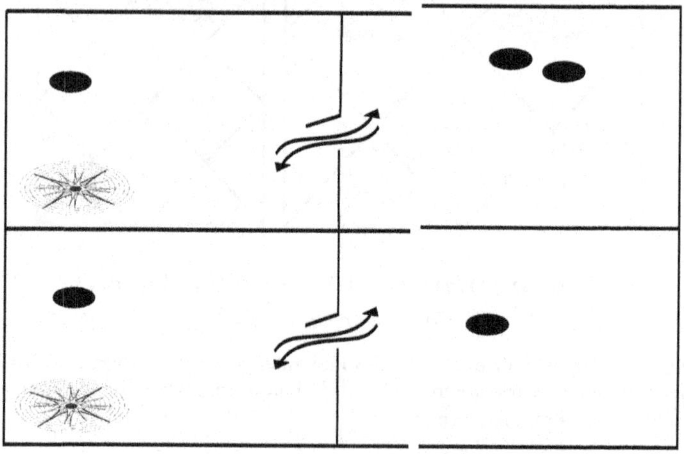

The Maharṣi's Birth Chart (South Indian)

Note: The *Maharṣi's* horoscope in the North Indian (above) and South Indian (below) format:

DOB = December 30, 1879; Rectified TOB = 12:19 a.m.; TZ = - 05:21 hours LMT; POB = Tiruchuzhi, Tamil Nadu, India (78°E 17′, 9°N 25′); Lahiri *ayanāmśa* = 22° 10′. The divisional charts appear on p. 74.

(i) The Asdt Lord Mercury (Me) is placed in the IIIH of profound interest and vitality but is weak on account of an exact affliction from the Most Malefic Planet (MMP) Mars (Ma), the *Mokṣakāraka* [significator of *Mokṣa*]. The strength of the *Mokṣakāraka* is at its very maximum in spite of the said affliction and is therefore sufficient for bringing about the fulfilment of the *Maharṣi's* destiny in a comparatively easy manner, as a strong VIIIH always bestows the so-called easy gains in life. This exact influence of the *Mokṣa* lord Ma on the Asdt lord Me acts in such a way as to blow out the personal self and give no scope for self-fulfilment, especially in the Me and Ma sub-periods.

(ii) The Asdt House MEP is closely, though not exactly, afflicted by the separative planet Saturn (Sa), which for a Virgo Asdt is a functional malefic (FM) ruling the VIH of *Karmayoga*. That the VIH in the spheres of *Dharma* and *Mokṣa* signifies *Karmayoga* is known to us from our version of Pandit Vamadeva Shastri's VA.

(iii) Sa's separative influence and affliction to the Asdt house does not end there; this influence and affliction also comes through the 10th aspect to the IVH of the *asmitā,* or I-am-ness. Its placement in the VIIH close to the MEP, though falling outside the orb of 1°, should suggest to us to make some allowance and expect this affliction to the VIIH to come into manifestation.

(iv) The separative influence of Sa very significantly comes onto the Su, placed in the IVH as a close affliction.

The Su's doubly separative influence is seen in the close affliction to the IVH of *asmitā* as well as the XH. The close influence of the Su on the IVH was crucial for the *Maharṣi's* Self-Realization. It was one of the important factors that created the grounds, as a necessary condition, for receiving the *prasāda* of *Ātmajñāna* [Self-Realization]. Such an influence of the Su on the IVH may be contrasted with the influence of the Su, again as

Mokṣakāraka, on the Asdt MEP in the case of *Śrī Shirdi Sai Baba* (who also had a Virgo Asdt) and on the IVH of *asmitā* in the case of the Master *Śrī J. Krishnamurti,* who had a Capricorn Asdt.

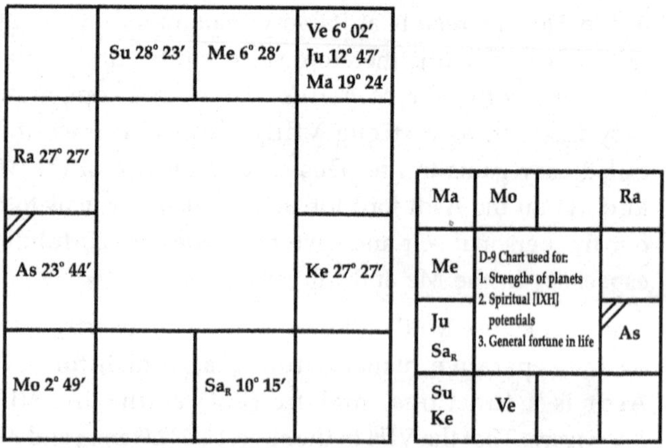
Su 28° 23′
Me 6° 28′
Ve 6° 02′
Ju 12° 47′
Ma 19° 24′
Ra 27° 27′
As 23° 44′
Ke 27° 27′
Mo 2° 49′
Sa_R 10° 15′
Ma
Mo
Ra
Me
D-9 Chart used for:
1. Strengths of planets
2. Spiritual [IXH] potentials
3. General fortune in life
Ju
Sa_R
As
Su
Ke
Ve

Rāśi and Navāṁśa Charts of Śrī J. Krishnamurti

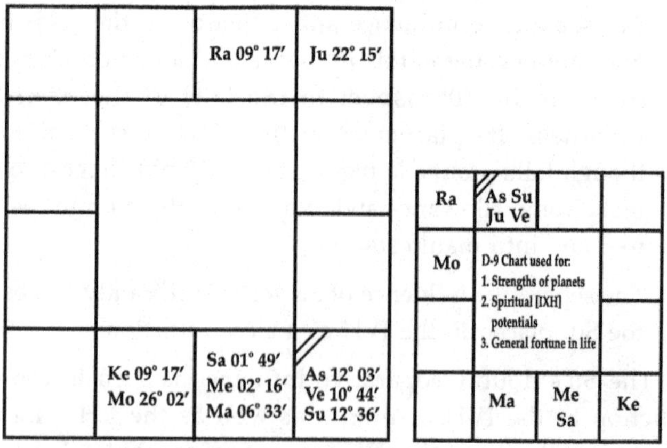
Ra 09° 17′
Ju 22° 15′
Ke 09° 17′
Mo 26° 02′
Sa 01° 49′
Me 02° 16′
Ma 06° 33′
As 12° 03′
Ve 10° 44′
Su 12° 36′
Ra
As Su
Ju Ve
Mo
D-9 Chart used for:
1. Strengths of planets
2. Spiritual [IXH] potentials
3. General fortune in life
Ma
Me
Sa
Ke

Rāśi and Navāṁśa Charts of Śrī Shirdi Sai Baba

Note: The natal charts of *Śrī J. Krishnamurti* and *Śrī Shirdi Baba* are used to clarify the role of the Su as a spiritual planet for these two Masters as well as for the *Maharṣi.*

In *Śrī Shirdi Sai Baba's* case, the Su not only made him a healer and doctor of herbal and psychic medicine, it also placed him in the state of oneness with God. In the case of the Master *Śrī J. Krishnamurti* however, though the Su was still the *Mokṣakāraka,* its placement close to the MEP of the IVH as the lord of the VIIIH of profundity, mysticism, and heterodoxy brought in these VIIIH characteristics into the teachings of that original but heterodox teacher.

Now that we have taken a look at all the afflictions in the horoscope of the *Maharṣi,* which we must deem to have been blessings in disguise, we may now turn to three influences of a strong Sa on the *Maharṣi's* life:

(i) A strong VIH lord Sa bestows profound enquiry in an unconventional field. Importantly, in the SA, as recently pointed out by Prof. V. K. Choudhry, the strong VIH lord Sa also creates the strong urge *"for delving deep into Ātmavicāra, and finding logical meanings and expressions of various facets of life"* (SA *sūtra*).

In both VA as well as the SA, it is the IIIH that bestows profound curiosity in both the arts and the sciences. However, in contrast to the profound curiosity bestowed by the IIIH, the influence of the strong VIH lord Sa on the *Maharṣi* not only pertains to the spiritual realm but also brings with it the element of delving deep into an unconventional field, as we shall explain below.

In view of Sa being the *Anugrahakāraka* in the *navāṁśa* chart, and in view of the *'Anugrahakāraka par excellence'* of the *rāśi* chart, Ju, being placed close to the MEP of the *Mūla Trikoṇa* house (MTH) of Sa, the deep delving necessarily occurs in the spiritual field.

(ii) The *Maharṣi's* life of chastity, celibacy, and renunciation arises from this spiritual Saturnian influence close to the VIIH MEP, as well as from the utter weakness of the planet Venus taken together with the spiritually strong *navāṁśa* chart, in which Sa is the *Anugrahakāraka.*

(iii) Again, as Sa's 3rd aspect closely afflicts the IXH of father and higher education, we must make allowance for this Saturnian influence to have also made its impact in those spheres of the *Maharṣi's* life, as there is unambiguous testimony for the same.

11. Jñāna, Kriyā, and Icchā Śaktis in the Horoscope

In Chapter III, Section 16, while introducing the houses in Hindu astrology, we became familiar with the various *Śaktis* of the Divine Mother manifesting in the outer spheres of the twelve houses. Here, we refresh our memory concerning the three *Śaktis* of the Divine Mother, but this time concentrating on how they enter into combinations, thereby creating the richness and diversity of human nature in pursuit of the four goals of human life. Finally, we apply these principles to the *Maharṣi's* horoscope.

The Divine Mother's life energy comes into manifestation as three distinct types of energies — *Jñāna Śakti, Kriyā Śakti,* and *Icchā Śakti.* Of these, *Jñāna Śakti* is *sāttvic, Kriyā Śakti* is *rājasic,* while *Icchā Śakti* is *tāmasic.* In Hindu astrology, the IVH, VH, and IXH are considered *sāttvic,* as the IVH signifies *Ātmā* while the VH and IXH are *Dharma* houses, connected to spiritual life and God. The three *sāttvic* planets are the *Ātmakāraka,* the Sun; the *Anugrahakāraka,* Jupiter; and the *Poṣakāraka,* the Moon (the planet of the Divine Mother).

If, in a horoscope, the *Kāma* Hs — the IIIH, VIIH, and XIH — are strong, then we must infer that the Divine Mother's *Icchā Śakti* is more in abundance. This makes the horoscope favourable for life fulfilment with regard to various aspirations, intentions, and goals pursued with tenacity and wilfulness. Such pursuit is very much part of the human drama in which the self finds its full expression. While the VIIH and Venus (its significator) may be considered to be more concerned with marital relationships and the seeking of comforts and luxuries, the other two *Kāma* Hs are very essential for any higher achievement in the sphere of vocation and profession as well as in the humanitarian and spiritual spheres.

The IIIH bestows profound interest and deep curiosity as well as a strong will and martial prowess with the strong urge to make alliances for the express purpose of achieving something substantial in the sphere of vocation. So too, the XIH bestows aspirations and sets humans on the path of seeking. Thus, though the *Kāma* Hs are generally concerned with seeking pleasure, desire fulfilment, and enjoyment, we must not lose sight of the vast benefits of these *Kāma* Hs for achieving something of value for the welfare of the world [*lokakalyāṇa*] as well.

If, on the other hand, one or more *Artha* Hs — the IIH, VIH, and XH — are strong, then the Divine Mother's *Kriyā Śakti* is strong in that individual's life; this bestows Divine grace for the achievement of professional goals, with the attendant merit, skill, and recognition coming to the *jīvātmā* concerned.

It can happen that the Divine Mother's *Icchā Śakti* can propel the *Artha* Hs; *Jñāna Śakti* can also propel the *Artha* Hs. In fact, any kind of combination of the Divine Mother's energies in the 'fields' of the houses is possible, and the decipherment of which energy of the Divine Mother has entered into which specific house makes each horoscope unique, interesting, as well as challenging.

In spiritual life, if the *Dharma* and *Mokṣa* Hs are strong (the IV, VIII, and XIIH are the *Mokṣa* Hs), then the Divine Mother's *Jñāna Śakti* is bound to be strong for the given individual. This might indicate sufficient Divine grace either for *Dharma,* a righteous spiritual life, or for *Mokṣa,* the highest kind of spiritual life, in which there cannot be any favouring and pampering of the *jīvātmā* by the Divine grace, but on the contrary, only Divine grace for bringing to a termination the 'life of individuality'.

Strong *Dharma* houses indicate Divine grace in the form of *Jñāna Śakti* for the pursuit of some God-centred spiritual learning [*vidyā*] and spiritual teaching or for engaging in *lokakalyāṇa* work for the spiritual welfare of the world at large. In view of the Hindu world of our ancients having turned somewhat undesirably secular, these classical manifestations of the strong *Dharma* Hs have now come to take on newer forms. Thus, in contemporary times, good advising skills, keeping the interests of clients at heart, and involvement in humanitarian and charitable activities with a view to bringing justice to one and all, must also be considered to fall in the sphere of the *Dharma* houses.

Strong *Mokṣa* houses signify Divine grace and *Jñāna Śakti* for seekers on the path of *Mokṣa* who are involved in some occult, spiritually esoteric, or research-oriented pursuits or who might be directly pursuing *Mokṣa* at the feet of some genuine Spiritual Master.

The Su and Ju are intrinsically spiritual and *sāttvic* planets, ruling *Dharma* signs in the natural zodiac, while Sa and Ke are the significators of the VIIIH and XIIH, both *Mokṣa* houses. For these reasons, a strong Su and/or Ju or even a strong Sa and/or Ke certainly serve to bring about spiritual fulfilment.

In the horoscope of *Śrī Ramaṇa Maharṣi,* Ma, as the strongest planet, signifies *Jñāna Śakti,* while Ju's impact on the *Artha* Hs and on the XIIH of *Mokṣa* connotes *Jñāna Śakti par excellence* for these Hs. What kind of energy of the Divine Mother is carried by the other strong planet in the *Maharṣi's* chart, Sa? Sa, when ruling the VIH, normally carries the Divine Mother's *Kriyā Śakti,* which is *rājasic* in nature and therefore conducive for action and achievement. However, each of the *Navagrahas* also has what are called general significations, which have nothing to do with the particular house that the planet may come to rule in a given Asdt. Importantly, the planets in Hindu astrology also have what are called *guṇās* [intrinsic tendencies]. In this respect, Sa bestows more *tamas,* inertia, immobility, or inaction in the *Maharṣi's* life. We present further evidence in Section 16 of the *tāmasic* nature of Sa coming into manifestation in the first few years of the *Maharṣi's* stay in Tiruvannamalai.

We know, however, that the *Maharṣi* was dominantly *sāttvic,* and never displayed any of the *rājasic* dynamism and action that was so characteristic of his contemporary, *Mahātmā Gandhi.* This *sāttvic* nature of the *Maharṣi* must be explained: Sa's lordship of the *sāttvic* IXH in the *navāṁśa* chart as well as the placement of natal Ju in Sa's *Mūla Trikoṇa* house both indirectly add a strong *Jñāna Śakti* component into the *Kriyā Śakti* that Sa is supposed to deliver. Thus, on the whole, if we take the strong *navāṁśa* chart into account, the predominance of *Jñāna Śakti* over other *Śaktis* is quite in evidence (we must not forget that a strong *navāṁśa* chart also enhances the *Jñāna Śakti* in one's life).

12. Jupiter's Jñāna Śakti Par Excellence for Self-Realization in Virgo Ascendants

The fullest extent of *Jñāna Śakti* carried by a natal Ju for the Virgo Asdt manifests only when Ju's MTH is strong. In such cases, the individuals feel that they themselves are God. This was the case with *Śrī Shirdi Sai Baba,* whose strong spiritual Ju was placed in his XH. And this is a fact well known to his biographers and devotees (Sambasiva Rao). Put differently, the Self-Realization of *Shirdi Sai Baba* is of the classic *Upaniṣadic Ahaṁ Brahmāsmi* [I am *Brahman*] type. We must remember that this is different from *Śrī Ramaṇa Maharṣi's* Self-Realization, which did not come from the strong natal Ju of a Virgo Asdt (his natal Ju was weak), but rather from the exact influences of two strong *Mokṣakārakas,* Ma and Sa, on the Asdt lord and the Asdt house, respectively.

Additionally in the case of the *Maharṣi,* the *Mokṣakāraka* Su also impacted closely on the IVH of *asmitā*; thus, while the personal self was extinguished for the *Maharṣi,* it was not so for *Śrī Shirdi Baba.* In the case of *Śrī Shirdi Baba,* who also had a Virgo Asdt and a strong IVH, while Jupiter (the *Anugrahakāraka par excellence*) gave him the *Ahaṁ Brahmāsmi* Realization and a definitive feeling that he was God, yet, as there was no *Mokṣa* lord's influence in the IVH of the natal chart, he was not destined to be the kind of Self-Realized Sage that the *Maharṣi* was. It is on account of these fundamental differences that the teachings of these two spiritual luminaries, one, a perfectly Self-Realized Sage, and the other, a perfectly God-Realized Saint, were entirely different.

Both were undoubtedly on the *Nivṛtti mārga,* yet their equation with God and Absolute Reality was entirely different. *Śrī Shirdi Baba's* compassion sourced in his strong IVH, was such that he (as an embodiment of the Divine Mother) could not but help people with his amazing variety of blessings in the form of miracles and healings, which still continue on the physical plane long after *Śrī Shirdi Baba* has shuffled off his mortal coils. The *Maharṣi,* on the other hand, was the Self (Godhead or *Śiva*), and there was no 'individual' entity to perceive 'another' human being to whom help had to be rendered. His was an *advaitic* Realization, as he was one with the Godhead, *Aruṇācala Śiva.*

Ju, the lord of the IVH of *Ātmā* and I-am-ness, is placed weakly in the *Maharṣi's* VIH of *Karmayoga;* but from this weak position, as it aspects closely both the Hs of vocation (the IIH and the XH), there is noticeably a definite Jupiterean spiritual impact on these houses. Such a Jupiterean impact from the VIH onto the vocational Hs points to the chart being possibly that of a spiritual teacher, as Ju signifies the teacher or *Bṛhaspati,* but from the position of being a *karmayogi* in life.

As Jupiter's spiritual energy or *Jñāna Śakti* is seen entering into the airy signs of the Hs of vocation, we must conclude that this Virgo Asdt's *karmayogic* Jupiter is favourable for bringing *Jñāna Śakti* to the Hs of vocation, with a strong intellectual orientation. This is just one illustrative example of how, by blending both systems of Hindu astrology, VA and SA, we may obtain the benefit of insights and fruits of enquiry of both systems.

13. Other Spiritual Potentials

From the point of view of the SA as applied to the material spheres of *Artha* and *Kāma*, the *Maharṣi's* horoscope is characterized by its multiple and all-round 'afflictions', with only Sa and Ma, two FMs, emerging as strong planets with full planetary strengths. These afflictions can grant only hardships, adversities, and obstructions as a general pattern in life, and indeed this has been borne out by the *Maharṣi's* life.

The only other silver lining is seen in the best placement of the Mo in the XH, and this was responsible in bestowing upon the *Maharṣi* much compassion and worldwide fame and popularity in the latter half of his life. But even this well placed Mo, though the influence of the nodes on it is negligible, the SA considers somewhat weak on account of its old age. While the chances for a successful life in the spheres of *Artha* and *Kāma* are patently very bleak, we must ask ourselves the more pertinent question as to what other hidden spiritual potentials the horoscope holds in the spheres of *Dharma* and *Mokṣa*. This is the mystery we now unfold in our continuing astrological Pilgrimage into the *Maharṣi's* life.

Insofar as his spiritual life is concerned, in the *rāśi* chart, spiritual power or *Jñāna Śakti* is ensured by a strong VIIIH as well as Ju's close impact as *Anugrahakāraka par excellence* on two *Artha* Hs of vocation. As we shall see in Section 21, the *navāṁśa* chart (D-9) of the *Maharṣi* is saturated with Divine grace, while the *caturviṁśāṁśa* chart (D-24) and the *viṁśāṁśa* chart (D-20) also have the power to account for the many spiritual inclinations of the *Maharṣi*. The *Dharma* Hs being empty is very significant, in that the *Maharṣi* bypassed *Dharma* and took a direct leap to *Mokṣa*. The fully empty *Dharma* houses, which occur in earth signs for a Virgo Asdt, illustrate another noteworthy feature of the *Maharṣi's* life: they show that the *Maharṣi* had no 'spiritual mission' in the sphere of *Dharma* that he intended to realize on the earth plane.

14. Rectified Birth Time

Taking into account a number of significant events in the life of the *Maharṣi,* we have, through the processes of birth rectification, arrived at the rectified Time of Birth (TOB), which is 12:19 a.m. on December 30, 1879. Rectification of the TOB is a special analytical method in VA as well as in the SA whereby a presumably erroneous TOB is corrected or rectified by checking with a set of important milestones from the life of an individual. The *Maharṣi's* rectified TOB is at variance with what has appeared in the various biographical records of the past. Justification for this new rectified TOB comes from the rectified TOB being able to reproduce all the significant events in the life of the *Maharṣi,* including the 'monumental occurrence' of his Self-Realization [*Mokṣa*] and his *Mahānirvāṇa* on April 14, 1950.

B. V. Narasimha Swami, one of the early biographers of the *Maharṣi,* mentions in his work *Self-Realization,* that the *Maharṣi* was born at 1:00 a.m. Prof. K. Swaminathan, in his biographical sketch *Ramaṇa Maharṣi,* posits the time of birth at a little past midnight. Pandit Vamadeva Shastri (*Astrology of the Seers*) notes a TOB of 1:15 a.m. (LMT). It is also quite possible that since the work of these eminent biographers and the *Vedācarya,* some revisions of the TOB could have taken place, but as I've been unaware of such researches, I have had to approach the whole question of the correctness of the TOB afresh, from the point of view of astrological rectification. I have had to use a combination of methods — the SA and VA — to arrive at what seemed to me to be the correct TOB. This also naturally fixes the Asdt MEP. *Without the powerful and clearly formulated analytical methods of the SA, there was no way in which I could have attempted this birth rectification of the Maharṣi's chart, much less undertaken this Pilgrimage in the spiritual spheres of Dharma and Mokṣa.*

15. New Methods of Rectification of Birth Time

As essential life patterns and transit significant events (TSEs) of the *Maharṣi's* life, I have noted the following:

(i) His *Mokṣa,* undoubtedly, is the most important landmark in his entire life, and fortunately for us, the date when this happened can be ascertained from the estimates given by many biographers, to be around July 16, 1896 (in Madurai). As we shall see, this in itself is sufficient to determine the Asdt, which happens to fall in the sign Virgo.

(ii) The boy *Ramaṇa* took delight in sporting activities, like wrestling and swimming, which testifies to his vitality. This also suggests a Virgo Asdt, for then the Asdt lord placed in the sign Scorpio in the IIIH and under the close influence of Ma (the planet of *prāṇaśakti* and significator of the IIIH) would account for the boy's physical inclinations towards sports and physically vigorous activities. In passing, we may note that we have just touched upon one of the well-known primordial characteristics of the zodiacal sign Scorpio, as Scorpio represents the physical side of Martian energy.

(iii) The *Maharṣi* was a world teacher, showing humanity the way to *Mokṣa* through the path of *Ātmavicāra* or *Jñānayoga.* This serves to fix the *navāṁśa* Asdt as also the *caturviṁśāṁśa* Asdt.

(iv) He was blessed with intense devotion to his *Iṣṭadevata,* notwithstanding his illustrious illumination and wisdom on the path of *Jñānayoga* and *Ātmavicāra.* This fact helps us to fix the Asdt in the *viṁśāṁśa* chart (D-20), which pertains to surrender to God and devotion.

(v) His father passed away rather early in life, when he was just about twelve. The date of this loss is also known (February 18, 1892). This has helped verify that Ju rules the IVH of father and home life in his chart. (SA *sūtra*)

(vi) The *Maharṣi* had left home and wandered into the world at large to finally take refuge at the feet of *Aruṇācala Śiva* in Tiruvannamalai. Thus, he had to be separated from home and family life, and the date of this separation is also known (August 29, 1896). This suggests strong separative influences in the IVH of home life in the natal chart.

(vii) With the commencement of his life of renunciation, he had to face many hardships, including abject poverty. Sa's influence on the Asdt and Ma's exact affliction were the instrumental causes of such poverty and many accompanying hardships. This poverty-conferring nature of Saturn has been emphasized by Pandit Vamadeva Shastri (*Astrology of the Seers* 99).

(viii) The dates on which the *Maharṣi* underwent surgeries, in the late evening of his life, are also known (first week of February, March 27, August 8, and December 19, 1949).

(ix) The date of his *Mahānirvāṇa* is known to be April 14, 1950.

(x) Evidence is available to us in the *Maharṣi's* own words that the boy *Ramaṇa* never told lies and that he was recognized by his playmates and family members as having 'golden hands': whatever he touched turned out to flourish in life. His scrupulous honesty can be attributed to both the aspect of a strong *Nivṛtti* Sa on the Asdt house, as well as an exceptionally strong *navāṁśa* chart, which is one of the most important astrological variables for a genuine spiritual life. The placement of the Su so close to the MEP of the IVH of character conferred the signification of honesty in no lesser measure, as honesty, character, and integrity come from the Su and the IVH (in SA and the VA).

The *Maharṣi's* celibacy, chastity, renunciation, poverty after his sixteenth year, and the premature death of his father serve to roughly fix the Most Effective Point (MEP) of the Virgo Asdt (through the powerful analytical methods of the SA).

The Asdt of the *navāṁśa* chart changes every twelve minutes, while the *caturviṁśāṁśa* and *viṁśāṁśa* charts change their Asdts every four and five minutes, respectively. As we know the *Maharṣi* to be fully enlightened, we have a tremendous advantage in selecting the right Asdt for the *caturviṁśāṁśa* chart to account for the same, and this also helps us fix the Asdt MEP to within an accuracy of four minutes. The crucial importance of the *caturviṁśāṁśa* and *viṁśāṁśa* charts for the spiritual life has been emphasized in VA. Also, taking the overall life of the *Maharṣi* into account, we must ensure that the *navāṁśa* and *pañcāṁśa* charts (the latter governing intelligence and learning capacity) turn out to be profoundly spiritual.

In the SA, one does not deal with divisional charts beyond the *dvādaśāṁśa* (D-12), only because the *lagnas* of these charts change too swiftly, every few minutes even, resulting in our inability to ascertain them accurately, especially when the MEP of the *rāśi* chart itself may be inaccurate by a few minutes. Notwithstanding, I have considered the D-24 and the D-20 charts pertaining to the spheres of *Jñānayoga* and *Bhaktiyoga* only because it helped confirm that the Asdt MEP of the *Maharṣi's* chart had been accurately determined from the gamut of all his life events (TSEs) by the systematic application of many SA *sūtras.* In this way, through the four-step process of determining the Asdts of the four spiritual divisional charts, we arrive at the correct MEP for the Virgo Asdt to within a minute or so. The *Maharṣi's* TOB, rectified in just this way, has been found to then account for all the remaining significant events in his life.

16. An Avatār of Aruṇācala Śiva in the Sphere of Mokṣa

In Tiruchuzhi, the holy town of Bhuminatha, I was born to Sundara and his good wife Sundari. To rescue me from this barren worldly life, Arunachala Siva in the form of a hill famous throughout the universe, gave me His own state of bliss so that His heart might rejoice, so that His own being as Awareness might shine forth and His own power might flourish. (The Maharshi qtd. in Natarajan 85)

The *Maharṣi's Avatārarahasya* [secret of avatarhood] lay in his continuously silent but powerful reminder to mankind that the *summum bonum* of human life was not one kind of revolution or other on the physical plane – even if such a benevolent revolution were solely for the welfare of the world – but that it was *Mokṣa* or Self-Realization. And it was by living this highest truth practically from start to finish in the silent presence of the Self that he profoundly touched humanity's collective heart and turned it decisively in the forgotten direction of *Mokṣa.*

A *Mahāpuruṣa* [great human spirit] has a lofty mission, only because even such *Mahāpuruṣas* wish to achieve something concrete on the physical plane, never for themselves but certainly for the welfare of the world as a whole. The *Maharṣi* had already ceased to be any kind of individual – even a *Mahāpuruṣa* – from the day of his *Mokṣa* and, in this sense, was no more human but was *Aruṇācala Śiva* Himself, wearing but a human *veṣa* [mask]. It was in this sense that *Śrī Ramaṇa Maharṣi* was an *Avatār* in the sphere of *Mokṣa.*

Avatār is a household word for Hindus, and this term is inextricably linked up in Hindu consciousness with the two great epic heros *Śrī Rāmacandra* and *Śrī Kṛṣṇa Paramātmā,* who were *Avatārs* of *Viṣṇu,* the immanent God of the Hindu world. The word *Avatār* itself means 'a human embodiment of the Pure Consciousness of God' and is to be understood as the descent of the Divine in a human form, either to open the eyes of a spiritually blind humanity to some important forgotten timeless truth or to establish a new world order and a new form of the timeless *Sanātana Dharma* at a time when the old world order, having turned putrid, is fast approaching its inevitable decay and dissolution.

In *Mahātmā Gandhi,* we had an *Avatār* in the sphere of *Dharma,* but one who was treading the path of *Karmayoga.* On the other hand, in *Śrī Ramaṇa Maharṣi's* case, it was his destiny to have attained the highest goal of *Mokṣa* or Self-Realization, but through the miraculous 'door' of *Jñānayoga,* and through this attainment, to make humanity aware of this highest *summum bonum* of life.

The *Avatārs* of *Viṣṇu* are commonly known and, therefore, better studied and understood. On the other hand, the *Avatārs* of *Śiva* are not so much as even heard of, except for the *Nāyanmars,* the great *Śaivite* Saints, who are also not so well studied. It is even said that since *Śiva* is the unmanifest God, He does not manifest as *Avatārs. Rāma* and *Kṛṣṇa* were certainly *Avatārs* of the immanent God of the Hindu world, *Viṣṇu,* but the *Maharṣi,* as we shall come to see, was a very rare kind of *Avatār* of *Śiva,* the transcendent God of the Hindu world.

Let us examine the influences on the Asdt or the self of *Śrī Ramaṇa Maharṣi* with a view to grasping the nature of his avatarhood. Me, the Asdt lord, is not a strong planet but aspects the IXH of philosophy and teaching. In one sense, the *Maharṣi* was not even a spiritual teacher out on the stage of the world for all to see. That is why the Asdt lord Me is not more intimately connected with the IXH or Ju, the significator of the IXH, in the *rāśi* chart itself. The *Maharṣi* had even transcended that position by having become one with *nirguṇa Parabrahma* [transcendent Godhead]. However, as Ju is placed in the IXH of the *navāṁśa* chart and aspects the Asdt from this position, the *Maharṣi* was a Spiritual Master all right, but only in the deep recesses of the IXH, which the *navāṁśa* chart represents. For this reason, his destiny did not bring him out into the open. Rather, seekers gathered at his feet at his *āśrama,* in which surroundings he was indeed one of the greatest *advaitic* Masters *Sanātana Dharma* had ever produced.

In fact, the influences on the Asdt and Asdt lord come from the closely aspecting and strong *Nirvāṇakāraka* Sa and an exactly aspecting strong *Mokṣakāraka* Ma. Both these FMs, Sa and Ma, were responsible for stripping *Ramaṇa* of all his material bondages, even to his body, for on one occasion that occurred sixteen years after the *Mokṣa* experience, *Ramaṇa's* body actually died and 'he' was an unperturbed witness to the same.

In this sense, the strong FMs, Sa and Ma, were beautifully co-operative with the *Nivṛtti* [withdrawal from the world, as in renunciation] activity of the Su by totally wiping out the light of *asmitā* or I-am-ness. In assisting the Su and joining hands with it, the strong Sa and Ma could not but take *Ramaṇa* into a condition of abject poverty and mendicancy.

As researchers attempting to understand a transcendental truth, which we might not succeed in being able to capture in just one single mould, we must be prepared to make a departure from simplistic models and try to comprehend the richness of this transcendental truth with many complementary models at the same time. This would be akin to the well-known model of the *andha-hasti-nyāya,* in which several blind men, making a sensory contact with different parts of the body of an elephant, naturally report the elephant to have 'such and such' characteristics but with no two observers ever agreeing! The fuller picture naturally must emerge from an enveloping synthesis of many fragmentary perceptions.

Thus, it might actually be quite proper to understand the nature of *Maharṣi's* avatarhood using three independent perspectives. Proceeding along these lines, it would be correct to understand the *Maharṣi* as simultaneously being all these aspects of *Aruṇācala Śiva*: *Kālakāla* [the aspect of *Śiva* that vanquishes death or is the slayer of death]; *Dakṣiṇāmūrti* [*Śiva* as the Supreme Teacher who teaches through silence]; and *Bhikṣāṭana* [*Śiva* as the Supreme Spiritual Mendicant], but with practically no wandering to do and, on the contrary, thoroughly devoid of movement — like *Aruṇācala Śiva* Himself.

Let us briefly delve into *Aruṇācala Śiva's Kālakāla* manifestation to lend support to the suggestion that *Śrī Ramaṇa Maharṣi* was indeed this *Avatār* of *Aruṇācala Śiva.* According to the *Purāṇās,* when the *Ṛṣi Mṛkaṇḍu* was given the option by *Śiva* to choose between one noble son who would die at sixteen and many sons lacking in virtue, he chose the single noble son, whose devotion to *Śiva* was so great that when death made a visitation on him when he was just sixteen, *Śiva* in His aspect as

Bhaktaparādhīna [dependent on the devotee] burst forth from the *Liṅga* [formless stump-like *vigraha* of *Śiva*] and dealt a death blow to death itself. The truth of this *archetypal* manifestation of *Śiva* has even been sung and chronicled by the fourteenth century *śaivaite ācārya* and temple priest *Umāpati* (Smith, *The Dance of Siva* 201). The Divine entry of *Aruṇācala Śiva* into *Ramaṇa's* life on the day of that 'monumental occurrence' is very similar to this *archetypal* manifestation.

Extending this analysis to the two other aspects of *Aruṇācala Śiva,* we ought to identify the *Maharṣi* as each of these three aspects rather than take him to be only an incarnation of the God *Muruga,* the son of *Śiva,* as many learned Hindu pundits have done in the past. This was on account of the strongest planet in *Śrī Ramaṇa Maharṣi's* chart being Ma and the ruling Deity corresponding to this planet being *Subrahmaṇya Swāmi.*

In our analysis, using the framework of the SA, we see that Ma is extremely well-placed in spite of its exact affliction of the Asdt lord; its strength must be considered to be at the maximum. We must also deem Sa, the other strong planet in the *Maharṣi's* chart, by virtue of its orb of affliction being more than a degree and by its being located in an angular house, to have its full unmitigated strength in accordance with the *sūtras* of the SA.

Though the role of Ma was patently crucial as a *Mokṣakāraka* for the boy *Ramaṇa,* we must also make allowance for Sa to have had a significant role in bestowing *Mokṣa* and in dragging him on the *Nivṛtti mārga* towards solitude and seclusion.

In fact, Sa, being one of the strong planets in the *Maharṣi's* chart and having a malefic impact on the Asdt house and IVH, must be deemed as imparting to the *Maharṣi* all those Saturnian *Nivṛtti* qualities that Pandit Vamadeva Shastri has painstakingly enumerated. The *Bhikṣāṭana* form of *Śiva, another aspect of the Maharṣi's avatarhood,* was architectured, for the most part, by this exact malefic Saturnian influence of negation and renunciation.

In the words of Pandit Vamadeva Shastri:

> *Saturn is the yogi in meditation. He can give complete detachment and independence. He is the one who stands alone and goes beyond the limitations of the masses. . . . In this respect the power of Shiva, who is the lord of the yogis and the god of transcendence, works through Saturn.* (*Astrology of the Seers* 80)
>
> *Saturn gives bad luck, misfortune, difficult karma, or an unfortunate destiny. . . . Some souls, particularly those more advanced, may seek such things as a means of quicker spiritual growth. . . . Saturn causes poverty, deprivation and want.* (78)

The above significations of Sa have been almost classically fulfilled in the life of the Maharṣi. To understand the trials and tribulations to which *Ramaṇa's* body was subjected, we must focus on the close influence of Sa on the Asdt MEP and IVH. The highly malefic influence of Ma, the MMP, on the Asdt lord must also be considered in *Ramaṇa's* strange experiences of body and mind, which astrologers would identify as 'near-death experiences' given by the lord of the VIIIH.

The implosion of *Mokṣa* had left the body of *Ramaṇa* without a proper human 'owner', and for this reason, it is probably correct to say that though the body was subjected to all these trials and tribulations, there was no owner to stake a claim to them. Though *Ramaṇa* did declare and accepted later on that 'he' did pass through these trials and tribulations, his words cannot be taken at face value, and there is no way for us to grasp what 'his' experiences were actually like. The experiences, nonetheless, are explained by the SA and VA *sūtras* describing the effects of a malefic Sa on the Asdt, or the effects of the MMP on the Asdt lord.

Insects, mosquitoes, and vermin inflicted pain on the body of *Ramaṇa* when he lost body consciousness for long periods of time. Then he shifted to the outskirts of Tiruvannamalai, to a few places in succession. A biography of the *Maharṣi* by

A. R. Natarajan confirms this. This happened during the Sa-Su sub-period after *Mokṣa,* when *Ramaṇa* used to spontaneously slip into the state of *samādhi.*

> *. . . . Ramana just moved into the Patalalingam, an underground vault in the thousand pillared hall. It was dark and damp. . . . Only ants, vermin and mosquitoes flourished there. They preyed upon him and his thighs were covered with sores that ran with blood and pus.* (Natarajan 44)

The strange mystical adventures of body and mind and the 'death-like experiences' characteristic of the VIIIH befell *Ramaṇa* during this period, and his experiences are best described in the *Maharṣi's* own words. Here, we find good evidence for the *tāmasic* nature of Sa (and Ma) coming into manifestation; the 'astrological clock' showed that the Sa-Ma sub-period was in effect:

> *Days and nights would pass without my being aware of their passing. I entertained no idea of bathing or cleaning of teeth or other cleansing activities even when I had defecated and had no baths. The face got begrimed, the hair had become one clotted mass like wax and the nails grew long. When anyone thought that I should have food, I would stretch a hand and something would drop on my hand. My hands were not useful for any other purpose. I would eat and rub my hands on my head or body and drop again into my continuous mood. This was my condition for some years from the time of my arrival. For many years I ate only off my hand without using any leaf plate.* (qtd. in Natarajan 48)

In 1899, *Ramaṇa* shifted to *Virūpākṣa* cave, but for a period of six months he temporarily had to shift to *Pacchaiamman Koil* due to the outbreak of plague in Tiruvannamalai. In this description of his ascetic life in *Ramaṇa's* own words, one discerns both the 'obstructions' so characteristic of the VIIIH lord's influence on the Asdt lord — brought into relief in minute painful detail — as also the influences of a strongly malefic Saturn, thereby clearly illustrating the conditions of poverty and penury. But we must not fail to notice that these seemingly degrading external conditions to which the body was subjected were nothing at all to the *Maharṣi,* as in his consciousness, he was poised on the throne of uninterrupted bliss of the Self.

> *When I was at Pachaiamman Koil, I had a small towel which was tattered and torn, almost to rags, with threads having come out in most places. Once a cowherd boy made fun of this torn rag by telling me, 'The governor wants this towel'. I replied, 'Tell him I won't give it to him!' I never used to spread it out in public. I used to keep it rolled into a ball and wipe my body, hands or mouth as the occasion demanded with the towel so rolled up into a ball. I used to wash it and dry it in a place between two rocks, which place was never visited by any of those who were with me. Even my cod-piece was tattered. When the top end used to become worn out, I would reverse the cod-piece and use it with the bottom end topmost. When going into the forest, I would secretly mend my cod-piece with thread taken out of it with prickly pear thorn for needle.* (qtd. in Natarajan 54)

This is sufficient testimony that *Ramaṇa* lived like a mendicant in abject poverty (*Bhikṣāṭana* aspect of *Śiva*). In sharp contrast to providing these adversities, Sa, being *Nirvāṇakāraka,* also had an important role in architecturing the *Maharṣi's Mokṣa.* We even have proof that a strong Sa blessed the *Maharṣi* with Saturnian virtues — love of meticulous detail, concentration, and capacity for disciplined work — amidst all the sufferings it created for the *Maharṣi* on account of its lordship of the malefic VIH.

In the kitchen of the *āśrama* where the *Maharṣi* often worked as a *karmayogi,* these Saturnian virtues became all too evident. He could not tolerate careless work. He used to cook and was very meticulous in his standards of service and taste. This was a lesson for all those who came later to cook for the devotees and remained there as *sevaks.*

17. Structure and Function of the Process of Mokṣa

The *Maharṣi's* route to *Mokṣa,* if there is one to be discerned at all, or the process, if there was a process in evidence at all, are fascinating mysteries for astrologers.

Every kind of 'process' culminating in *Mokṣa* is naturally different from every other kind, but the *Maharṣi's* has an astonishing quality to it — its sudden emergence without any *sādhana,* its precedence by twenty minutes of profound and penetrative enquiry into the nature of death and the self. The structure and nature of this incredible process can be grasped in astrological terms and this will, in fact, be one of our memorable milestones in this Pilgrimage.

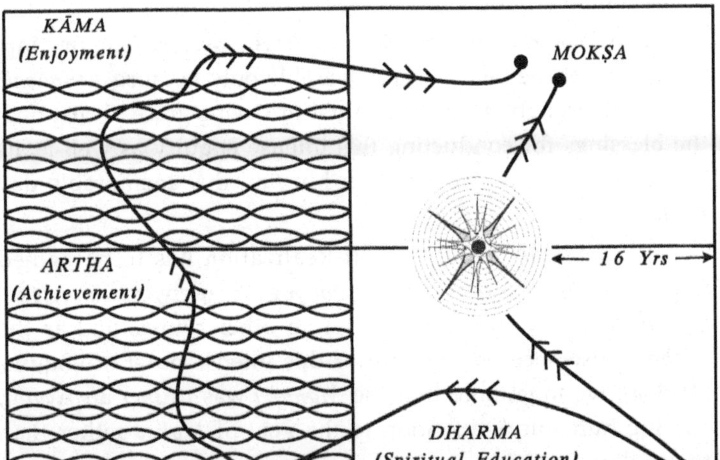

The Maharṣi's Route to Mokṣa

Note: The above figure illustrates the unheard-of 'short cut' to *Mokṣa* that the *Maharṣi* took on account of the blessings of *Aruṇācala Śiva.* In traditional Hindu society, seekers secured the blessings of *Mokṣa* only after they had completed their pilgrimage through the mundane spheres of *Artha* and *Kāma.* In the *Maharṣi's* case, he was spared the agony of travelling through the mundane spheres of *Artha* and *Kāma.*

When the door of *Jñāna* had suddenly opened up for the *Maharṣi* in his sixteenth year, it was as if the gates of heaven had swung open for him in a most unexpected manner, without giving him the slightest foretaste of what was to come into his life. He was certainly no ardent seeker like *Ādi Śaṅkara* or the *Buddha*. In fact he had never even asked God in this life that he be given Self-Realization! However, once at this 'gate', he was unconditionally granted the Divine grace for conducting a profound *maraṇavicāra* [enquiry into death] that lasted for twenty minutes. And as he passed this 'entrance test' there and then with flying colours, he was forthwith dramatically ushered into the kingdom of the Self, with a full-blown Realization that he was indeed that Self or the Godhead, the transcendental Source of all creation.

The *Maharṣi's maraṇavicāra* and *Ātmavicāra* [enquiry into the nature of the Self] became possible only because *Aruṇācala Śiva* had, through His sudden burst of Divine grace, thrust both the blessings for conducting this intense enquiry as well as its immediate fruit of *Mokṣa* upon him, on that memorable day itself.

In fact, this 'route' to Self-Realization has to be named appropriately as a branch of *Jñānayoga,* namely, *maraṇavicāra* and *Ātmavicāra,* to set it apart from other routes, and as the *Maharṣi* also secured the fruit of this intense burst of enquiry (*Mokṣa*), we must note that the *Maharṣi* was in fact an *Avatār,* turning humanity's attention to the goal of *Mokṣa* rather than the goal of *Dharma.*

The strange quality to the Maharṣi's Mokṣa was that there was no Guru who had initiated him through a dīkṣa [initiation]; Ju was too weak for a Guru to have manifested in his life. This is to be contrasted with Śrī Shirdi Sai Baba, whose strong Ju had blessed him with a great and powerful Guru. For the Maharṣi, there was no mantra sādhana, no yoga, no awakening of chakras and nadis, no rising of Kuṇḍalinī, no seeing of lights and visions, no mystic experience nor even a 'death experience' or even samādhi, and yet the illusory little self — the me and the mine — suddenly fell away, unmasking the truth of who he was. It is difficult to visualize a more direct and faster route to Mokṣa.

The testimony for the complete absence of any kind of *sādhana,* both before *Mokṣa* as well as after it, comes from the *Maharṣi* himself:

> *I have never done any sadhana. I did not even know what sadhana was. Only long afterwards I came to know what sadhana was and how many different kinds of it there were.* ***It is only if there was any object or anything different from me that I could think of it. Only if there was a goal to attain, I should have made sadhana towards that goal. There was nothing which I wanted to obtain.*** *I am now sitting with my eyes open. I was then sitting with my eyes closed. That was all the difference. I was not doing any sadhana even then. As I sat with my eyes closed, people said I was in samadhi. As I was not talking, they said I was in mouna. The fact is I did nothing. Some Higher Power took hold of me and I was entirely in Its hands* (emphasis mine). (qtd. in Natarajan 31)

There is another signification of the strong Sa that impressed itself on the *Maharṣi's* life in no small measure. Light on this aspect of Sa as the lord of the VIH is thrown by the SA. The VIH lord, when strong, and especially when making an impact on the Asdt, not only confers on the individual all the Saturnian traits we have been describing but also creates in that individual the urge for profound enquiry — delving deep into *Ātmavicāra* or finding logical meanings and expressions for the various enigmatic spiritual truths of life (SA *sūtra*).

In VA, it is well known that the IIIH *per se* is the house of profound interest and curiosity. As the *Icchā Śakti* of the Divine Mother drives this house, the profound interest given by the IIIH carries with it the intoxication of enjoyment and absorption, whereas the profound enquiry given by Sa as the VIH lord is driven rather by the Divine Mother's *Kriyā Śakti,* which confers greater wilfulness. Therefore, the individual in question prefers to bring an alternative approach and a new understanding to unconventional fields rather than passively accept the truth given by traditional authorities.

However, the new approach arising in this way through the energy of the VIH lord might not find adequate recognition. Thus, the new teaching of *Śrī Ramaṇa Maharṣi* in the sphere of *Jñānamārga* was profound enquiry into the nature of the Self and came as a blessing both from Sa as the VIH lord as well as from Ma, the VIIIH lord, the *Mokṣakāraka.*

These additional insights into Sa's influence come from Prof. V. K. Choudhry's SA. It is also recognized in the SA that like the VIIIH lord, even the VIH lord can confer research and occult interests. However, as the *rājasic Kriyā Śakti* drives the VIH, there is an additional element of impatience and rushing energy that is likely to make the works of the VIH vulnerable to damage, *but only in the event of more sāttvic influences not being present in the chart.* In the *Maharṣi's* case, we have already seen that the *Kriyā Śakti* flowing through a strong Sa includes a large component of *Jñāna Śakti.* These subtle differences between the profound enquiry of the VIIIH and VIH are part of the insights of the SA.

18. Afflictions in the Maharṣi's Horoscope Created Spiritual Blessings

The *Maharṣi's* horoscope has so many afflictions (see Section 10) that on the face of it, it might come as a rude shock that this is indeed the chart of a great *Avatār.* Apart from the two strong FMs Ma and Sa, there are no strong FBs from the SA point of view. Moreover, all four of the angular Hs are afflicted almost exactly, and worst of all, both the Asdt as well as the Asdt lord are exactly afflicted. All of this means that the *Maharṣi* was, from the astrological point of view, almost crucified and held captive by the life force of the Divine Mother so that, in fact, he could achieve practically nothing through his own personal exertions.

There is thus seen to be an 'all-round conspiracy' in the mood of God at the time and place of the *Maharṣi's* birth insofar as his achievements in the spheres of *Artha* and *Kāma* are concerned. We may remind ourselves here that in Hindu astrology in the spheres of *Dharma* and *Mokṣa* (see Chapter III, Section 18), the horoscope shows the mood of God at the time and place of birth, and this mood can either be favourable for enjoyment and achievement or unfavourable for the same. For the *Maharṣi,* it precluded a life in the spheres of *Artha* and *Kāma.*

Rather than view this as a handicap and a denial of all opportunities, we must see in this all-round conspiracy in the mood of God, a Divine plan, which while being highly unfavourable for success in mundane life, had, in fact, opened up the doors of *Mokṣa* for the *Maharṣi!* As the door to enjoyment and achievement in the outer world had been slammed shut through these multiple afflictions, the *Maharṣi* had no option but to turn inwards — which is actually what he was obliged to do during the 'monumental occurrence' on the day of his illumination — and in this process, make the monumental discovery that he was the Self of the whole world (see Section 24, wherein this 'occurrence' is described in detail). Thus, all the afflictions in hindsight seem to be just the right ingredients and spiritual blessings in disguised form, necessary for the making of this *Avatār* in the *Nivṛtti* sphere of *Mokṣa.*

There is a Christian *sūtra* that throws abundant light on this strange astrological paradox on the duality of life. This astrological *sūtra* may be put in the following enigmatic form: *In every affliction is concealed a blessing and in every blessing is the inherent potential for a fall.* It is on account of this paradox that those destined to become one with God often have to suffer the worst kinds of hardships and perhaps even poverty. It is said, "*Blessed are the meek, for they shall inherit the kingdom of God* (Christian *sūtra*)." Interpreted astrologically, this would mean that the meek are those with afflictions in their charts, and these afflictions and planetary weaknesses deny the material world while blessing us with the highest bliss of *Mokṣa.*

For the *Maharṣi,* for whom the earth was to become heaven and the kingdom of God was to be here on earth, it was but inevitable that he had to be humbled in the sense meant in the Christian *sūtra.* The so-called afflictions in his chart are but a reflection of the price he had to pay on the material plane for securing and deserving *Mokṣa*! Thus it is that the ones who have these kinds of all-round afflictions are the recipients of the highest blessings, for it is only for them that the *prasāda* of *Mokṣa* seems to be reserved.

19. The Maharṣi vis-à-vis the Mahātmā

In one sense, *Mahātmā Gandhi* was on the *Pravṛtti mārga,* but he was also on the *Nivṛtti mārga* insofar as his unceasing self-critical introspections were concerned. By contrast, the *Maharṣi* was entirely on the *Nivṛtti mārga.* The achievements of the *Mahātmā* on the *Pravṛtti mārga* were visible to the whole world, and he therefore came to be recognized as an *Avatār,* whereas the *Maharṣi,* treading the *Nivṛtti mārga* and being in *antarmukha* for practically the whole course of his life, never really emerged on the horizon as a national hero, a crusading champion for the cause of some pressing social reform nor even a great patriot in the mould of *Swāmi Vivekānanda. He did not have the engines of desire still running in his consciousness to be able to seek out any kind of role for himself on the world stage. A Mahāpuruṣa can have a mission, but Ramaṇa as Aruṇācala Śiva, the transcendent God of the Hindu world, could not possibly seek a role for himself, for he was already the Self in all its infinite glory.*

Notwithstanding the *Maharṣi's* more subdued spiritual impact, his irresistible spiritual message of awakening to the Self, intended for the whole of humanity, was certainly one that went more irresistibly and directly into human souls, especially for all those sensitive spiritual seekers who could see that a moral or political revolution on the physical plane was not necessarily the highest and most beneficial goal for humankind but that there was a still higher spiritual life for the species.

We must thus recognize that *Ramaṇa Maharṣi* was the embodiment of *Mokṣa,* and we can rejoice in the recognition that this was also the true goal of *Mahātmā Gandhi,* for which his *satyāgraha, ahiṁsā,* and *lokakalyāṇa seva* were all forms of *sādhana,* as he himself had a number of times made abundantly clear:

> *I do not consider myself worthy to be mentioned in the same breath with the race of prophets. I am a humble seeker after truth. I am impatient to realize myself, to attain moksha in this very existence. My national service is part of my training for freeing my soul from the bondage of flesh. Thus considered, my service may be regarded as purely selfish. I have no desire for the perishable kingdom of earth. I am striving for the Kingdom of Heaven which is moksha.* (*What is Hinduism?* 17)

For the reason that we did not see much 'activity' and much outward concern in the *Maharṣi* for the pathetic plight of a spiritually blind humanity, we must not be quick to pass him by. By the example of his life, he was the embodiment of *Sanātana Dharma* in its highest spiritual sphere of *Mokṣa.* From this point of view then, it would be proper to view *Mahātmā Gandhi* as the embodiment of *Sanātana Dharma* in the spiritual and political sphere of *Dharma.*

While one *Avatār* was busy fighting *adharma* in the land with the spiritual weapons of *ahiṁsā* and *satyāgraha* and attempting to establish moral and social order [*Dharma*] in our social and political life, the other *Avatār* was not even trying to create order or *Dharma* in the inner life! No! He was far far away from all these concerns of the virtuous and the compassionate. He was established on the innermost throne of the Self by the Divine grace of his *Iṣṭadevatā, Aruṇācala Śiva,* and was constantly blessing the world through his benevolent gaze from that exalted position of himself being *Aruṇācala Śiva*!

20. No Prior Spiritual Inclinations

There was no obvious proof that *Ramaṇa* was spiritually inclined until his sixteenth year, when he was suddenly blessed with *Mokṣa.* When his biographer B. V. Narasimha Swami had once questioned the *Maharṣi* about the spiritual disposition of the boy *Ramaṇa* prior to *Mokṣa,* the *Maharṣi* provided the following truthful answer:

> *At that time, I had no idea of the identity of that current of my personality with personal God or 'Iswara' as I used to term him. I had not even heard of the Bhagavad Gita or other religious works. Except Periapuranam and the Bible class texts, the Gospels and Psalms, I had not read any other religious books. I had just seen, with my uncle, a copy of Vivekananda's Chicago address but had not read it. I could not even correctly pronounce the Swami's name but pronounced it Vyvekananda, giving the 'I' the 'y' sound. I had no notions of religious philosophy, except the current notion of God that he is an infinitely powerful person, present everywhere, though worshipped in special places in images representing him and other ideas which are contained in the Bible text or Periapuranam which I had read.* (qtd. in Natarajan 26)

To these spiritual credentials, we may add another important observation the *Maharṣi* had himself made elsewhere, namely, his honesty — he never lied. There were no spiritual events other than these. The placement of the Su in the IVH, making a close impact on the MEP of that house, was crucial for the boy *Ramaṇa* being utterly honest, as the Su is a significator of character as well as honesty. A strong *navāṁśa* chart also reinforced this trait of honesty.

We must not miss here a very significant feature in the horoscope of the *Maharṣi,* tallying with the complete absence of any signs of early spiritual development in the boy *Ramaṇa,* who was later to flower into the *Maharṣi*: there were no planets placed in the VH of *Iṣṭadevatā* and the IXH of *Guru,* God, and grace. Had there been especially benefic planets in one or both of these *Dharma* Hs, this would have manifested as some spiritual qualities in the boy *Ramaṇa.*

This may be contrasted with the chart and life of the Master *Śrī Śrī Bhagavān,* who had strong spiritual inclinations such as wanting to be in solitude and wanting to meditate even as a child. Similar prominent spiritual tendencies such as a compassionate nature and astral sensitivity to subtler planes of consciousness have also been known to exist in the life of the other Master *Śrī J. Krishnamurti* right from his childhood. By mentioning the contrasting examples of these two Masters, by no means am I suggesting that they were more spiritually evolved than the *Maharṣi.* Each *Avatār* and each great Master is a special manifestation of God; for our part in this astrological Pilgrimage, we have the challenge of coming into empathy with each Master, thereby attempting to understand how the *Śaktis* of the Divine Mother have been shaping and sculpturing their respective approaches and teachings.

21. Candra Lagna, Sūrya Lagna, and the Navāṁśa Chart

When the *Maharṣi's* horoscope is viewed with regard to *Candra lagna,* one comes upon spiritual or *Dharma* potentials that were not evident at all when viewed with regard to *Janma lagna. This is usually done in VA but ignored in the SA on account of the latter's greater precisional clarity in reading the Janma lagna itself.* In VA, the view from the *Candra lagna* and *Sūrya lagna* gain importance as in the spiritual spheres one is not so much on the physical plane to which the *Janma lagna* refers, but rather, on the subtler planes of consciousness. The astral body [*Candra lagna*] and the causal body [*Sūrya lagna*] acquire greater importance for the spiritual life.

With respect to the *Candra lagna* in the *Maharṣi's* chart, Sa is *Anugrahakāraka,* and Sa's exact aspect energizes the IVH of *asmitā,* while Ju's fifth aspect as well as ninth aspect energizes the IH and VH. Thus, the chart shows a spiritual orientation of the astral body and consciousness even though the personality in the outer life did not reveal these potentials until *Mokṣa* had come to pass.

In my experience of studying horoscopes in the spheres of *Dharma* and *Mokṣa,* I have found that it does happen that the outer personality as revealed in the *rāśi* chart can be far from spiritual and might even be ostensibly antagonistic to God, whereas the soul or the astral body as revealed by the *navāṁśa* chart can be highly spiritual. In VA, the *navāṁśa* chart is taken to signify the mission of the soul; the outlook and the mission of the outer personality is explained more by the *rāśi* chart.

In the light of these subtle considerations, we see that behind the mask of the seemingly unspiritual personality of the boy *Ramaṇa,* there was well-concealed an astral body and a causal body (soul), which were both quite drenched in Divine grace with their faces turned towards God. Here, then, is an example of an astrological insight that could not possibly have come from a biography of the *Maharṣi.*

Again, with regard to the *Sūrya lagna,* the Su as the IXH lord occupies the Asdt and blesses the Asdt MEP almost exactly. Thus, the spiritual power of the chart comes into view. The Asdt lord with regard to *Sūrya lagna,* by virtue of its placement in the IIIH close to the MEP, makes an impact on the MEP of the IXH of God and grace as well.

As the Mo is the planet of subconsciousness and the feeling nature, these spiritual potentials in the horoscopes of the astral body and the causal body actually came to the fore in the form of a profound newly discovered devotion to God. But the 'monumental occurrence' was needed in order to unleash this hidden potential. We have therefore abundant proof of the deeply spiritual nature of the soul, especially if we take into account the *navāṁśa* chart. With so many spiritual assets, it should not be surprising to us that the mission of this *Ātmā* [soul] during its earthly sojourn revolved effortlessly and naturally only around *Ātmavicāra,* as the sure means to Self-Realization.

The *navāṁśa* chart has extraordinary importance in Hindu astrology, and we may picture it to be more or less like the *garbhagṛha* [*sanctum sanctorum*] of the IXH of the *rāśi* chart. The IXH in the *Maharṣi's rāśi* chart is closely afflicted by Sa, the FM ruling the VIH. As even Ju, the significator of the IXH, is weak for this Virgo Asdt in view of the IXH not having an MT sign, our only hope of the IXH figuring significantly in the *Maharṣi's* life is through a strong *navāṁśa* chart.

Fortunately, the *navāṁśa* chart, which is the most important among all divisional charts, indicates an exceptionally strong spiritual orientation in the *Maharṣi.* It has a Gemini Asdt with the Mo placed in the Asdt, and with the *Anugrahakāraka* Ju aspecting the Asdt and the Mo from the highly auspicious IXH therein. Sa, another *Anugrahakāraka* for the *navāṁśa* chart, also aspects the Asdt, the Mo, and Ju, which is placed in the *Mūla Trikoṇa* house of Sa. In addition, Ju also aspects the Su, which is placed in its own *Mūla Trikoṇa* house.

Some astrologers justifiably consider the *navāṁśa* chart as the fruit if the *rāśi* chart is likened to the tree. Sometimes, the *navāṁśa* is likened to the spinal cord if the *rāśi* chart is likened to the body. All such perceptions point in one way or other to one thing only — the extraordinary significance of the *navāṁśa* chart, especially in the lives of spiritual people. Thus, the excellent placement of the spiritual planets with regard to the Asdt of the *navāṁśa* chart holds one of the important keys to the spiritual mystery of the *Maharṣi's* life and makes him a teacher on the path of *Jñānayoga* or spiritual understanding and wisdom.

The essence of the *Maharṣi's* teaching lay in the profound *Ātmavicāra* or enquiry into the nature of the 'I'. For this mission of a spiritual teacher, we could not have a better Asdt than Gemini for the D-9 chart, as Gemini bestows an absorbing and profound interest and orientation towards knowledge. The vocation of the teacher figures because Ju's aspect on the Asdt, the Mo, and the Su is from the most spiritual of all the houses, the IXH of the *navāṁśa* chart. The third sign Gemini, ruled by the *rāśi* chart's Asdt lord Me, which was also placed in the IIIH of Scorpio, points to the profound interest and enquiry with which the IIIH and Gemini are intimately connected.

Although the *Dharma* houses in the *rāśi* chart are empty, and although the IXH as well as its significator are weak, yet, as the placements of spiritual planets in the *navāṁśa* chart are excellent, this chart is saturated with Divine grace. Thus, the potential for being an enlightened teacher is beyond dispute. The teachings are indicated by the chart to be Jupiterean (spiritual) and also Saturnian, related to the *Nivṛtti mārga* and detachment, and centred around some profound enquiry.

22. The Boy Ramaṇa's Personality

In a biographical work on the *Maharṣi*, A. R. Natarajan has thrown light on some aspects of the boy's personality. *Ramaṇa* seems to have enjoyed a certain 'gift', which people described as his 'golden touch'. In his native Tamil language, someone with 'golden hands' has a special blessing, which s/he can transmit to the world, by just 'touching'. This is best described by the *Maharṣi* himself. The boy also had a passion for physical and sporting activities.

> *At all times and in all games, I used to win invariably, were it wrestling or swimming or even domestic chores. If my aunt began preparing appalams (a typically Tamilian flat round preparation made from rice and lentils, usually fried and eaten), or such like, she would call me and ask me to put my hand on it first. She had great faith in me because I would do everything according to her wishes and never told lies.* (qtd. in Natarajan 24)

We may understand this blessing of golden hands as being sourced in two independent astrological variables in the *Maharṣi's* chart. In VA it is understood that if a certain potential in the horoscope is destined to come to fructification in the outer life, that potential will recur in two, three, or even four independent ways. It is on the basis of such a recurring pattern that we may become certain of its fructification. The *Maharṣi's* Asdt is in the *Hasta nakṣatra,* which has the following signification: *Hasta nakṣatra* people are known to have some special advantage, skill, or blessing in the use of their hands. But this is not the whole story.

The Asdt lord Me is placed in the IIIH, signifying hands, and is exactly influenced by the strong MMP Ma from the VIIIH. When there is such an instance of 'good fortune', we need to look for a strong IXH or a strong Ju (the significator of the IXH) and a strong *navāṁśa* chart to see what the possible source of the good fortune could be. Two other sources in Hindu astrology of what astrologers call 'easy gains' are a strong Mo as a representative of the Divine Mother, who nurtures and nourishes, as well as a strong VIIIH.

If we look at all these possible sources of good fortune, we find that the *navāṁśa* chart is saturated with Divine grace; in addition, there is a 'strong' Mo, which is not only well-placed but is also blessed by two *Anugrahakārakas* in the *navāṁśa* chart. The Mo is also in the Asdt of the *navāṁśa* chart and is the lord of the XIH of the *rāśi* chart. All these facts, taken along with the strong lord of the VIIIH, which gives easy gains, would account for the boy *Ramaṇa* always winning in all his IIIH activities.

After all, the Mo is the lord of the XIH of fulfilment of goals and ambitions, of aspirations, and of gains, and the position of the Mo in the *rāśi* chart and *navāṁśa* chart fully accounts for how Grace always favoured the boy *Ramaṇa* even when he was on the *Nivṛtti mārga.* The IIIH signifies hands, and since the power of vitality coming from Ma is seen to fully enter into the boy *Ramaṇa's* body represented by Me, we must suppose that Me's placement in the IIIH and significantly in the sign Scorpio, which represents the physical side of Ma's energy, endowed the boy *Ramaṇa* with the physical prowess of Ma, thereby accounting for his strong inclination and success in all sports activities.

The power of the boy *Ramaṇa's* memory was recognized at school, especially his detailed knowledge of abstruse Tamil grammar. This capacity, in the SA, comes from a strong VH, the Mo, and Me. Me, being the planet of analytical processing, carries the power of memory, whenever strong in a horoscope. For a Virgo Asdt, as the VH has no MT Sign, a strong Ju as significator of the VH also gives a strong memory. Though the *Maharṣi's* Ju was not strong, its close impact on the IIH of the intellect and concentration gave him Divine grace for a good memory.

Again, in the *caturviṁśāṁśa* chart (D-24) pertaining to education and to *Jñānayoga* in the spiritual life, we see the close impact of Ju on the Asdt and on the Asdt lord Me placed in the VH therein. Finally, as the Virgo Asdt's lord is Me, the planet of analytical processing, Virgos have an advantage where memory power is concerned. The confluence of all these factors resulted in the *Maharṣi's* good memory.

Another characteristic of the boy *Ramaṇa* was that he could not easily be roused from sleep; his family members and others had great difficulty in waking him. This very strange difficulty in rousing him from the depths of slumber was well attested to by the *Maharṣi* in later years:

> *I was a heavy sleeper. When I was at Dindigul in 1891 a huge crowd had gathered close to the room where I slept and tried to rouse me by their shouting, roaring and knocking at the door in vain, and it was only by getting into my room and giving me a violent shake that I was roused from my torpor.* (qtd. in Narasimha Swami 16)

In the SA as well as in VA, sleep comes under the dominion of the XIIH, the house of the unmanifest, the unconscious, rest, sleep, and relaxation. In the *Maharṣi's* horoscope, the lord that grants sleep, namely, the Su, is placed close to the MEP of the house of waking consciousness, namely, the IVH of *asmitā* or I-am-ness. The Su is a massive body and the fructification it grants is proportionate to its royal massivity and abundance. Thus, the placement of the Su in the fourth house of waking consciousness naturally extinguishes the light of waking consciousness or creates a 'loss' of waking consciousness in proportion to the massivity of the Su.

In addition to this mechanism of the infusion of sleep into waking consciousness, there is also the *tāmasic* influence of Sa on the house of waking consciousness as Sa afflicts the IVH closely. Ju, which basically decides how 'bright' the light of waking consciousness is, is also seen to be weak, having been placed weakly in the VIH. These cumulative influences made it very difficult for the boy *Ramaṇa* to be a light sleeper. In other words, only in a Virgo Asdt with the Su placed close to the MEP of the IVH would it be possible to account for the strange 'death-like' sleep of the boy *Ramaṇa.*

23. Maraṇavicāra Leads to Full Self-Realization

On February 18, 1892 (Sa-Ke sub-period), *Ramaṇa's* father passed away. The boy *Ramaṇa* was then only twelve years old. The impact of his father's death upon the young *Ramaṇa* comes to our notice through A. R. Natarajan's biography. That he had puzzled over this shocking loss is known to us from the journalist Paul Brunton's description, which appears in this biography.

> *On the day his father died* ***he felt puzzled by death and pondered over it, whilst his mother and brothers wept****. He thought for hours and after the corpse was cremated he got by analysis to the point of perceiving that it was the 'I' which makes the body to see, to run, to walk and to eat. "I now know this 'I' but my father's 'I' has left the body"* (emphasis mine). (qtd. in Natarajan 22)

The approach to life via the intellect and enquiry so typical of Virgo Asdts finds a confirmation in the foregoing description. This is very reminiscent of *Ādi Śaṅkara,* who lost his father and *Guru* at all too tender an age. The philosophical impact of death in human life is beautifully portrayed in G. V. Iyer's film on

Ādi Śaṅkara, in which the boy *Śaṅkara* is seen to be accompanied constantly by two 'friends'. One friend was Death and the other was *Prajñāna,* the intelligence of the enlightened. The importance of 'dying' to every human experience and 'living with death' has also been emphasized by the Master *Śrī J. Krishnamurti.* Apart from Ma's affliction to the Asdt lord resulting in 'dying' becoming the central theme of *Ramaṇa's* life, Sa's separative influences on the IXH, the Su, and the IVH were also responsible for the premature death of *Ramaṇa's* father and his subsequent profound interest and enquiry into the same.

On July 16, 1896, at Madurai, after *Ramaṇa* had completed his sixteenth year, a spontaneously arising strange and intensely profound enquiry into the nature of death overtook him, leaving him, at the end of the process, a mature Self-Realized Sage. This is so incredible an occurrence that spiritual seekers would simply be dumbfounded by the immense gravity of it, and above all, its sheer impossibility. This occurred in the Sa-Su sub-period and lasted only for about twenty minutes. It was a profound enquiry into the meaning of death. Was this 'death' only for the gross human body or did it also extended to the spirit or the 'I' that *Ramaṇa* felt himself to be?

There was surely not a 'death experience' as such nor even a 'near-death' experience on the said date, but an intense spurt of spontaneous profound enquiry had overtaken the boy and gently landed him on the shores of Self-Realization – an absolutely unheard-of happening.

What followed in the wake – weeks and months – after this 'monumental occurrence' was the *Maharṣi's* stabilization in Self-Realization, which Self-Realization *per se* had already come to pass with its full-fledged maturity on that very day of days. This was the decided view of the great *Ramaṇa* himself. We first examine the *Maharṣi's* own account of *maraṇavicāra* as a prelude to a Hindu astrological examination of the same.

It was about six weeks before I left Madurai for good that the great change in my life took place. It was quite sudden. I was sitting alone in a room on the first floor of my uncle's house. I seldom had any sickness, and on that day there was nothing wrong with my health, ***but a sudden violent fear of death overtook me****. There was nothing in my state of health to account for it, and I did not try to account for it or to find out whether there was any reason for the fear.* ***I just felt 'I am going to die' and began thinking what to do about it****. It did not occur to me to consult a doctor, or my elders or friends; I felt that I had to solve the problem myself, there and then.*

The shock of the fear of death drove my mind inwards and I said to myself mentally, without actually framing the words: ***'Now death has come; what does it mean****?* ***What is it that is dying****?* ***The body dies'****. And I at once dramatized the occurrence of death. I lay with my limbs stretched out stiff as though* **rigor mortis** *had set in and imitated a corpse so as to give greater reality to the enquiry. I held my breath and kept my lips tightly closed so that no sound could escape, so that neither the word 'I' nor any other word could be uttered. 'Well then', I said to myself, 'this body is dead. It will be carried stiff to the burning ground and there burnt and reduced to ashes. But with the death of this body am I dead? Is the body I? It is silent and inert but I feel the full force of my personality and even the voice of the 'I' within me, apart from it. So I am Spirit transcending the body. The body dies but the Spirit that transcends it cannot be touched by death. That means I am the deathless Spirit'. All this was not dull thought; it flashed through me vividly as living truth, which I perceived directly, almost without thought-process.* ***'I' was something very real, the only real thing about my present state, and all the conscious activity connected with my body was centred on that 'I'. From that moment onwards the 'I' or Self focussed attention on itself by a powerful fascination****. Fear of death had vanished once and for all. Absorption in the Self continued unbroken from that time on* (emphasis mine). (qtd. in Arthur Osborne *The Teachings* 2)

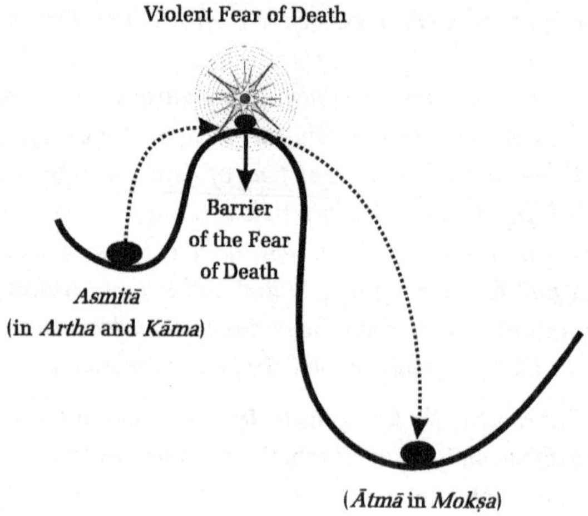

The Miracle of Self-Realization

Note: This figure conveys the process of *Mokṣa* that the *Maharṣi* has described in the above paragraphs. Significant was his surmounting the barrier of the fear of death and thereafter descending beautifully into the valley of Immortality.

Although the 'I' of *Ramaṇa* had gotten permanently dissociated from his body and from the idea of an ownership of that body, yet this Self-Realization was so profoundly non-verbal that the boy, because he did not then possess the special spiritual vocabulary from the sacred texts, was unable to articulate his new condition with full clarity. Another thing that was unknown to the boy *Ramaṇa* was the fact that he had attained the highest Realization that the traditional scriptures expounded. He was at a loss to 'know' this fact, because the instrument and faculty of knowing, I-am-ness, had also been lost, for this was synonymous with the loss of individuality. It was only after coming into contact with standard scriptural texts that the young Sage was able to understand and articulate his Realization with perfect clarity. The following two testimonies bring home this point to us.

Śrī V. S. Ramanan, president of *Śrī Ramanasramam,* in writing a Publisher's Note to *The Song of Ribhu* in 2003 makes it clear that the traditional spiritual significance of the boy *Ramaṇa's* Self-Realization in the context of the Hindu spiritual tradition had dawned on *Ramaṇa* only a year or so after its occurrence, having come into contact with classical works on *Mokṣa* such as the *Ribhu Gīta* as well as other *Vedāntic* texts. As an eighteen-year old Sage, the *Maharṣi* was then living in the mango grove near *Gurumurtham,* and it was his attendant Palaniswami who procured these works for the *Maharṣi* from the Nagalinga Swami library. In *Śrī* V. S. Ramanan's words:

> *The Maharshi later told of his surprise upon hearing an exact description of his own exalted state in verses recited from this Ribhu Gita. Until then he had no idea that what had happened to him during an intense, brief enquiry into his own being at his Madurai house, had been experienced by others and was much sought after by seekers of Truth from time immemorial.* (*The Song of Ribhu* Publisher's Note)

The *Maharṣi* had also said:

> *At Tiruvannamalai, as I listened to Ribhugita and other works I picked up these facts and discovered that these books were analysing and naming what I had previously felt intuitively without analysis and name. In the language of the books, I should describe my mental or spiritual condition after the awakening, as Suddha Manas or Prajnana* [*i.e.,* the Intuition of the Illumined]. (Narasimha Swami *Self Realization* 20)

This *Prajñāna* of the *Maharṣi* could thereafter eloquently expound the *advaitic* Realization, which the *Maharṣi* was living every moment of his life. He was a *Tyāgarāja* [king among renunciants], and as he desired absolutely nothing from the world, he transmitted to every thirsty seeker who came to his door this very same *advaitic* truth without ever diluting it with even the slightest inessential 'coating' – even in those circumstances when his *advaitic* truth remained intangible and unintelligible; whereas it was only the 'coated' version that seemed to go home and was actually relished by seekers! We shall have occasion to meet with one or two illustrative examples of this strict uncompromising adherence to the *advaitic* truth even when it was not intelligible.

There were many testimonies for *Ramaṇa* having lost his self. From among these one may be cited here as it seems particularly striking. *Ramaṇa* had absolutely no plans of his own, in howsoever subtle a form – a most definitive hallmark of the loss of the self.

As the *Maharṣi* had no motive arising from the self, he always spoke the truth without ever toning it down. He adhered to the *advaitic* truth of his Realization, sometimes 'not even understanding' the difficulties that arose from others' naturally dualistic perceptions. Thus, *Śrīmūrti upāsana* [worship of the formful aspect of *Bhagavān*], considered indispensable in *Bhaktiyoga,* never found any favour with him as is clear from the following guidelines of the *Maharṣi.* He did not use the flexible integrative approach used by *Ādi Śaṅkarācārya* in which both *advaita* as well as *dvaita* with God are brought together into a single unified *darśana* [spiritual world view].

> *You must learn to realize the subject and object as one. In meditating on an object, whether concrete or abstract, you are destroying the sense of oneness and creating duality.* (qtd. in Natarajan 258)

On another such occasion, rather than descend from the highest summit of *advaita* to the lower levels of *dvaita,* which alone is expected to be intelligible to ordinary people, the *Maharṣi* is instead seen asking the *dvaitin* to rise to his own *advaitic* level:

Uma Devi, a Polish lady who had opened her heart to the blessings from Hinduism, sought ardently a vision of *Śiva,* who was her beloved Lord. "*Ramaṇa* clarified to her the importance of direct perception of the Self through self-enquiry: *A vision depends on the subject. It would appear and disappear. It is not inherent, not first hand. . . . Therefore enquire 'Who am I?' Sink deep within and abide as the Self. . . .*" (qtd. in Natarajan 267)

24. Ingredients of the 'Monumental Occurrence'

(i) There was a sudden violent fear of death to begin with. This was the trigger for the ensuing process. The *Maharṣi* realized that death had in fact arrived, but strangely, there was a bypassing of both surrender to death as well as resistance to death stemming from fear. Instead, the challenge of the reality of death was met by a very strange detached response: *Ramaṇa* got absorbed there and then in a short but rather intense and penetrative enquiry into death. Death had arrived psychologically, and this was recognized by his faculty of knowing, the I-am-ness.

(ii) Shock of the fear of death, which had triggered this enquiry, made the consciousness turn inwards. This nearly impossible step was due to the grace of God. The non-verbal enquiry followed only because the *Maharṣi's* consciousness could turn inwards. In other words, this was a *prasāda* from God and had its astrological origin in the aspect of the planet of Divine grace, natal Ju, falling on transit (Tr) Me in the sign Gemini. Simultaneously, the aspect of Tr Ju fell on natal Me placed in Scorpio. These synchronous aspects of Ju on Me resulted in the *Maharṣi's* Realization.

(iii) As part of the intense penetrative inner enquiry, the *Maharṣi* simulated bodily death and realized that it brings only the body to an end, leaving the imperishable Spirit untouched.

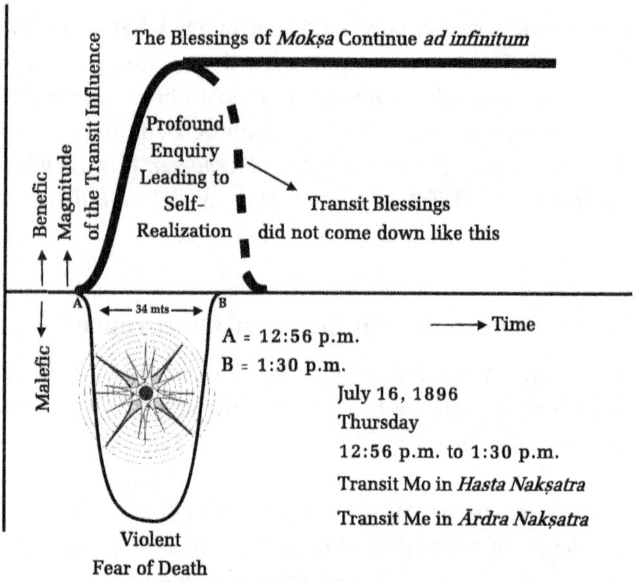

Maharṣi's Mokṣa

Note: The Process of *Mokṣa* involved two simultaneously occurring transit significant events (TSEs). As the *asmitā* was being ripped off by the *Mokṣakārakas* Ma and Sa, a violent fear of death was unleashed in the *Maharṣi.* This challenge was met with an equanimous profound enquiry into the nature of death and self, and grace was available for the same. The cumulative result was the *prasāda* of *Mokṣa.*

(iv) Thus, the Realization dawned that 'he' was the deathless Spirit. With this, the Self, which had been disguised till then as the 'the personal self', lost all its identity and 'imagined association' with the body, the human personality and the ego, and fell back into its original pristine state — the Self of the whole world, *Śiva.*

(v) With the Realization of the Self as it actually is, that is, without any association with the body or the mind, fear of death entirely vanished for the rest of the *Maharṣi's* life.

25. An Actual Death Experience Versus the 'Monumental Occurrence'

Ramaṇa's body had actually 'died' in 1912 at Virūpākṣa cave, but was miraculously resuscitated. I mention this genuine 'physical death experience' of the *Maharṣi,* which came to pass some sixteen years after the 'monumental occurrence' of *Mokṣa* as an immediate sequel to *maraṇavicāra,* merely to drive home the point that what happened to the *Maharṣi* on the day of Self-Realization was certainly not in the nature of a 'near-death experience'. Rather, it was in the nature of an unimaginably profound, non-verbal, inner enquiry into death and self, and this had brought forth the blessed fruit of Self-Realization.

The *Maharṣi's* actual physical death experience in 1912 in his own words:

> *Suddenly the view of natural scenery in front of me disappeared and a bright white curtain was drawn across the line of my vision and shut out the view of nature. I could distinctly see the gradual process. At one stage I could see a part of the prospect of nature yet clear, and the rest was being covered by the advancing curtain. It was just like drawing a slide across one's view in the stereoscope. On experiencing this I stopped walking lest I should fall. When it cleared, I walked on. When darkness and faintness overtook me a second time, I leaned against a rock until it cleared. And again for the third time, I felt it safest to sit, so I sat near the rock. Then the bright white curtain had completely shut out my vision, my head was swimming, and my blood circulation and breathing stopped. The skin turned a livid blue. It was the regular death-like hue and it got darker and darker. Vasudeva Sastri took me in fact to be dead; held me in his embrace and began to weep aloud and lament my death. His body was shivering.*
>
> *I could at that time distinctly feel his clasp and his shivering, hear his lamentation, and understand the meaning. I also saw the discolouration of my skin, and I felt the stoppage of my heartbeat and respiration, and the increased chilliness of the extremities of my body. Yet my usual current was continuing without a break in that state also. I was not afraid in the least, nor felt any sadness at the condition*

of my body. I had closed my eyes as soon as I sat near the rock in my usual posture, but was not leaning against it. The body which had no circulation, nor respiration maintained that position still. This state continued for some 10 or 15 minutes. Then a shock passed suddenly through the body, circulation revived with enormous force, as also respiration; and there was perspiration all over the body at every pore. The colour of life reappeared on the skin. I then opened my eyes, got up and said, 'Let us go'. We reached Virupaksha cave without further trouble. That was the only occasion on which both my blood circulation and respiration stopped. (qtd. in Natarajan 75)

Therefore, some sixteen years after the 'monumental occurrence' of *Mokṣa* (July 16, 1896) at the tortoise rock in 1912, *Ramaṇa's* body actually clinically died, and he was an unperturbed witness to the same. Because the body that died was not actually 'his' in the sense meant by humans, this could not have been the ghastly experience it would have been for someone who had the feeling of ownership over the body. The point of invoking this experience is only to make it known that Self-Realization on July 16, 1896 was certainly not accompanied by this kind of a truly awesome physical death experience.

26. Self-Realization Leads to Renunciation

On August 29, 1896, some six weeks after the monumental occurrence, the *Maharṣi* renounced his life as a school pupil and as a member of his uncle's family and turned himself over to his beloved God *Aruṇācala Śiva.* (His father had passed away prematurely when he was just twelve, and he was thus obliged to live with his uncle's family in Madurai.) As he had ceased to be 'human' from the very day of his illumination, conformity to human society with its strong emphasis on survival values and conventions must have become an intolerable burden for him. In response to possible lack of communion with the people at home, he at last acted in tune with what the Spirit was bidding from within. The call from God was quite unmistakable, as testified to by the boy *Ramaṇa* himself through the note he left behind before departing from home:

> *I have, in search of my father and in obedience to his command, started from here. This is only embarking on a virtuous enterprise. Therefore none need grieve over this affair. To trace this out, no money need be spent.* (qtd. in Narasimha Swami 24)

Very significantly, as he had been dispossessed of the illusion of a human personality, he did not even sign this note as 'so and so'. Thus began a voyage into the depths of the unknown, not volitionally undertaken by a tremulous and hurt school boy, but rather, through a Divine ordination. Future and past are perceived by one in bondage to time, but here was a sixteen-year old Sage for whom time had already fallen out of life; renunciation – for want of a better word – was what he, as the embodiment of *Aruṇācala Śiva,* wished. He was just going back 'home' – to the place from where he had come in the first place.

After travelling for three days, on September 1, 1896, the boy *Ramaṇa* reached 'home'. Presenting himself forthwith in the sacred presence of his 'Father', he announced his arrival: *"Oh God, obedient to Thy call, here have I come, deserting all"* (qtd. in Narasimha Swami 36). The finality of this homecoming was to be seen in the tenure of years for which he settled in the proximity of *Aruṇācala Śiva* in Tiruvannamalai, not feeling the necessity to leave this abode on even a single occasion. The *Maharṣi* lived there for the full span of fifty-four years as a living embodiment of the highest blessings of *Mokṣa* that *Aruṇācala Śiva,* the transcendent God, had bestowed upon him.

Astrologically, from July 16, 1896, that is, the day of the monumental occurrence, *Ramaṇa* had entered into the *Nivṛtti mārga;* till then, for the first sixteen years of his life, he was indeed only in the *Pravṛtti mārga* like the vast majority of humans. The transition from the *Pravṛtti mārga* to the *Nivṛtti mārga* happened abruptly, and for the ensuing fifty-four years, he was indeed its living embodiment.

Astrologically, if destiny is to unfold in the *Pravṛtti mārga,* then the *Artha* and the *Kāma* Hs and their lords ought to be strong, and the *daśās* of these lords must figure during the lifetime of the individual, and that too, during youth and the time spent as a householder. On the other hand, if destiny is to unfold in the spheres of *Dharma* and *Mokṣa,* that is, in the *Nivṛtti mārga,* then the *Dharma* and *Mokṣa* Hs and their lords must be strong, and correspondingly, their *daśās* must figure during the individual's lifetime.

It is interesting to examine the *Maharṣi's* chart for its potentials in the spheres of *Artha* and *Kāma.* From the point of view of the SA, the group of marriage Hs, the VIIH, IIH, IVH, VIIIH, XIIH, and Ve, are all weak in the *Maharṣi's* horoscope (with the exception of the VIIIH), being closely or exactly afflicted. Thus, the 'mansion of marriage' was already in a broken down condition in the initial mood of God at the time of birth. For the *Maharṣi,* this mood was such that all Hs and their lords in the material spheres of *Artha* and *Kāma* were weak, with the single exception of the VIH lord Sa. This would have given very little scope for the *Maharṣi* to act through the self and make an impact upon the world, except through some selfless *Karmayoga.* We do know that even this afflicted self, which is the main engine of action in any human life, was also abruptly annihilated by Divine ordination, thus wiping out all traces of individuality and with it, also life in the material spheres of *Artha* and *Kāma.*

Most importantly, the Asdt H as well as the Asdt lord were under severe affliction. The Asdt H was under almost exact affliction from Sa, the ideal planet for taking people onto the *Nivṛtti mārga.* Sa, which powerfully afflicts the IH, VIIH, IVH and IXH, taken along with a very weak Vẹ and a strong spiritual *navāṁśa* chart, also accounts for the *Maharṣi's* immaculate celibacy and chastity, which is often a concomitant of the lives of Sages on the *Nivṛtti mārga.*

The Asdt lord Me suffers an exact affliction from the most malefic planet (MMP) Ma. Thus, as both the Asdt H and the Asdt lord are under severe affliction, *Ramaṇa Maharṣi's jīvātmā* is practically like the figure of Christ, 'crucified' in its freedom to make any move on the *Pravṛtti mārga.* The Asdt H and the Asdt lord are like the captain of the *Navagraha* team, and when the captain is under the severest of afflictions or disabling influences, then the achievement of the team is reduced in proportion.

Another factor that kept the *Maharṣi* out of the *Pravṛtti mārga* is the near exact affliction of the four angular Hs. Sa afflicts, as an FM for the Virgo Asdt, the IH, IVH, VIIH, and the IXH. The Su, as another FM, closely afflicts both the IVH and XH. The angular Hs are called *Lakṣmī sthānas* and are *the Hs of psychological becoming* in contrast to the *Viṣṇu sthānas,* which are the *Dharma* Hs or the Trines. These are the IH, VH, and IXH, *the Hs of being or sattvaguṇa.*

In VA, it is held that for an individual to be able to achieve something of substantial value on the physical plane, there must be planets in angular Hs or these Hs must not be afflicted. In the *Maharṣi's* case, the immense fame and truth of his compassion became known throughout the world because the Mo was placed in the strongest of all angular Hs, the XH, and the *navāṁśa* chart was strong. The *Maharṣi's* Mo was powerful, being placed just two days after *paurṇami* in the excellent *Punarvasu nakṣatra,* which in VA is known to be favourable for going back 'home' to the Supreme Light.

Thus, apart from the Mo, which brought him into public prominence, the energies of the Divine Mother had all retreated inwards, leaving the *Maharṣi* very little scope for active work on the *Pravṛtti mārga* in the likeness of *Mahātmā Gandhi.* The *Maharṣi's* relationship with the energies of the Divine Mother are beautifully summarised in the following *sūtra,* found in a work on *Durgā Saptaśati.*

> *I dance, and all that you perceive are its manifestations. If you like, you can watch me dance, or if you like, you can make me stop. He who can make me stop, I make him a Seer, a man of wisdom, one of intuitive vision, my husband, Lord Śiva, the consciousness of infinite goodness.* (qtd. in Saraswati Invocation)

Having discovered his original identity with the Supreme *Śiva* as the unmanifest Godhead, the Pure Consciousness of infinite goodness, there was no way for the *Maharṣi* to once again 'commence creation' by sending out His Consort the Divine Mother on her voyage of *māyā* and *līlā* [illusion and Divine play]. It is not that he was unclear as to whether these powers were available to him. On one occasion, he had very clearly said, *"For granting boons, the jñāni's powers are same as Īśvara's or God's"* (qtd. in *Timeless in Time* 354). Yet he disassociated himself from the miraculous because he was *Śiva,* the Godhead, on the *Nivṛtti mārga.*

His was a fiery Jupiter energizing airy signs; this made him a teacher who encouraged *Ātmavicāra.* (For the occurrence of psycho-physical Divine miracles, one needs a fiery Jupiter energizing earthy signs underlying *Dharma* or *Kāma* Hs.) His disinterested stand towards miracles is another solid proof that he had lost all sense of a separative individuality with its attendant identity of the me and the mine. Papaji (affectionate name for the Master *Śrī* H. W. L. Poonja), a *Jīvanmukta* through the Divine grace of the *Maharṣi,* is seen in the following passage confirming this very important facet of the *Maharṣi's* life:

> *He never performed any miracles and never even accepted any responsibility for those that seemed to happen either in his presence or on account of a devotee's faith in him. The only 'miracles' he indulged in were those of inner transformation. By a word, a look, a gesture, or merely by remaining in silence, he quietened the minds of people around him, enabling them to become aware of who they really were. There*

> *is no greater miracle than this.* (qtd. in Godman *Nothing Ever Happened* I: 145)

The *Maharṣi's* austere renunciation was well known, even in the matter of handling money, which was certainly needed for keeping his *āśrama* in a smoothly running condition. While *Śrī Ramakrishna Paramahamsa* can be taken as an embodiment of *kāmini-kāñcana tyāga*, meaning total renunciation of association with the opposite sex and with wealth and gold, *Ramaṇa Maharṣi's* life is not only an illustration of the highest form of *kāmini-kāñcana tyāga* (the *Maharṣi* having become one with *Parabrahma* – something that was denied to *Śrī Ramakrishna Paramahamsa*), the *Maharṣi* went further in his renunciation in that any kind of mission for setting right a world perceived to be unhappy and imperfect could not arouse him to action from his profound equanimity, the fruit of his direct *advaitic* Realization.

The *Maharṣi's tyāga* came from a valorous Su in the IVH as well as from a strong Saturnian influence. A strong Ma bestowed the immense courage necessary for detachment as well as renunciation. As an example of *kāñcana tyāga*, we cite the following circumstance from the *Maharṣi's* life:

> *Uddandi Nayanar, who was the first regular devotee to be attached to Ramana, was suddenly called away in 1897 to the headquarters of the ascetic order to which he belonged. Seven years later, he returned with a hundred rupees as his offering. The Master refused to accept it, since he had no use for money and would not touch it. Nayanar left the money with a devotee asking him to utilise it for any good cause of which the Master approved. It was spent on printing the translation of the Vivekacudamani.* (Natarajan 69)

Through the *Maharṣi's* mighty renunciatory inclination to retreat to *Virūpākṣa* cave beyond the reach of curious onlookers, we may understand the extent to which he was held back by the infinite tranquility and bliss of the *Ātman*.

Virūpākṣa Cave

He entered the *Virūpākṣa* cave as a twenty-year old lad in 1899, and remained there for a seventeen-year period. *Virūpākṣa Deva,* a saint of the thirteenth century, had lived and died there. Many momentous events in the *Maharṣi's* life occurred during this period. His first oral *upadeśa* to his illustrious disciple, *Vāsiṣṭa Gaṇapati Muni,* was given here on November 18, 1907. This was a milestone in the *Maharṣi's* life, for on this day he broke his eleven-year silence. It was also *Vāsiṣṭa Gaṇapati Muni* who truly discovered the immeasurable value of the *Maharṣi* and began to address him with the highest reverence and devotion as '*Bhagavān Śrī Ramaṇa Maharṣi*'. It may also be noted that because of *Gaṇapati Muni's* profound devotion and *Sanskrit* scholarship, he was asked by the *Maharṣi* to compose, in the course of a single night, the classic on the Divine Mother, *Umā Sahasram.*

At *Virūpākṣa* cave, the *Maharṣi* communicated the experience of his enlightenment through his spiritual instructions to Gambiran Seshier and Sivaprakasam Pillai. It was also while at *Virūpākṣa* that the *Maharṣi* translated into Tamil *Ādi Śaṅkara's* classic on enlightenment, *Vivekacūḍāmaṇi.*

The *Maharṣi* spent his *Virūpākṣa* years on the extreme *Nivṛtti mārga,* and it would be good to understand the provision for his being on the *Nivṛtti mārga* in the mood of *Īśvara* at the time of birth. The IIH and the IVH pertain to family life, and in the *Maharṣi's* chart, the IVH comes under the strong influence of two separative planets: Sa as the lord of the VIH, and the Su as the lord of the XIIH, both FMs for the Virgo Asdt. Both Sa and the Su closely afflict the IVH. Further, the IVH lord is weak, having been placed in the *duhsthāna,* the VIH.

Again, the IIH lord Ve is very weak, being in extreme 'infancy', while the IIH is closely afflicted by the MMP Ma. These multiple factors were responsible for separating the boy *Ramaṇa* from home life and from his parents. This separation, which was to be permanent, occurred in the Sa-Su sub-period, one most favourable for such a separation.

Virūpākṣa cave became the natural abode of the *Maharṣi* for seventeen long years from 1899, only because the strong Sa afflicting the Asdt and the IVH in the *Maharṣi's* chart necessitated his being placed in a typical *Saturnian environment* such as a solitary cave or a hermit's abode. *Virūpākṣa* cave was just such an environment.

Saturnian influences are also discernable in the *navāṁśa* chart, which is highly pertinent for the *Maharṣi* in view of his life having moved into the *Dharma* and *Mokṣa* spheres. In the *navāṁśa* chart, Sa, as *Anugrahakāraka* and as a detachment giving planet, exactly influences the lagna, the Mo, and Ju, which is the lord of the IVH in the *rāśi* chart. From the placement of the *Anugrahakāraka par excellence* in the VIH of service, we may infer that the *Maharṣi's* heart, signified by the lord of the IVH, was in service and *Karmayoga.* All these influences combined together paved the way for the monumental renunciation of the *Maharṣi.*

27. Devotion Coexisted with the Seriousness of Self-Realization

Even before the boy *Ramaṇa* departed for Tiruvannamalai, that is, during the six weeks he stayed in Madurai after the 'monumental occurrence', his new-found intense devotion to the Lord came to the fore, as he has clarified himself:

> *One of the new features related to the temple of Meenakshi and Sundareswara. Formerly I would go there rarely, go with friends, see the images, put on sacred ashes and sacred vermillion on the forehead, and return home without any perceptible emotion. After the awakening into the new life, I would go almost every evening to the temple. I would go alone and stand before Siva, or Meenakshi, or Nataraja, or the sixty three saints for long periods. I would feel waves of emotion overcoming me. The former hold (alambana) on the body had been given up by my spirit, since it ceased to cherish the idea I-am-the-body (dehatmabuddhi). The spirit, therefore, longed to have a fresh hold (alambana) and hence the frequent visits to the temple and the overflow of the soul in profuse tears. This was God's (Iswara's) play with the individual spirit. I would stand before Iswara, the controller of the Universe and the destinies of all, the Omniscient and Omnipresent, and pray for the descent of His grace upon me so that my devotion might increase and become perpetual like that of the sixty three saints. Mostly I would not pray at all, but let the deep within flow on and into the deep without. Tears would mark this overflow of the soul and would not betoken any particular feeling of pleasure or pain.* (qtd. in Narasimha Swami 19)

This devotional state of mind after July 16, 1896 is, on deeper examination, unintelligible to us; for if enlightenment were really nothing but Self-Realization, then when the Self had been realized and had discovered its Absolute Sovereignty, what need was there to seek fresh anchorage in an external formful Deity, which was anyhow only an image of that very Self? Or was it only the 'thinking aspect of the Self', the little self, which may be nothing more than a *veṣa* or 'cloak of *māyā*' on its essential nature of Absolute Sovereignty, that was attempting to create, according to its natural function, a cogent order in the very limited sphere of thought and feeling, and in this attempt, sought out temples, which were the various abodes of its Sovereign Lord? Here is an enigma for us to ponder over. A fully enlightened Sage, an embodiment of the Realization of non-duality, is seen here involved in intense devotion to his Lord, which presupposes the operation of duality. How are we to resolve this contradiction astrologically?

Even later in life, in the course of his fifty four-year stay in Tiruvannamalai, the *Maharṣi* came to be identified as a Sage whose heart always overflowed with love and devotion. His shedding tears of compassion before devotees on so many occasions is very well recorded. He was full of compassion for all living creatures. Thus, the necessity to astrologically account for his compassionate and devotional nature becomes all the more compelling.

There is one other thing that deserves special mention: The *Maharṣi's* compassionate hospitality was evident to all observers of his dispassionate involvement in the activities of the *āśrama.* He took an active interest in ensuring that all seekers of truth who came to the *āśrama* were provided meals there. This comes from the Mo's influence upon the IVH of home, mother, and hospitality. The Mo is the planet of the Divine Mother, the planet of compassion, nurture, and hospitality. The IVH lord for Virgo Asdts, Ju, is another planet of compassion, and in the *navāṁśa* chart, which is a kind of *garbhagṛha* of the IXH, there are planetary aspects bestowing compassion, piling up on the *navāṁśa lagna.*

Like *Ādi Śaṅkara,* who broke with so-called tradition in order to attend to the last rites of his beloved mother *Āryamba,* the *Maharṣi,* in his immeasurable sensitivity to the sufferings of Hindu women, had given the highest blessings to his mother in the form of the *prasāda* of *Jīvanmukti* prior to her departure from the physical plane on May 19, 1922. The *Maharṣi's* mother had lived in his *āśrama* till her end. Here again, the compassion of the *Maharṣi* is seen to overflow, crossing all conventional boundaries and extending to all people near and dear who had reposed their trust in him. Many animals at the *āśrama* were also recipients of the Divine grace of his compassion.

Very significantly, as though to remind us of this facet of the *Maharṣi,* today there stands on the sacred premises of *Śrī Ramaṇāśrama* the *Mātṛbhūteśvar* temple, which has the distinction of being the only temple in the world for an enlightened mother.

28. Astrological Light on the Maharṣi's Devotion

The benefic planets placed in the VH usually bestow *Bhakti* or strong devotion. Or, if the IVH lord is placed in the IXH, then too a person can have a spiritual and devotional nature. In the *Maharṣi's rāśi* chart, there are no planets in the VH. The Mo could also be an asset in this regard, for the Mo is a planet of feeling and empathy and is the significator of the IVH of emotions. However, the Mo too does not impact on the VH. Moreover, the house in which the Mo is placed is afflicted closely by the Su, an FM. There must have been some other hidden factors then, probably in the divisional charts, that accounted for the newly discovered devotion of the *Maharṣi* after the 'monumental occurrence'.

The resolution to this enigma lies in the *viṁśāṁśa* divisional chart (D-20) pertaining to surrender and *Bhakti.* We may notice that it is fully drenched in Divine grace, quite apart from the *caturviṁśāṁśa* chart (D-24), which is also fully blessed by the *Anugrahakāraka* Ju. These two divisional charts pertain to different aspects of the spiritual life: the former to *Bhaktiyoga,* the latter to *Jñānayoga.* An individual who reaches Realization through devotion and surrender will have a relatively stronger *viṁśāṁśa* chart, while one who comes to Realization through the blessing and fruit of *Ātmavicāra* or enquiry into the nature of the 'I' will have a very favourable *caturviṁśāṁśa* chart.

Strangely, in the *Maharṣi's* case, although he had reached Realization through the route of *maraṇavicāra* and *Ātmavicāra,* his devotion and surrender [*Bhakti*] to the Divine was equally intense, as suggested by his *viṁśāṁśa* chart and by a strong Mo, the planet of devotion and feeling, both in the *navāṁśa* chart as well as the *rāśi* chart. It is for this reason (of overflowing *Parabhakti)* that he sought refuge in the Lord *Aruṇācala Śiva,* and it is for the very same reason that he surrendered himself unconditionally at the *sannidhi* of *Aruṇācala Śiva.*

In the *viṁśāṁśa* chart, the Asdt lord Su is under the influence of two *Anugrahakārakas,* Ma and Ju. The former rules the IXH in this divisional chart, while Ju rules the VH therein. As Ju is already *Anugrahakāraka par excellence* in the *rāśi* chart, these cumulative spiritual influences in the *viṁśāṁśa* chart have the effect of strongly spiritualizing the Su, which signifies surrender therein. Very significantly, the Ju-blessed Mo also aspects the Asdt of the *viṁśāṁśa* chart, and thus, there is an intensification of *Bhakti.*

In passing we may also take a look at how the mood of *Īśvara* at the time of the *Maharṣi's* birth provided for his spontaneous self-restraint in speech. In truth, we cannot separate this aspect of the *Maharṣi's* life from his spiritual and devotional nature. The *Maharṣi's* conspicuous silence in the state of *Jñāna* for an unbroken period of eleven years arose from a weak lord of the IIH of *vāk* or speech, and a weak Me, the significator of speech, on account of its exact affliction from the MMP Ma. The IIH, which bestows the Divine grace for oral communication and *vāk,* is seen to be closely afflicted by the MMP Ma. In the SA, it is very significant that Me is also considered the significator of the IIH of speech. Ma's aspect to

Me in the *Mokṣa* sign Scorpio creates a necessary condition for *Mokṣa* as well as imposes obstacles on speech, which in the *Maharṣi's* case, took the form of a spontaneous self-restraint in speech (*mouna*).

29. Unmoving Like Śiva

One of the hallmarks of the *Maharṣi's* life was the complete absence of all travel from the time he arrived at the abode of *Aruṇācala Śiva* as a lad of sixteen on September 1, 1896. Since then, for an unbroken period of fifty four years, the *Maharṣi* had absolutely no urge or inclination to stir out of this holy abode. This is in sharp contrast to the life of *Parivrājakasanyāsis,* who wander from place to place in an attempt to keep all attachments to any one fond place at bay. The *Maharṣi's* inner silence must have been so immense that 'thought' had no impetus to seek any kind of change or excitement. The horoscope of the *Maharṣi* accounts for this extraordinary fixity of abode.

The Su, the most massive of *sthira* lords, occupies the heart of the IVH of home, house, and *Ātmā.* The IVH lord Ju is in another *sthira rāśi,* while Sa, ruling the MT sign of Aquarius, another *sthira rāśi,* also aspects the IVH of abode. These three confluent influences of fixity coming upon the IVH imparted the quality of *sthiratva* to the *Maharṣi's* abode. In this sense, he was unmoving like *Aruṇācala Śiva* Himself.

30. Necessary and Sufficient Conditions for Mokṣa

In studying Hindu astrology in the sphere of *Mokṣa,* my methodology has consisted in first ascertaining whether there are what may appropriately be called *necessary conditions* for the fructification of *Mokṣa* already present in the natal chart, which we know to be nothing but the mood of God at the time and place of birth. As in the discipline of mathematics, where the occurrence of the *necessary condition is by itself insufficient,* here too, in the second stage of investigation, we search for *sufficient conditions*, which, building up on the assets of the necessary conditions, serve to bring to flower the potentiality already present in its embryonic form therein.

The *sufficient conditions*, of course, arise in a surprising and emergent fashion in the mood of God on a certain fortunate day as a transit significant event (TSE). Then, these sufficient conditions are powerful enough to harvest the crop for which the mood of God at the time of birth did the sowing. This will be our line of approach to the study of *Mokṣa* in Hindu astrology as well. Both *the necessary and the sufficient conditions* involve the *asmitākārakas* on the one hand and the *Mokṣakārakas* on the other. We must now make our acquaintance with these new variables, which become pertinent in the Hindu astrology of *Dharma* and *Mokṣa*.

31. Asmitākārakas, Mokṣakārakas, Mokṣayogas

In VA, the IVH, VIIIH, and XIIH are considered *Mokṣa* Hs. The meaning of this rather cryptic *sūtra* is the following: The IVH is the *asmitāsthāna*, where the 'self' as individuality or the 'small aperture of light of the I-am-ness' resides. The VIIIH lord as well as the XIIH lord are, by contrast, the *Nivṛtti* lords, capable of extinguishing that light of I-am-ness, thereby bestowing *Mokṣa* or enlightenment. This clear distinction between the IVH of *Mokṣa* on the one hand and the VIII and XII Hs of *Mokṣa* on the other will give us tremendous clarity into the whole process of *Mokṣa*. As Sa is the significator of the VIIIH of *Mokṣa* and as Ke is the significator of the XIIH of *Mokṣa*, both these planets are noted in VA as being *Mokṣakārakas* or *Nirvāṇakārakas*.

In *Śrī Nisargadatta Maharaj's* principal conversations on Self-Realization, he draws our attention time and again to the I-am-ness [*asmitā*]. Through meditative introversion and the successful bringing home of the 'galloping horses of thought' that are ever on the lookout for sensory gratification in the outside world, we will come to realize that the I-am-ness or *asmitā* is the 'irreducible lump of our individuality', even though it is not a particularly irksome state of being in our day to day existence.

Śrī Maharaj's approach has been to draw our attention repeatedly to the fact of our being the I-am-ness as a prerequisite to its transcendence, which, according to him, occurs automatically, that is, through Divine grace once we stay poised as the I-am-ness for reasonably long periods of time. I-am-ness is a state of being, although definitely only of individuality, whereas when the 'galloping horses of thought' are given free rein, we are thrown into a much more extroverted state of becoming. Put differently, the I-am-ness state of being is one of *sattvaguṇa* in which we may be prone to declare 'I am happy', whereas our other states of consciousness have far greater 'contamination of duality' built into them as they are *rājasic* by contrast.

As *Śrī Maharaj* has pointed out, the I-am-ness, which the *Yogasūtras* of *Patañjali* refer to as *asmitā,* is a kind of small aperture through which the light of the infinite *Ātmā* or Self shines, thus projecting the infinitely splendorous world in front of our eyes. I have identified this crucial state of consciousness as the essence of *sattvaguṇa* of the IVH of Hindu astrology (see Section 16, Chapter III). When this I-am-ness is extinguished during a TSE, in lieu of the small aperture of the I-am-ness, a flood of *Ātmic* Light comes into existence because the *Mokṣakārakas* rip apart and tear asunder the membrane of the I-am-ness with its small aperture. I use this pictorial language in an attempt to bring the *Mokṣa* process into greater relief.

Thus, when one or more of the IVH lord, IVH MEP, Asdt lord, Asdt MEP, the Su as *Ātmakāraka,* the Mo as *manahkāraka,* or Me as *buddhikāraka* come under the close influence of the powerful *Mokṣa* lords of the VIIIH and/or the XIIH, or when they come under the close influence of the significators of *Mokṣa* Sa or Ke, then alone do the blessings of *Mokṣa* come to pass. This is the most generalized *sūtra* on *Mokṣayogas.* (See the Glossary for the clear definition of the astrological terms *manahkāraka* and *buddhikāraka.*)

As a prelude to the study of the *sufficient conditions* for *Mokṣa,* we now identify the *necessary conditions* that were already present in the mood of God at the time of birth in the *Maharṣi's* chart.

The *asmitā* or I-am-ness, which is the most characteristic feature of our individuality, is carried by many astrological variables. The Su, though a first rate *Ātmākāraka* or the significator of the Self (as *Jīvanmuktas* know), is also tainted by the 'covering' of the *asmitā* before *Mokṣa* comes to pass. So too, the Mo, the significator of the IVH of I-am-ness, also denotes this 'covering'. In addition and very importantly, the IVH and IVH lord Ju also carry this taint of the *asmitā.* The Asdt lord, especially if this is Me as in the case of the Virgo Asdt, also carries the taint of I-am-ness. As we learn from *Patañjali's Yogasūtras* and the classic *advaitic* teaching of *Śrī Nisargadatta Maharaj,* the essence of the self or *jīvātma* is held in the taint of the *asmitā* or I-am-ness.

Now, the separative planets in *Vedic* astrology are the Su, Sa, Ra, Ke, and the lord of the XIIH. The *Mokṣakārakas* for the Virgo Asdt are Ma ruling the VIIIH and the Su ruling the XIIH. We may also remember that the signs Cancer, Scorpio, and Pisces are *Mokṣa* signs in VA, and accordingly, when a *Mokṣa-yoga* is formed in one of these fruitful *Mokṣa* signs, the auspiciousness and certainty about the fructification of that *Mokṣayoga* is all the greater.

When one or more of these malefic separative planets or *Mokṣakārakas* influence and afflict those planets that carry the taint of *asmitā,* there is the possibility of the covering being ripped off. Thereupon, the *Ātmā* becomes unmasked and begins to shine in all its infinite glory. This miraculous event usually happens as a transit significant event (TSE) and is the *sufficient condition* for *Mokṣa* on the day of illumination, whereas the *necessary conditions* are already clearly seen in the mood of God at the time and place of birth.

32. Necessary Conditions for Mokṣa

The following are the *necessary conditions* for *Mokṣa* present in the mood of God at the time and place of the *Maharṣi's* birth:

(i) Me, the 'builder' (to use the phraseology of Edgar Cayce) and the planet that creates the illusion that we are the thinker (and that we are the body – for a Virgo Asdt) is placed in the *Mokṣa* sign of Scorpio and is involved in an exact affliction from the most powerful *Mokṣakāraka* Ma. This shows that there is a potentiality for Ma to rip off the covering of *asmitā* on Me and this ripping off may occur during a favourable TSE on a certain fortunate day.

(ii) The IVH carries the taint of *asmitā,* and two first-rate separative planets are seen influencing the MEP of the IVH closely: Sa's tenth aspect afflicts the IVH closely, while the Su, another *Mokṣakāraka* and separative planet, is seen to be placed close to the MEP of the IVH.

In recognition of the virtue of Sa being a significator of the VIIIH, the SA tells us that Sa functions like a *Nirvāṇakāraka* in those charts where it is an FM. The SA, however, also insists that unless Sa is an FM, it does not manifest its separative influence. Thus, for a Virgo Asdt, Sa definitely has the scope of functioning like a separative planet and therefore also as a *Nirvāṇakāraka.*

(iii) Sa's tenth aspect is seen to closely afflict the natal Su placed in the IVH, and this too holds the potential for ripping apart the veil on the Su, thereby allowing it to shine with all its *Ātmaprabhā* [effulgence of the Self].

(iv) Sa, a first-rate separative planet, makes an almost exact impact and affliction on the Asdt MEP. This is another necessary condition for being separated from the personal self.

(v) In addition, as the IVH and IIH are weak and afflicted by the FMs in the chart, we see that the tethers of bondage serving to tie the *Maharṣi* to home and family life are extremely tenuous and have therefore the possibility of breaking quite easily during a favourable TSE.

(vi) Equally significant is the MMP Ma's close aspect to the IIH of bondage to family and wealth and to the fourth sign of Cancer, which also carries the taint of the *asmitā.*

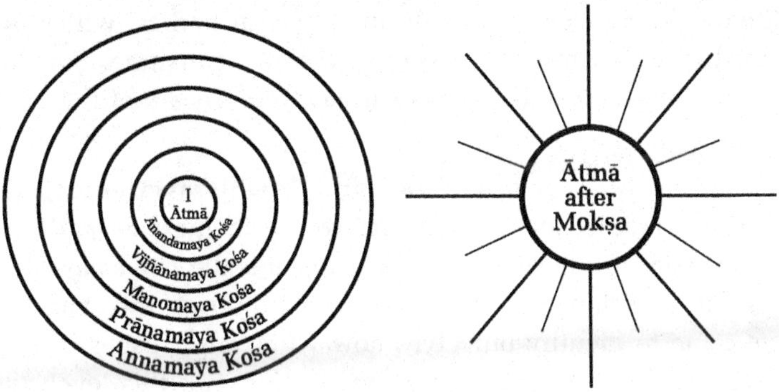

The Five Sheaths Covering the Ātmā and the Ātmā after Mokṣa

The figures above illustrate how an *asmitākāraka* such as the Su or the lord of the IVH undergoes a metamorphosis into an *Ātmakāraka* during the process of *Mokṣa,* when the veils carried by the *asmitākārakas* are ripped off by the *Mokṣakārakas.*

The astrological variables that represent the various *anātmās* [false selves] may be collectively called *asmitākārakas* or significators of *asmitā* [feeling of I-am-ness]. The Asdt lord, and Asdt MEP represent the *anātmā* of the *annamayakośa.* The IVH lord, IVH and Mo signify the *manomayakośa.* The IIIH, IIIH lord, and Ma signify the *prāṇamayakośa.* The VH, VH lord, Ju, and Me signify the *vijñānamayakośa,* while the same VH, VH lord, and Ve signify the *ānandamayakośa,* especially when Ve is placed in the VH. Note, however, that the root of all these *asmitās* is the witness consciousness, the I-am-ness, which is in the IVH and the Mo. During the process of *Mokṣa,* these consecutive sheaths are ripped apart (see Section 16, Chapter III).

For a clearer understanding of the *asmitākārakas,* we shall briefly recall the *Upaniṣadic* multi-sheath model of our human consciousness. In this model, the five sheaths encasing the *Ātmā* are to be understood as our series of *anātmās* [false selves] arising at different levels of our being. At the grossest level, we identify ourselves only with our physical bodies, which are constituted entirely by the food that we consume. For this reason, this *anātmā* is called *annamayakośa* [sheath of the 'food body'].

With some *yogasādhana* and breath awareness, we discover another identity for ourselves at the next deeper level as our vital breath or *prāṇa.* This *anātmā* is the *prāṇamayakośa.* As our consciousness deepens further through introversion, we come to identify ourselves now with consciousness *per se,* especially with the current of our feelings. At this level, the *anātmā* is called *manomayakośa.*

If our consciousness deepens even more through various meditational practices such as being a mere witness to the goings on in consciousness, our identity shifts yet again and we come to identify ourselves with the flux of our insights, understanding, and wisdom. At this level, our *anātmā* is called *vijñānamayakośa.* Beyond this level, when even these *sāttvic* vibrations in the consciousness in the form of streaming insights subside, we come upon our last subtle identity, which is called *ānandamayakośa* or the 'bliss body'. Transcending even this final sheath of bliss or *ānanda* is the pristine *Ātmā,* the Self of the whole world.

When the *Maharṣi's* chart is read with respect to the *Candra lagna,* we see many spiritual influences radiating from Ju, the general significator of grace, as well as from Sa, the lord of the IXH. With regard to the *Surya lagna,* Sa conjuncts the IVH of

I-am-ness as well as the IH of the self, while the Su as the IXH lord blesses the Asdt H. Thus, both from the point of view of the SA as well as from the point of view of VA, there are a number of *necessary conditions* for the occurrence of *Mokṣa* already evident in the mood of God at the time and place of the *Maharṣi's* birth.

33. Insights of the Systems Approach into the Maharṣi's Mokṣa

The date of the *Maharṣi* losing all association with body and mind seems to be a little uncertain in many of the records; it is placed at roughly six weeks prior to his departure from Madurai, which date is known accurately to be August 29, 1896. In Prof. K. Swaminathan's biography, it is speculated that the day of Liberation fell on July 16, 1896, a Thursday; while in the biography by A. R. Natarajan, this extraordinary day is mentioned to be July 17, 1896. In B. V. Narasimha Swami's biography, there is again uncertainty regarding the actual date of the monumental occurrence.

In such cases where an ambiguity prevails as to the actual date of *Mokṣa,* the SA comes to our rescue with its powerful analytical methods applicable to TSEs and serves to accurately determine the actual moments of the *Maharṣi's Mokṣa,* which commenced a little after mid-day on July 16, 1896 and lasted for something like half an hour. This is the suggestion I would like to make with regard to the actual timing of the blessings of *Mokṣa,* which has remained unsettled till now.

In attempting to narrow down the slice of time within which we are deeming the process of *Mokṣa* to have been both triggered and also completed, it is best to remember the insight of another enlightened Master, Papaji, concerning the limitations of the significance of the time of enlightenment. It was Papaji's good fortune to receive the *prasāda* of *Mokṣa* from the *Maharṣi* directly through an unpremeditated *nayana dīkṣa.* This is a method of spiritual initiation in the Hindu *sampradāya* [tradition] in which the enlightened Master passes on his illumination through an intentional and benevolent gaze directed at the eyes of the disciple. In such a *nayana dīkṣa,* the eyes — both the Master's as well as the disciple's — function as the 'windows of the *Ātmā*'. Papaji reminds us of the futility of attempting to understand the process of *Mokṣa* as something that transpires in time:

> *Enlightenment, is not something that happens in time, or at a particular time. It is the understanding that time is not real. It is an understanding that transcends time completely. Enlightenment and bondage are both concepts that exist only as long as time exists. When time goes, these concepts also go.* (qtd. in Godman I: 127)

In the light of this timely and pertinent caution, we must avoid the temptation of attempting to place an undue emphasis on the fact that there was a 'process' that transpired in time and that holds the real key to the essence of *Mokṣa* — just because this is how it appears from the point of view of the unenlightened state. Rather, the critical slice of time we are identifying as representing the process of *Mokṣa* must instead be taken to point to that metamorphosis whereby the boy *Ramaṇa* became entirely free of time; for after that monumental occurrence, the boy would never be in a position to understand what time was all about. Thus, the *Maharṣi's* enlightened state may be characterized as being entirely devoid of the contamination of time in the sense of the *jīvātmā* [the personal self] having a secure continuity in time. With the culmination of the process of *Mokṣa,* the illusion of a 'running' time as well as the illusion of the *jīvātmā* as a separately existing body-centred entity comes to an end.

As we have already rectified the *Maharṣi's* time of birth (TOB) and made it fully capable of reproducing the event of his *Mahānirvāṇa* (April 14, 1950) as well as many other significant life events, we can depend on this reliable TOB to read from the

Viṁśottarī daśā system the exact sub-period during which this auspicious event came to pass. Both the *Maharṣi's Mokṣa* as well as the renunciation of his home and family occurred in the Sa-Su sub-period, which commenced on May 21, 1896 and continued till May 3, 1897 (see the Table on p. 86 Section 23, Chapter III). The *sufficient conditions* for *Mokṣa* were fulfilled on the July 16, 1896.

With the monumental occurrence, the curtain was abruptly dropped over the *Maharṣi's* life in the mundane spheres of home and family. Thereafter, as there was no individuality left in life, only the eternal life inhabited the body and spoke the eternal truth of *Mokṣa.* The abrupt ending of the imagined association with the body and mind may actually be taken to be *Mokṣa.*

From the manner in which the boy *Ramaṇa* began to live his life thereafter, it is abundantly clear that every trace of attachment and association with the body had been annihilated, leaving only the Supreme Light of the *Ātmā* to shine in its pristine purity. In our study of the TSEs of his life, we cite evidence for the separate entity of the personal self, having been completely wiped out, leaving not even the slightest vestige of that taint.

In the SA, the orb of affliction from the MMP Ma is 2°, that is, whenever the affliction pertains to an afflicted planet that is otherwise 'strong'. If, on the other hand, the afflicted planet is weak, then by the criteria of the SA, this weak afflicted planet succumbs to a transit affliction when the reducing orb of affliction reaches the critical threshold value of 5°. The actual orb of affliction between the afflicting *Mokṣakāraka* and the afflicted *asmitākāraka* thus depends on the strength of the *asmitākāraka,* both in its natal as well as transit positions. These are some general SA *sūtras* that we now apply to the *Maharṣi's* transit (Tr) chart corresponding to July 16, 1896, 12:56 p.m., that is, corresponding to the commencement of the process of *Mokṣa* (see charts on p. 191).

The Asdt lord Me is placed in the IIIH and in the eighth *Mokṣa* sign of Scorpio. This placement was behind many of the spiritual characteristics of the *Maharṣi* — his *Mokṣa* as well as his approach of profound enquiry into life and Reality. The exact sphere in which his profound interest comes into manifestation is decided by the following factors: the sign Scorpio in which the IIIH falls, and the exact influence of the MMP Ma on the Asdt lord Me.

We know that the eighth sign Scorpio has the following primordial characteristics: It is a deep and mysterious sign, generally covering the occult spheres of life including death and *Mokṣa,* as also profound enquiry and a penetrative kind of intelligence. The MMP's exact affliction on Me served not only to weaken Me by bringing every kind of obstacle on the path of the *Maharṣi's* life but also to create a passion for profound enquiry leading to *Mokṣa,* as Ma is a strong *Mokṣakāraka.* The *Nirvāṇakāraka* Sa in the natal chart is also seen to almost exactly afflict the natal Asdt.

The *Maharṣi's* profound and penetrative non-verbal inner enquiry began initially in the face of a sudden and violent fear of death. This profound enquiry did not cease with that, but rather, came to constitute the very heart of the *Maharṣi's advaitic* teachings. We see this arising astrologically only for a Virgo Asdt, with the Asdt lord Me placed in the IIIH and in the sign Scorpio and exactly involved in an affliction from the death- and Immortality-conferring planet Ma.

The natal chart and the transit chart (corresponding to the TSE of *Mokṣa*) are always juxtaposed by astrologers in this fashion to facilitate the study of three kinds of aspects and conjunctions, which arise during the transit in an emergent fashion. This is called the triple transit triggering influence, arising first from the natal planets to the transit planets, second from the transit planets to the natal planets, and third from the transit planets to themselves. As the relevant laws of planetary aspects are well known, they are not being specifically mentioned here.

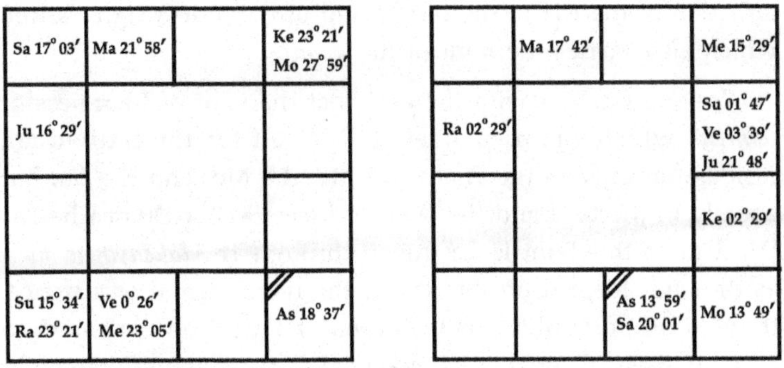
Sa 17° 03′
Ma 21° 58′
Ke 23° 21′
Mo 27° 59′
Ju 16° 29′
Su 15° 34′
Ra 23° 21′
Ve 0° 26′
Me 23° 05′
As 18° 37′
Ma 17° 42′
Me 15° 29′
Ra 02° 29′
Su 01° 47′
Ve 03° 39′
Ju 21° 48′
Ke 02° 29′
As 13° 59′
Sa 20° 01′
Mo 13° 49′

The Maharṣi's Natal and Mokṣa Transit Charts

The principles of Hindu astrology (Section 18, Chapter III) tell us that the Tr chart corresponding to the monumental occurrence conveys to us the mood of God at just that moment when the highest blessing of *Mokṣa* was about to descend on the boy *Ramaṇa*. Our task is now to decipher and understand the implications of this mood of God. The following group of TSEs collectively create the *sufficient conditions for Mokṣa* and portray the pertinent mood of God.

34. Sufficient Conditions for Mokṣa

TSE 1: Tr Ma's Affliction to the Fourth Sign Cancer and the IIH

On July 16, 1896, when Tr Ma was fully strong in its own MT sign at 17°42′, its eighth afflicting aspect was approaching a weak natal Me, which was at 23°05′ in Scorpio. SA astrologers will know that the closeness of this orb of affliction could not have been one of the crucial factors in extinguishing the mind as signified by Me. This was not, then, an important TSE among the group of six synchronous TSEs that were cumulatively responsible for architecturing the exact kind of *Mokṣa* that was the *Maharṣi's* good fortune to receive. However, what was much more significant for the *Mokṣa* process was Tr Ma's exact affliction of the IIH of the family and of the fourth sign Cancer, which also carries the taint of the *asmitā*.

We are familiar with the idea that the taint of I-am-ness or *asmitā*, which signifies a separative self for the individual, resides not only in the Asdt lord Me, the Mo, and the Su, but equally in the IVH and the IVH lord (see Section 30 of Chapter IV). Unless this taint is destroyed through Tr *Mokṣayogas* such as the ones formed on the day of the monumental occurrence, there is no possibility for the *Ātmā* or Pure Consciousness to become disengaged from its imagined association with the body and personality.

We must realize that the *Maharṣi's Mokṣa* was not just any kind of *Mokṣa*. Rather, it had a most definitive hallmark in that it took the form of a challenge and response, in the sense in which this fundamental principle has been systematically used by British historian Arnold J. Toynbee. However, while Toynbee applied this principle to civilizations, we are concerned here with its application to an individual in his personal life in the context of a psychological crisis.

TSE 2: Anugrahakāraka Ju's Blessings on Me

The *jīvātmā* or the self had come face to face with the shock of a violent fear of death, and it was this which constituted the challenge for the *jīvātmā*. The response was, as we have already emphasized, not a meek submission or surrender, nor the invocation of God and His name in that perilous hour, nor even an attempt to beat the shock of that violent fear by yelling and fleeing from the scene of action. It was none of these, but took an entirely unexpected form.

Paradoxically, courage and a profound intellectual clarity with equanimity in enquiry marked the response to the enormity of this challenge. *Thus, fearless enquiry was the response to the challenge of the shock of the fear of death.* A strong transit Ma, the significator of will and courage, gave the *Maharṣi* the blessing of fearlessness and immense courage on that day, although this was not all. A strong Me, the Asdt lord transiting the strongest of the angular Hs, the tenth, and in the third sign Gemini, supplied both additional courage as well as the profound intellectual enquiry that was needed to respond to the challenge.

The sign Gemini is highly favourable for profound enquiry and courage by virtue of its being a *sāttvic* airy sign and being the third in the natural zodiac. In fact, this is one of the primordial characteristics of Gemini (Section 11, Chapter III). On the day of the *Maharṣi's* illumination, Tr Me was strong and came under the exact aspect of natal Ju from another airy sign, Aquarius. As Ju is *Anugrahakāraka par excellence* and the giver of wisdom and Realization, being the IVH lord for Virgo Asdts, its aspect falling exactly upon a strong Tr Me in Gemini supplied all the Divine grace needed for propelling the profound inner enquiry to its natural terminal limit of Self-Realization.

This profound inner non-verbal enquiry was the route along which the *Maharṣi* travelled to *Mokṣa.* We see this route being opened up for him on that day of days through two remarkable synchronous Tr blessings, which came upon the intellectual planet Me. Natal Me was in the eighth sign Scorpio, in the IIIH of the natal chart, while Tr Me was strong in the third sign Gemini and in the XH. Natal Ju exactly aspected a strong Tr Mercury in the third sign, while an exalted Tr Jupiter almost exactly aspected a weak natal Me in the IIIH. Thus, there was abundant Divine grace on that day to propel the engine of intellectual enquiry Me, which was commissioned to execute this rarest of rare intellectual tasks.

The extent of Tr exalted Ju's blessing coming upon the natal weak Me is governed by the first part of the following SA *sūtra*:

> *The exaltation of functional benefic planets in transit at the time of forming close conjunction/aspect generate considerably good results. Similarly the debilitation of functional malefic planets in transit at the time of forming close conjunction/aspect is very painful and is for longer durations.* (Choudhry, *Significant Events* 30)

Likewise the strength of natal Ju's blessing upon a strong Tr Me is governed by the following pertinent SA *sūtra*:

> *Whenever any strong transit functional benefic planet forms close conjunction with or becomes closely aspected by a natal functional benefic planet(s), it triggers significant happy incidents pertaining to the planet involved.* (Choudhry, *Significant Events* 29)

In the present context, 'a significant happy incident' would be 'an understatement' for the flood of Divine grace that the *Maharṣi* was destined to receive during the process of *Mokṣa.* An understatement in the present case, only because two synchronous Tr blessings from Ju, the *Anugrahakāraka par excellence,* upon the intellectual planet Me, magnified and intensified the Divine grace by unimaginable proportions. However, the above two SA *sūtras* applied concurrently do portray the immensity of Divine grace.

Having understood the route that was opened up for the *Maharṣi,* we must next understand how the self was blown out in these Tr afflictions through *Mokṣayogas.*

TSE 3: Tr Ma's affliction of Tr Ju

Tr Ma threw its close fourth aspect on Tr Ju, which carries the *asmitā,* and this Tr affliction in the *Mokṣa* sign Cancer served to rip off the veil of I-am-ness that Tr Ju was naturally wearing. Once the veil of I-am-ness was ripped apart, what remained as the residue was the *Ātmā* or the Self. Natal Ju was weak, and even though Tr Ju was exalted, its attendant debility in the *navāṁśa* chart and its weak dispositor made it weak even in Tr (SA *sūtra*). Thus, the orb of affliction of Tr Ju from the afflicting MMP Tr Ma was understandably around 4°06′. Tr Ma's close aspect on Tr Ju, the *asmitākāraka,* was a typical *Mokṣayoga,* and was an important *sufficient condition* for *Mokṣa.*

It is interesting to observe in this group of synchronous TSEs that while the *asmitā* was being ripped off through the afflictions of the *Mokṣakāraka* Tr Ma and the *Nirvāṇakāraka* Tr Sa, the penetrative enquiry blessed by Ju was also concurrently in progress. The final fruit of these two distinct synchronous processes was Self-Realization.

TSE 4: Tr Sa's Separative Influences on the Asmitākārakas

Tr Sa's tenth separative aspect on Tr Ju, the *asmitākāraka,* afflicts the latter within an orb of less than 2°, and this affliction was to take effect even though on that day Tr Ju had actually crossed the tenth aspectual 'landmine' that Tr Sa had laid in the *Mokṣa* sign Cancer. Tr Sa had greatly slowed down during its retrograde motion and had turned direct on July 15, at 8:57 p.m., but was still perfectly stationary at 20°01′ in Libra. The cumulative effect of Ma's aspect as well as Sa's aspect on Tr Ju and on the fourth sign Cancer was to unmistakably wipe out the association with body and mind and establish the sixteen-year old lad in his natural state of Pure Awareness.

Significantly, in view of Tr Ma being strongly placed in its own MTH on July 16, from 12:56 p.m. onwards, while the orb of affliction from Tr Sa to Tr Ma was well outside the critical value of 1°, Tr Sa itself suffered an exact affliction from natal Ma and this magnified and intensified the maleficity of Tr Sa's aspects. Even though Tr Sa was debilitated in the *navāṁśa* chart, its separative influence and power as *Nirvāṇakāraka* was not diminished on account of this weakness, which the SA makes clear. Thus, Tr Sa's affliction of the IIH, IVH, the fourth sign Cancer, and Tr Ju was more 'destructive' insofar as its potential for giving detachment, *Nirvāṇa,* and renunciation were concerned.

As the fourth sign Cancer, the IVH, and Tr Ju all carry the taint of *asmitā,* this Saturnian affliction only served to rip apart such taints, instilling tremendous fear or terror in the process of dismantling the personal self. The magnification of fear arose not only from the Tr MMP's close affliction of Cancer but more so from Tr Sa's affliction of the three *asmitākārakas* (because of natal and Tr Ma's affliction to Tr Sa). *What the boy Ramaṇa experienced was a violent fear of death, which we may understand as arising from a malefic Saturn-induced fear, while death creeps into the picture because of the death-giving MMP Ma's concurrent affliction of the fear-inducing FM planet Sa.*

The SA *sūtra* that governs the magnitude of the loss such an afflicting Sa brings upon the afflicted *asmitākāraka* Ju is the following:

> *Malefic transit impact of slow moving functional malefic planets like Jupiter, Saturn, Rahu, and Ketu are more pronounced when, during the course of their close conjunctions/aspects, they move more slowly as compared to their normal speed or become stationary. This is true both for natal and transit influences.* (Choudhry, *Significant Events* 30)

The magnified maleficity of Tr Sa, which its third and tenth aspect carry, tells us that planets and house cusps within the orb of 1-2° of these Saturnian aspects will definitely suffer this profoundly magnified affliction. Note that we have already seen in TSEs 1 and 3 that Tr Ma's doubly malefic aspect exactly afflicts Cancer apart from closely afflicting the *asmitākāraka* Tr Ju. It was this highly malefic affliction that did to perfection the job of extinguishing once and for all, all traces of the personal self or the light of I-am-ness.

That Sa is quite capable of bringing into manifestation such sudden and violent changes is brought home to us in the telling astrological vision of the American 'sleeping prophet' Edgar Cayce.

In Saturn we find the sudden or violent changes: those influences and environs that do not grow, as it were, but are sudden by that of change of circumstances materially, or by activities. . . . of others. (Sidney Kirkpatrick *Edgar Cayce* 275)

TSE 5: The Mokṣa-Bestowing Aspect of Natal Ma on Tr Ju

The natal *Mokṣakāraka* Ma was exactly aspecting Tr Ju, an *asmitākāraka,* and on account of the strength of natal Ma, this Tr affliction was fully strong and therefore able to peel off the taint of I-am-ness from the *asmitākāraka* Tr Ju.

In view of the cumulative aspects of the *Mokṣakāraka* Ma and *Nirvāṇakāraka* Sa on Tr Ju, and very significantly in the *Mokṣa* sign Cancer, it would be reasonable to suppose that the self of the boy *Ramaṇa* just dropped off, thus establishing him in the pristine state of Pure Awareness, which therefore is represented by Tr Ju from this point onwards in its continuing transit journey.

As it was the aspect of the Tr Ju that fell on natal Me, the wisdom of Ju, which is never revealed fully if the person is not enlightened, went on to illumine the *Maharṣi's* intelligence and intellect, represented by Me. Thus, the Jupiterian aspects created the Realization or illumination that *Ramaṇa Maharṣi* had. However, this Realization cannot be separated from the *Mokṣa* experience, which was partly bestowed by Tr *Mokṣakāraka* Ma on both natal Me as well as Tr Ju and partly also by Tr Sa on the three *asmitākārakas* mentioned in TSE 4.

Summing up, while the actual separation of Pure Awareness from its material associations and bondages was achieved through the confluence of the Tr afflictions of the *Mokṣakāraka* Ma and the *Nirvāṇakāraka* Sa, the Realization, which was the fruit of these various *Mokṣayogas,* was nothing but blessings that the *Anugrahakārakas* natal Ju and Tr Ju bestowed upon Tr and natal Me, respectively. However the *Mokṣayogas* involving

Tr Ju did give the fruit of liberating the *Ātmā* from its imagined association with the body and personality. In this sense, *Mokṣa* was the extinction of the illusion of the personal self, which was lurking in the Asdt lord Me as well as in Ju as both were only *asmitākārakas.*

In passing, we may mention that the whole process of *Mokṣa* transpired when the Tr Mo was in the *Mokṣanakṣatra Hasta.* Likewise, Tr Me was in the *nakṣatra Ārdra,* which was ruled by a destructive aspect of *Śiva,* namely, *Rudra.* One of the primordial characteristics of *Ārdra* in VA is passionate thinking as well as death; these significations figured prominently as Tr Me was moving through the *Ārdra nakṣatra.* The Asdt MEP in the *Maharṣi's* natal chart was also in the *Mokṣanakṣatra Hasta.*

35. The Maharṣi's Personal God, Aruṇācala Śiva

In examining the chart of the *Maharṣi,* we have to proceed with considerable trepidation, for while the *Maharṣi* had arrived at Self-Realization through his *Ātmavicāra* and taught the same as the sure means to Self-Realization, he was also paradoxically and inexplicably profoundly devoted to his *Iṣṭadevatā Aruṇācala Śiva,* just as a devotee with a personal self would be bonded to his personal God [*Iṣṭadevatā*] while still traversing the spheres of *Artha* and *Kāma.* One must thus understand how the duality inherent in the *Bhaktimārga* between the devotee and his/her personal God is fully reconcilable with the *advaitic* [non-dual] oneness implied by the *Maharṣi's* Self-Realization.

> *Aruṇācala, Thou form of grace itself! Once having claimed me, loveless though I be, how canst Thou let me now be lost, and fail to fill me so with love that I must pine for Thee unceasingly and melt within like wax over the fire? Oh nectar springing up in the Heart of devotees! Haven of my refuge! Let Thy pleasure be mine, for that way lies my joy, Lord of my life!* (qtd. in *Collected Works* 98)

The personal God or *Iṣṭadevatā* of *Ramaṇa Maharṣi* was, of course, *Aruṇācala Śiva.* The *Iṣṭadevatā* in his horoscope is the Sun, which signifies the Self [the *Ātmā* or the *Paramātmā*] on the one hand and is a *Mokṣakāraka* as the lord of the XIIH of Liberation on the other. Now, the Virgo Asdt actually has two potential *Mokṣakārakas,* Ma as the lord of the VIIIH, and the Su as lord of the XIIH. In the *Maharṣi's Mokṣa,* we have seen how it was Ma and Sa that had acquired the function of *Mokṣakārakas* on the day of the monumental occurrence; whereas the Su, though potentially also a *Mokṣakāraka,* was not used by God for the purpose of bestowing *Mokṣa.* There was, however, another role reserved for the Su; this role was not connected with *Mokṣa* as such, but had to do more with the personal God or the *Iṣṭadevatā* of the *Maharṣi.*

Now we must introduce as a *sūtra* of *Vedic* astrology that if a *Mokṣa* lord – irrespective of whether it is the lord of the XIIH or lord of the VIIIH – comes to occupy a natal position close to the MEP of the IVH, this constitutes one of the important *necessary conditions* for *Mokṣa.* However, if the same *Mokṣakāraka* comes to occupy a natal position in the VH of the *Iṣṭadevatā* without afflicting the MEP of that house, then the individual concerned sees this *Mokṣakāraka* only as a Deity, that is, as a Divine presence different from the self.

On the other hand, if the *Mokṣakāraka* settles close to the MEP of the IVH of *asmitā* or *Ātmā* and afflicts that house closely, then the individual will see the 'self' itself as the Supreme Deity, and indeed, this was the case with *Ramaṇa Maharṣi.* The IVH is one of *Jñāna* or Self-Realization, whereas the VH is the house of *Bhaktiyoga* and God-Realization. When *soumya* planets [FBs] settle here close to the MEP, then the person will 'see' the *Iṣṭadevatā* in a benefic or *soumya* form. When *krūra* planets [FMs] settle in the VH without afflicting the MEP, then the *Iṣṭadevatā* is of the *krūra* form, typical examples of which are *Kālīmātā* and *Narasiṁha Swāmi.*

In Self-Realization, the Deity is not different from the Self; both become one and the same. This was the case with the *Maharṣi,* and the Deity was both the *Paramātmā* as well as *Hṛdayakamalavāsa.* This Deity was *Aruṇācala Śiva.*

In the Hindu spiritual tradition, one is usually introduced to a personal God either through one's parents or through one's Spiritual Master. The *Iṣṭadevatā,* as a result of worship offered on a daily basis, begins to guide the individual steadily but surely through all the stages of life: *Dharma, Artha* and *Kāma.* If the individual has emotionally, intellectually, and spiritually flowered as a result of deliberate and focussed pilgrimage in these three spheres of life, then s/he automatically becomes a *Brahma-jijñāsu* or a *Mumukṣu,* and when he or she seeks after *Mokṣa* passionately, the beloved *Iṣṭadevatā* also readily grants this boon in the last stage of life.

It is very noteworthy that in the case of the *Maharṣi,* while he was still pursuing a secularised version of *Dharma* — as in the days of the Raj, the spiritual education given through *Gurukulāśramas* had already come to be replaced by our modern secular schools — an unknown God abruptly entered into his life, and blessing him with *Mokṣa,* thereafter developed an unbreakable bond of solidarity between Himself and His beloved devotee. In other words, the traditional sequence of events were turned upside down, *Mokṣa* coming first and the raptures with the *Iṣṭadevatā Aruṇācala Śiva* coming thereafter. From this we may suspect that the boy *Ramaṇa,* in the eyes of his *Iṣṭadevatā Aruṇācala Śiva,* must have somehow admirably qualified for the *prasāda* of *Mokṣa* even though such high qualifications were not at all apparent to his near and dear!

As *Aruṇācala Śiva* began His blessings with *Mokṣa* and only thereafter became the beloved *Iṣṭadevatā* of the *Maharṣi,* we are led to speculate whether this particular *Iṣṭadevatā* has any special propensity and attraction towards the benevolent act of bestowing *Mokṣa.* The spiritual tradition in Tamil Nadu throws light on our pondering. Indeed, it is maintained in the annals of tradition that this particular God *Aruṇācala Śiva* does indeed have a 'passion' for bestowing the blessing of *Mokṣa* on seekers. The amazing thing in the *Maharṣi's* case was that he was not a seeker at all, and yet, *Aruṇācala Śiva* placed him forever and ever on the throne of Immortality unconditionally.

36. Astrological Insights into Maharṣi's Mahānirvāṇa

Since the day of *Mokṣa,* as the self of the *Maharṣi* had ceased to exist and therefore gave way for the *Ātmā* to be his true Self, the illusion of time itself vanished for the *Maharṣi,* though certainly not for his body. Thus, the body's vulnerability to diseases was still being governed by his astrological clock time, and this, in spite of the fact that for his Self, astrological clock time had altogether ceased.

In the *Maharṣi's* natal chart, strong afflictions to the Asdt lord Me and to the Asdt house by the two strong FMs, Ma and Sa, were bound to take their toll insofar as bodily disease was concerned, even though these afflictions were also the very blessings that brought the *Maharṣi* the *prasāda* of *Mokṣa.*

Once, when the *Maharṣi* was asked about the kind of 'suffering' that *Jñānis* [liberated beings] undergo, he clarified the matter, quite clearly, using a telling analogy.

> *All pains, even physical, are in the mind. Everybody feels the pain of a cut or a sting, but a jnani whose mind is sunk in bliss feels it as in a dream. His resembles the case of two lovers in the story who were tortured together, but did not feel the pain because their minds were in ecstasy gazing at each other's face.* (qtd. in Natarajan 294)

In Sections 10 and 16 of Chapter IV, we saw the damage that a malefic Sa can cause whenever there are close afflictions in the horoscope. Sa is also well known in VA to be a disease-causing planet, capable of inflicting pain and suffering. When sarcoma came upon the *Maharṣi,* the 'experience' of 'his' pain may be discerned from his own description:

> *Appa [Father]! Who could conceive that such a disease as this could be in this world? When a hiccough comes the whole body splits like flashes of lightning in a cloud!* (qtd. in Natarajan 295)

And again, "*There is not a spot which has not been painful to touch*" (*ibid*).

True to the Hindu ideal of self-sacrifice, the *Maharṣi,* even in this condition, never allowed either the convenience of the devotees nor the smoothly running routine of the *āśrama* to be disrupted on account of his own intense suffering.

> *Many people come from great distances for the darśan and cannot wait till evening; they must not be disappointed.... If you pin the devotees to only these hours, the time may not suit some of them who will be greatly inconvenienced.* (qtd. in Natarajan 296)

Thus, without the schedule being broken, there was *darśan* for an hour in the morning and again for another hour in the evening, right until the time became ripe for *Aruṇācala Śiva* to depart from the temporary abode of the *Maharṣi's* body [*Mahānirvāṇa*]. The final moment arrived on April 14, 1950 at 8:47 p.m.

In terms of the astrological 'seasons of time', the Su-Ma highly malefic *daśā-bhukti* period had commenced on March 19, 1950. What is more, within this period, Me, the Asdt lord signifying the body, had entered on April 5, into the VIIIH of death. On July 16, 1896, the mood of God was one of descent such that all traces of individuality had to be wiped out so as to make 'room' for the presence of *Aruṇācala Śiva,* in that physical abode that all knew to be the boy *Ramaṇa's* body. He had come as *Kālakāla,* the slayer of death, and remained for the highest kind of *lokakalyāṇa* as both *Bhikṣāṭana* as well as *Dakṣiṇāmūrti,* the Supreme Teacher who teaches through silence.

On April 14, 1950, the mood of God was quite another. It favoured *Aruṇācala Śiva* ascending, by withdrawing from the physical abode that He had consciously occupied for an uninterrupted period of fifty four years. That the moods were so very different is seen from the following transit afflictions, which, occurring synchronously, brought the physical vehicle to its naturally intended limit of exhaustion.

(i) Tr nodes at 14°18′ in Pisces and Virgo (Ra and Ke, respectively), which had in fact become direct and also stationary since April 10, began to closely afflict the Asdt house.

(ii) Tr nodes also began to closely afflict natal Sa, the *Āyuṣkāraka,* placed in Pisces, the 12th sign.

(iii) Tr Me at 18°03′ in Aries in the VIIIH began to suffer a close Tr affliction from the MMP Ma, placed natally in its own MTH at 21°58′. It should be noted that the VIIIH is the house of death.

(iv) Tr Ma, which was retrograde in Virgo at 1°11′, exactly afflicted the Tr Su, placed very weakly in the VIIIH of death at 0°56′.

(v) Tr Ma also afflicted Tr Mo at 1°11′ in Pisces.

(vi) Tr Sa, which had turned retrograde in the XIIH at 20°12′, began to closely afflict natal Ju, which signifies the arteries and the heart, placed weakly in the natal VIH at 16°29′. It also afflicted the sign Leo, which signifies the heart and stomach.

(vii) Tr Sa from the XIIH of Leo at 20°12′ also began to closely afflict the IXH, which signifies the arterial system and therefore, produced the affliction creating the condition of low productivity of blood (SA *sūtra*).

The cumulative result of these synchronous afflictions was the withdrawal of *Aruṇācala Śiva* from the physical vehicle.

Blessed were all those devotees who were fortunate enough to have a last *darśan* of *Aruṇācala Śiva* almost on the verge of His decisive departure from His manifested world. Some three months prior to the day of *Mahānirvāṇa,* the *darśan* couch of the *Maharṣi* had been moved into the verandah, as the *Maharṣi* now found it impossible to move to the hall. The last *darśan* is best described in the words of Swami Satyananda, who was attending to the *Maharṣi* at that time:

> *On the evening of April 14, 1950, we were massaging Sri Ramana's body. At about 5 o'clock, he asked us to help him to sit up. Precisely at that moment devotees started chanting 'Arunachala Siva', 'Arunachala Siva'. When Sri Bhagavan heard this, his face lit up with radiant joy. Tears began to flow from his eyes and continued to flow for a long time. I was wiping them from time to time. I was also giving him spoonfuls of water boiled with ginger. The doctor wanted to administer artificial respiration, but Sri Bhagavan waved it away. . . . Sri Bhagavan's breathing became gradually slower and at 8:47 p.m., it subsided quietly.* (qtd. in Natarajan 298)

The presence of *Aruṇācala Śiva,* which shone through the gaze of *Śrī Ramaṇa Maharṣi's* eyes and resided in the *Maharṣi's* silence, as well as in his words, tears, and gestures, is still available to humanity fully in many varied forms: through the *Maharṣi's advaitic* teachings, his abode at Tiruvannamalai, the space he sanctified for fifty four years, and especially the *samādhisthal,* where the *Maharṣi's* mortal remains were enshrined in accordance with scriptural injunctions.

We will now have to make a transition to another mostly unrecognized abode of the *Maharṣi,* the inner destination of *Aruṇācala Śiva,* to which he ceaselessly urged us to go, through the route of Self-enquiry. The *Maharṣi,* being a Master *par excellence* on the path of *Jñāna* or *Ātmavicāra,* never gave a chance even to his best and most accomplished disciples to get attached to him. Even his enlightened devotee, Papaji, was asked to return so that he was free to re-enter the world and act in consonance with the promptings of the Self within.

If, parting from the beloved *Maharṣi* could be so difficult for Papaji, how much more difficult should it have been for countless devotees, who neither had the courage nor the extraordinary gifts that Papaji was blessed with?

We reproduce below the last poignant conversation Papaji had with the *Maharṣi.* It was to be his last *darśan* of *Aruṇācala Śiva.*

> *I am far too attached to your physical form. I cannot leave you. I love you so much I cannot take my eyes off you. How can I leave?*
>
> *"I am with you wherever you are," was his answer.*
>
> *I immediately understood the deep significance of his remark. The 'I' which was my Master's real nature, was also my own inner reality. How could I ever be away from that 'I'? It was my own Self, and both my Master and I knew that nothing else exists.*
>
> *I accepted his decision. I prostrated before him and for the first and only time in my life I touched his feet as an act of veneration, love and respect. He didn't normally let anyone touch his feet, but this was a special occasion and he made no objection. Before I rose, I collected some of the dust from beneath his feet and put it in my pocket to keep as a sacred memento. I also asked for his blessings because I had an intuition that this was our final parting. I somehow knew I would never see him again.* (qtd.in Godman I: 159)

37. The Presence of Śiva and Śakti in Sages and Avatārs

On account of multiple afflictions in the *Maharṣi's* case, *Mokṣa* was accompanied by the cessation of the activity of the Divine Mother so that in this case of *advaitic* Realization, there was no scope for any kind of 'mission' for the *Maharṣi,* as some *Avatārs* — his illustrious contemporaries, *Mahātmā Gandhi* and *Śrī Aurobindo* — had.

In the *Maharṣi,* only *Śiva* was left after *Mokṣa;* the only remnants of *Śakti* were *Jñāna Śakti,* with *Icchā Śakti* and *Kriyā Śakti* being rendered practically void. With the Divine Mother returning to her consort *Śiva,* and with the play of *māyā* and duality thus coming to an end, there was no opportunity whatsoever for *Icchā Śakti* and *Kriyā Śakti* to have any manifestation. By contrast, in the case of his contemporaries *Mahātmā Gandhi* and *Śrī Aurobindo,* there was the functionality, mission, and relationship with the world as the 'other' on account of *Śakti* still being active. Thus, these *Avatārs* were never fully on the *Nivṛtti mārga,* which was the *mārga* of *Śrī Ramaṇa Maharṣi* as well as of *Śrī Nisargadatta Maharaj.* This differentiation in the presences of *Śiva* and *Śakti* in the charts of Sages and *Avatārs* is extremely important for understanding who they were, how they functioned, what they taught, and how they lived through their earthly sojourn.

As *Śakti,* the consort of *Aruṇācala Śiva,* had to return home to her beloved, how she related to her beloved as *Śrī Ramaṇa Maharṣi* is best portrayed in the Divine Mother's own words from a work on *Durgā Saptaśatī:*

> *I dance, and all that you perceive are its manifestations. If you like you can watch me dance, or if you like you can make me stop. He who can make me stop, I make him a seer, a man of wisdom, one of intuitive vision, my husband, Lord Śiva, the consciousness of infinite goodness.* (Saraswati Invocation)

It was *Śrī Ramaṇa Maharṣi's* destiny that the Divine display and the sportive play of *līlā* and *māyā* of the Divine Mother was called to a halt in the field of his life for the highest spiritual welfare of the whole world.

38. Waving of the Lights [Maṅgalahārati] to Aruṇācala Śiva and the Beloved Masters

With the inevitable feeling of sadness in our hearts at the *Maharṣi's Mahānirvāṇa* and our empathetic entry into Papaji's shoes at the time of his poignant leave-taking, this astrological Pilgrimage into the life and *Mokṣa* of *Śrī Ramaṇa Maharṣi* comes to its natural end. Now it is the appropriate time for us to offer our leave taking *praṇāms* [obeisance] to this illustrious *Avatār* of that transcendent God of the Hindu world, *Śiva.*

In the Preface and in the earlier chapters of the Pilgrimage, we had identified more or less three classes of readers whom we cited as kindred fellow pilgrims who might chance to undertake the Pilgrimage with us. First, there were my cultural kinsmen, the English-educated Hindus who have strongly come under western intellectual and cultural influences, which have had their origin in the western *apotheosis* of science and technology and the concomitant unspiritual outlook on life.

The second group consisted of Hindu astrologers, also my kinsmen in the learning of this Hindu *vidyā*. The third class consisted of my spiritual kinsmen, *Brahma-jijñāsus* and *Mumukṣus* on their respective paths of *Jñāna* and *Bhakti*. Administering the 'Hindu medicine', promoting a 'Hindu homecoming', creating a taste for Hindu astrology in the spheres of *Dharma* and *Mokṣa* and an attendant yearning for *Mokṣa* inspired by the illustrious example of *Śrī Ramaṇa Maharṣi,* these were our goals at the commencement of the Pilgrimage.

It is indeed possible at this stage that some scales of *avidyā* are still clouding our vision, and that the 'lump' of *asmitā* or the feeling of being a separate self might also be lingering in our hearts without there being any sign of the descent of that grace for receiving the highest *prasāda* in life. Yet, if we pause to wonder, we shall find that we cannot deny that *Aruṇācala Śiva* and the four beloved Masters have touched the right cord in the celestial instrument of our hearts. Now it is time to take leave from the *satsaṅg* with the Masters.

Before we gladly gulp down that parting draught of the 'Hindu medicine' that the uncompromising beloved Master *Śrī Nisargadatta Maharaj* is now about to administer to us, we offer our gratitude and devotional adoration to him, not only for giving us a stern admonition regarding the danger of our self-conceit about ourselves, but also for giving us some much-needed encouragement for uplifting our possibly dejected and disconsolate selves at this crucial hour as our Pilgrimage draws to a close.

> *As long as you feel competent and confident, reality is beyond your reach. Unless you accept inner adventure as a way of life, discovery will not come to you.* (qtd. in *I Am That* 499)

> *The experience is unique and unmistakable. It will dawn on you suddenly, when the obstacles are removed to some extent. It is like a frayed rope snapping. Yours is to work at the strands. The break is bound to happen. It can be delayed, but not prevented.* (*I Am That* 502)

The final destination or *garbhagṛha* [*sanctum sanctorum*] of this Hindu Pilgrimage has been the Self-Realization and the *Mahānirvāṇa* of *Śrī Ramaṇa Maharṣi.* Thus, 'death', physical as well as in its highest aspect of Immortality, has been common to both these events. As the Sage of *Aruṇācala* in the ripeness of his wisdom never chose to communicate to humanity what Self-Realization had actually meant for someone like him and whose self was extinguished, we are obliged to seek at least a partial glimpse of a kindred 'experience' from the life of another of our beloved Masters.

Ever since merging with *Śiva* as *Kālakāla,* the slayer of death, the *Maharṣi* had come to live with death as an inalienable part of life. Though the Master *Śrī J. Krishnamurti's* portrayal of what it was like for him to live with death might necessarily be different from what this might have meant for the *Maharṣi,* nevertheless it does give us a deeper understanding – however incomplete – of the role of death as the *Maharṣi's* constant companion and beloved.

In his masterly motion picture on *Ādi Śaṅkarācārya's* life, director *Śrī* G. V. Iyer portrayed this highest mystic truth of having to live with death by showing *Ādi Śaṅkarācārya* as always accompanied by an anthropomorphic form of death from the time of his early boyhood till his very end. Death was thus beautifully portrayed as *Ādi Śaṅkarā's* constant companion and beloved friend.

All Hindu Masters on the *Nivṛtti mārga* have acknowledged having to constantly live with death. *Śrī J. Krishnamurti* would not agree to the following portrayal of death from his own encounter with it during his mystic life as being, by any stretch of imagination, 'a medicine from Hindu stock', although I am choosing to make it one in view of the universality of the *Nivṛtti* Masters having had to constantly live with death.

In offering this penultimate draught of the 'Hindu medicine', we discharge our profound debt of gratitude and offer our devotional adoration to the Master *Śrī J. Krishnamurti*, for it was his 'Hindu medicine' of *seeing*, administered to me by my Master *Śrī Śrī Bhagavān* in a more potent form, that had certainly rid me of the madness of worldliness and ambition. Looking back, I think the enhanced potency came simply from the deep concern and compassion the sensitive philosopher-friend and beloved Master *Śrī Śrī Bhagavān* had for me. This penultimate draught of Hindu medicine is evocative of the *Maharṣi's* life of perfect detachment and renunciation:

> *It was there, the very essence of death. The essence of self is death but this death was the very essence of life as well. In fact they were not separate, life and death. This was not something conjured up by the brain for its comfort and ideational security. The very living was the dying and dying was living. . . . It was there, in reality, in fact, as intense and demanding as the honk of a car that wanted to pass. As life would never leave, nor can be set aside, so death now would never leave or be put aside. It was there with an extraordinary intensity and with a finality.* (Krishnamurti *Notebook* 66)

While it was the destiny of *Śrī J. Krishnamurti* to make repeated forays and attempts to ford 'the river of death' in the course of his mystic flights, *Śrī Ramaṇa Maharṣi,* by virtue of being an embodiment of *Aruṇācala Śiva,* seems to have finished with death once and for all, if we are to go by his life and written compositions, and is instead seen to be poised peacefully on the shore of Immortality, which lies beyond the river of death. In this sense, the significance of death for the two Masters would have been entirely different. The horoscope of *Śrī J. Krishnamurti* created the blessings of '*dying and the otherness*', whereas, the horoscope of *Śrī Ramaṇa Maharṣi* created the blessings of Immortality, which lies beyond death.

As *Brahma-jijñāsus* and *Mumukṣus* who are true to the *Vedic* ethos of perceiving the same eternal Self behind the teachings and the 'auspicious physical forms' of the three beloved Masters, and also profoundly touched by their selfless lives, even though all three have now departed from the physical plane, it is now in the fitness of things for us to offer with devotional ardour our wholehearted *praṇāms* and *Maṅgalahārati* to *Aruṇācala Śiva* as well as the three beloved *advaitic* Masters, as embodiments of the eternal Self: *Śrī Ramaṇa Maharṣi, Śrī Nisargadatta Maharaj,* and *Śrī J. Krishnamurti,* through our full-throated chants of the *mṛtyuṁjaya mantra,* but with a courageous and clear-sighted setting aside of the Master *Śrī J. Krishnamurti's* possible annoyance at the same!

Aum Trayambakaṁ Yajāmahe
Sugandhiṁ Puṣṭi-vardhanam |
Urvā-rukam-iva Bandhanāt
Mṛtyor-mukṣīya mā-'mṛtāt || *(Mahānārāyaṇa Upaniṣad)*

We worship Lord Śiva, the three-eyed one,
Who is full of fragrance and who nourishes all beings,
May He liberate us from death, by bestowing Immortality,
Even as the cucumber in its ripeness is spontaneously liberated
— from its bondage to the creeper.

At this auspicious moment of homage to the beloved Masters, may my beloved *Jyotiṣācāryas*, Prof. V. K. Choudhry and Pandit Vamadeva Shastri; kindred elders; benefactors; circle of seekers of astrological guidance; my tribesmen the English-educated Hindus, astrologers, *Brahma-jijñāsus,* and *Mumukṣus;* my publisher and his teammates; readers; well-wishers; my own teammates, family and friends – may they all, who are also the manifestations of the eternal Self, be equally protected and blessed by *Aruṇācala Śiva* and the four beloved Masters for their selfless and untiring labours for the material and spiritual upliftment of the world!

Aum Sarve Bhavantu Sukhinaḥ |
Sarve Santu Nirāmayāḥ ||
Sarve Bhadrāṇi Paśyantu |
Mā-Kaścit duḥkha-bhāg Bhavet ||
Aum Śāntiḥ Śāntiḥ Śāntiḥ

Aum: May all have the bliss of equanimity in their hearts!
May all be free from disease!
May all see only the grace that brings prosperity!
May none have any kind of suffering!
May peace prevail at all times!

In the early 1970s, my beloved Master *Śrī Śrī Bhagavān* had sent me a letter from Coimbatore in which he had narrated his response to the spectacle of humanity hurrying along the road down below as he watched this strange movement of life with dispassionate eyes from an overlooking terrace parapet high above. In the letter, he had raised the unsettling but pertinent question:

People are all busily hurrying past, but busy about what?

I was to understand by this that humanity was in the feverish grip of some worldly madness, of always being caught up in the incessant process of doing and becoming, and that this was at the very root of their frenzied involvement in the world, with all the inevitable consequences of pleasure and pain.

The following concluding line of my Master's letter came to be etched on the impressionable tablet of my heart, even as an astrologer would engrave a *mantra* or *yantra* on a *kavach,* and has remained there as a memorable blessing all these decades without ever becoming tarnished:

> *As I write this, the world comes up before me and I am filled with anxious tears.*

Deeply moved, even at this distant moment in time, by this musing which betokens the Master's unwavering and relentless concern for the world and its strange ways, and with a clear recognition that this beloved Master *Śrī Śrī Bhagavān* is but a new manifestation of that eternal Self, in the form of an inimitable blessing *Avatār,* for bringing about the welfare of the world [*lokakalyāṇa*] in all the four spheres of life: *Dharma, Artha, Kāma,* and *Mokṣa;* we now perform the auspicious waving of the lights [*maṅgalahārati*] to him as well as to beloved *Śrī Śrī Amma,* true to the Hindu ethos, with our hearts joyfully chanting their *mūlamantra* as an expression of our devotional adoration and abiding gratitude for their Divine grace:

Aum Sat-Cit-Ānanda Parabrahma Puruṣottama Paramātma |
Śrī Bhagavatī sameta Śrī Bhagavate Namaḥ ||
Aum Sat-Cit-Ānanda Parabrahma Puruṣottama Paramātma |
Śrī Bhagavatī sameta Śrī Bhagavate Namaḥ ||
Aum Sat-Cit-Ānanda Parabrahma Puruṣottama Paramātma |
Śrī Bhagavatī sameta Śrī Bhagavate Namaḥ ||

Aum Śāntiḥ Śāntiḥ Śāntiḥ

Obeisance to:
Sat-Cit-Ānanda Parabrahma [the Godhead, *Śiva*],
Who is the unmanifest Source of all manifestations, and Whose Absolute Reality is Beingness — Awareness — Bliss [*Sat-Cit-Ānanda*];

Obeisance to:
Him in His aspect as the Supreme Spirit [*Puruṣottama*];

Obeisance to:
Him in His aspect as the Supreme Soul [*Paramātmā*], Who enlivens all embodied souls;

Obeisance to:
Śrī Śrī Bhagavān and *Śrī Śrī Amma,*
Who are the embodiments of the Supreme *Śiva-Śakti.*

May the blessings of *Śrī Śrī Amma-Bhagavān* always pervade our lives as Divine peace.

❀❀❀❀❀❀❀

ASTROLOGICAL SYMBOLS

1. *Vedic* astrology = VA
Systems Approach to *Vedic* astrology = SA

2. Time of Birth = TOB
Place of Birth = POB
Date of Birth = DOB
Time Zone = TZ
LMT = Local Mean Time

The above are the birth details in any birth chart. By horoscope is meant the *rāśi* chart and the *navāmśa* chart as well as the entire gamut of the divisional (div) charts.

Navāṁśa chart = D-9
Daśāṁśa chart = D-10
Viṁśāṁśa chart = D-20
Caturviṁśāṁśa chart = D-24
Pançāṁśa chart = D-5
Dvādaśāṁśa chart = D-12

3. Sun = Su
Moon = Mo
Jupiter = Ju

Mars = Ma
Saturn = Sa
Venus = Ve
Mercury = Me
Rāhu = Ra
Ketu = Ke

4. Houses = Hs
First House = IH
Second House = IIH, etc.
Ascendant = Asdt
Most Effective Point = MEP
Mūla Trikoṇa house = MTH
Mūla Trikoṇa sign = MTS
Transit = Tr
Transit Significant Event = TSE
Debilitation = deb, Exalted = exalt
Daśā = major period, *Bhukti* = minor period or sub-period

Dharma Hs are IH, VH, and IXH.
Dharma signs are Aries, Leo, and Sagittarius.

Artha Hs are IIH, VIH, and XH.
Artha signs are Taurus, Virgo, and Capricorn.

Kāma Hs are IIIH, VIIH, and XIH.
Kāma signs are Gemini, Libra, and Aquarius.

Mokṣa Hs are IVH, VIIIH, and XIIH.
Mokṣa signs are Cancer, Scorpio, and Pisces.

Angular Hs are IH, IVH, VIIH, and XH.
Trinal Hs are IH, VH, and IXH.

Duhsthānas or malefic Hs are VIH, VIIIH, and XIIH.
Malefic signs are Virgo, Scorpio, and Pisces.
Cara rāśis are *Meṣa, Kataka, Tula,* and *Makara.*
Sthira rāśis are *Vṛṣabha, Siṁha, Vṛścika,* and *Kumbha.*
Dwisvabhava rāśis are *Mithuna, Kanyā, Dhanus,* and *Mīna.*

5. MTSs and Non-MTSs:
Aries is the MTS of Ma.
Cancer is the MTS of the Mo.
Leo is the MTS of the Su.
Virgo is the MTS of Me.
Libra is the MTS of Ve.
Sagittarius is the MTS of Ju.
Aquarius is the MTS of Sa.

Accordingly, if Taurus, Gemini, Scorpio, Capricorn, and Pisces are the signs that underlie particular Hs in the SA, those Hs do not have lords. Only the houses falling in the MTSs mentioned above have house lords. *This sharp distinction between the MTSs and non-MTSs is a characteristic hallmark of the SA.*

6. *Navagrahas* refers to the nine *grahas* [planets] listed above.
Functional Benefic planet = FB
Functional Malefic planet = FM
Most Malefic Planet = MMP

7. We use the *Vimṣottari daśa-bhukti* system of clock time in the SA, and the *Lahiri Ayanāmśa,* used by the government of India.

BIBLIOGRAPHY

Śrī Ramaṇa Maharṣi's Mokṣa is based on authentic information from the following standard sources.

Choudhry, V. K., and Rajesh, K. Chaudhary. **Systems Approach for Interpreting Horoscopes**. 3rd ed. New Delhi: Sagar, 2002.

Choudhry, V. K., Prof. **How to Identify Significant Events (Through Transit)**. Rev ed. New Delhi: Sagar, 2003.

Dikshit, Sudhakar S., ed. **I Am That – Talks with Sri Nisargdatta Maharaj**. Trans. Maurice Frydman. 3rd ed. Mumbai: Chetana, 1993.

Durga Saptasati. Trans. Swami Satyananda Saraswati. 1994. 1st ed. New Delhi: Motilal Banarsidas, 1995.

Frawley, David (Vamadeva Shastri). **Astrology of the Seers – A Guide to Vedic/Hindu Astrology**. 1st Indian ed. New Delhi: Motilal Banarsidas, 1992.

Gandhi, Mahatma. **What is Hinduism?** New Delhi: National Book Trust, 1994.

Giri, Sri Swami Yukteswar. **The Holy Science**. 1963. 8th Indian ed. Calcutta: Yogoda Satsanga Society of India, 1990.

Godman, David. **Living by the Words of Bhagavan**. 2nd ed. Tiruvannamalai: Sri Annamalai Swami Ashram Trust, 1995.

—. **Nothing Ever Happened**. 3 vols. Boulder: Avadhuta Foundation, 1998.

Govindan, Marshall. **Kriya Yoga Sutras of Patanjali and the Siddhas – Translation, Commentary, and Practice**. Bangalore: Babaji's Kriya Yoga Order of Acharyas Trust, 2000.

Kirkpatrick, Sidney D. **Edgar Cayce, An American Prophet**. New York: Riverhead-Berkley-Penguin Putnam, 2000.

Krishnamurti, Jiddu. **Krishnamurti's Notebook**. London: Victor Gollancz, 1976.

—. **Meditations**. Chennai: Krishnamurti Foundation of India, 2000.

Maharshi Parasara. **Brihat Parasara Hora Sastra**. Trans., comm. and anno. Girish Chand Sharma. Vol. 2. New Delhi: Sagar, 1995.

Muruganar. **Non-Dual Consciousness—The Flood Tide of Bliss, Sri Ramana Anubuti**. Trans. Robert Butler. Bangalore: Ramana Maharshi Centre for Learning, 1998.

Narasimha Swami, B. V. **Self Realization**. Tiruvannamalai: V. S. Ramanan, President, Sri Ramanasramam, 2002.

Natarajan, A. R. **Timeless in Time – Sri Ramana Maharshi, a Biography**. Bangalore: Ramana Maharshi Centre for Learning, 2002.

Osborne, Arthur, ed. **The Teachings of Sri Ramana Maharshi in His Own Words**. Tiruvannamalai: T. N. Venkataraman, President, Sri Ramanasramam, 1988.

Rajaram, Navaratna S., and David Frawley (Vamadeva Shastri). **Vedic Aryans and the Origin of Civilization – A Literary and Scientific Perspective**. 1955. 3rd ed. New Delhi: Voice of India, 2001.[1]

Ramanan, V. S. **Song of Ribhu**. Trans. Ramamoorthy, H, and Nome. Spec. ed. Tiruvannamalai: V. S. Ramanan, President, Sri Ramanasramam, 2003. Pulisher's Note.

Sambasiva Rao, Ammula. **Life History of Shirdi Sai Baba**. Trans. Thota Bhaskara Rao. New Delhi: Sterling, 1977.

Smith, David. **The Dance of Shiva – Religion, Art, and Poetry in South India**. 1944. 1st Indian ed. New Delhi: Manas Saikia for Foundation Books, 1998.

Sri Ramanasramam. **The Collected Works of Sri Ramana Maharshi**. 9th ed. Tiruvannamalai, 2004.[2]

Swāmī, Śrī Vidyāraṇya. **Pañcadaśī**. Trans. Swāmī Swāhānanda. Madras: Sri Ramakrishna Math, 1967.

Swaminathan, K. **Ramana Maharshi**. New Delhi: National Book Trust of India, 1975.

The Hymns of Sankara. Comp. T. M. P. Mahadevan. Delhi: Motilal Banarsidas, 1980.

Taimni, I. K. **The Science of Yoga**. 1961. Chennai. The Theosophical Publishing House, Ninth Reprint 1999.[3]

Toynbee, Arnold. **A Study of History**. 1972. London: Oxford University Press, 1976.[4]

❀❀❀❀❀❀❀

[1] See also Feuerstein, Georg, Subhash Kak, and David Frawley. **In Search of the Cradle of Civilization**. New Delhi: Motilal Banarsidas, 1995.

[2] See 'Eleven Verses to Sri Arunachala' (100, stanza 10).

[3] The witness consciousness 'I AM' is described by this author, without the capitals, i.e., as 'I am'.

[4] See page 341 in Part VII, dealing with Universal Churches.

GLOSSARY OF SANSKRIT TERMS

Adharma That which is a violation of *Dharma* or virtue.

Adhikāri A spiritual aspirant who has a certain competency through her/his intellectual, emotional, and psychic endowments, where a particular spiritual path is concerned. The term refers to one who is qualified and entitled to function with authority in a specific area of the spiritual life, to which s/he is temperamentally suited.

Adhikāri-bhedha-nyāya The principle [*nyāya*] by which the spiritual path is held to be different [*bhedha*] for each *adhikāri* based on his/her temperament and spiritual maturity. This principle goes against a massified approach to spiritual development and implies a greater care in the selection of spiritual paths for individuals, with due consideration of their innate propensities and aptitudes.

Advaita As a noun as well as adjective, it stands for a non-dual system of philosophy and world view that goes hand in hand with experiential Self-Realization. It implies the cessation of duality, that is, ending the sharp separation and distinction between the observing subject and the observed object as in the perfect *advaitic* state of Self-Realization.

Advaita Vedānta The highest esoteric non-dual [*advaita*] Hindu philosophy of the *Upaniṣads* which are taken to be the terminal limit of the *Vedas* [*Vedānta*]. It is founded on the *advaitic* state of Self-Realization and also reconciles it with the 'reality' of the perceived world of duality experienced prior to Self-Realization. Also refers to the Hindu world view [*darśana*] upheld by *Ādi Śaṅkarācārya* (788-820 CE).

Aham Brahmāsmi Sourced in the sacred texts of the Hindus, the *Upaniṣads,* it describes the state of God-Realization and Self-Realization of *Ṛṣis.* This is a great *advaitic* saying in that it establishes an identity between the Self [*Ātmā*] in humans and the infinite power behind creation [*Brahman*]. *Aham asmi* means I am. When this *advaitic* Realization becomes a reality, the individual realizes that the seemingly inconsequential self is, indeed, when unmasked, the eternal Self or *Ātmā.*

Ahimsā The prefix 'a' in *Sanskrit* denotes negation. *Himsā* means cruelty or violence. The *Dharmic* principle adopted by *Mahātmā* Gandhi during the freedom struggle. It tantamounts to not only non-cruelty and non-violence as an approach to life, but also implies a reverence towards all forms of life.

Anātmā *Anātmā* means, not the *Ātmā,* but only a false self. A person's identity as a personality, in the family or in society are apt examples of only *anātmās.* Her/his true undiscovered identity is of course the *Ātmā.*

Andha-hasti-nyāya The principle [*nyāya*] of contradictory and fragmentary perceptions, as in the illustrative example of an elephant [*hasti*] being 'discovered' by blind [*andha*] men. Each describes the reality of the elephant entirely differently and no two agree as to what the elephant really is! However, the total true picture of the elephant emerges from a synthesis of these multiple contradictory and fragmentary perceptions.

Annamayakośa The body [*kośa* or covering sheath] that is made up of food [*anna*], namely, the physical body.

Antarmukha Introversion, spiritual seclusion, or withdrawal from the world with a view to gather spiritual strength through study, contemplation, meditation, etc..

Anugrahakāraka Significator [*kāraka*] of grace [*anugraha*].

Artha The second of the goals of life in traditional Hindu society, devoted to the earning of wealth, gaining of professional skill, and eminence, name, and fame; deemed to be an important achievement of the *jīvātmā* in the course of its earthly sojourn, even as a solid preparation for entering into the later stages [*āśramas*] of life, which were structured to be more austere and spiritual.

Aruṇācala Name of the sacred hill in Tiruvannamalai (*acala* signifies rest or the negation of movement as in a mountain). Therefore, *Aruṇācala* signifies a mountain or a hill that is an embodiment of fiery reddish light [*aruṇa*] symbolizing enlightenment. This is the colour of the hill around sunrise. *Śiva* is the transcendent God of the Hindu world, beyond sensory perceptions of time and space. The *Maharṣi* and Hindu *Śaivite* tradition held *Aruṇācala* to be an embodiment of *Śiva*.

Asmitā I-am-ness, referred to in the *Yogasūtras* of *Patañjali* as one of the taints standing in the way of *Mokṣa* and denoting a sense of selfhood, which is felt to be distinct and different from the world and all observed objects therein.

Asmitākāraka Significator of the sense of selfhood or *asmitā*.

Asmitāsthāna The place [*sthāna*] of *asmitā* in Hindu astrology, namely, the IVH.

Asura A personification of one of the cosmic malefic life energies in the *Purāṇas*, and represented by a functional malefic planet (FM) in Hindu astrology.

Avatār A Divine embodiment of *Brahman* in human form but with the human consciousness inextricably interwoven with the Divine consciousness. It is this 'descent of Divine grace' that functions through the *Avatār*, empowering the *Avatār's* work for the welfare of the world [*lokakalyāṇa*].

Avatārarahasya The mystery or secret-knowledge [*rahasya*] behind the coming of an *Avatār*.

Avidyā Ignorance, one of the five taints in *Patañjali's Yogasūtras.* Meant as primordial ignorance manifesting as the sense of selfhood [*asmitā*] supposing itself to be separate from the rest of the world. That the perceived duality is ignorance can be known only after *Mokṣa.*

Ayanāṁśa The angular segment or shift [*aṁśa*] between the position [*ayana*] of the vernal equinox and the beginning of the sign Aries amounting, in May 2008, to 23° 58′. This is also the mismatch or the extent of displacement between the Sidereal zodiac and the Tropical zodiac.

Ācārya Preceptor or accredited Spiritual Teacher in Hindu society (usually within a well-defined framework of spiritual tradition), holding a position of authority.

Ālambana Supporting ground or foundation.

Ānanda Bliss, one of the three primordial manifestations of *Parabrahma* or Absolute Reality.

Ānandamayakośa In the *Upaniṣadic* model of human consciouness, this is the interior-most sheath [*kośa*] or covering over the *Ātmā.* The nature of this sheath is bliss [*ānandamaya*].

Ārdra The name of the sixth *nakṣatra* in the zodiac, in the sign Gemini.

Āryamba *Ādi Śaṅkarācārya's* mother.

Āśrama A centre for pursuing spiritual growth and good works for the welfare of the world, not however through *rājasic* activity inspired by selfish goals, but by being poised in the gentle and relaxed *sāttvic* state in which alone concern for the world is natural and spontaneous.

Ātma Jñāna Realization [*Jñāna*] of the Self [*Ātmā*] in *Śrī Ramaṇa Maharṣi's* teachings.

Ātmakāraka Significator of the *Ātmā* or the Self. In VA, the Sun is the significator of the *Ātmā.* The IVH also signifies the *Ātmā* after *Mokṣa,* and the *asmitā* prior to *Mokṣa.*

Ātma Prabhā The effulgence [*Prabhā*] or glory of the Self [*Ātmā*], which is self-luminous and is the light of the world.

Ātma Vicāra Enquiry [*Vicāra*] into the nature of the Self [*Ātmā*], synonymous with the teachings of *Śrī Ramaṇa Maharṣi.*

Ātmā, Ātman Referred to as the *Puruṣa* in the *Yogasūtras* and as the Self by *Śrī Ramaṇa Maharṣi;* stands for the infinite Absolute Reality behind the body and the individualized consciousness. Also, sometimes used to refer to the individual self, when pointing to its true nature.

Āyuṣkāraka Significator [*kāraka*] of longevity [*āyuṣ*] in VA and the SA, namely, Saturn.

Bhagavad Gīta An important Hindu scripture, extracted from the Hindu epic, the *Mahābhārata,* being the comprehensive teaching of the Hindu *Avatār Śrī Kṛṣṇa* given to *Arjuna* on the *Kurukṣetra* battlefield. It literally translates as 'Song [*Gīta*] of the Lord [*Bhagavān*]'.

Bhaja Govindam A composition of *Śrī Ādi Śaṅkarācārya,* devotional and overflowing with the power of detachment and surrender to God and presenting the perishable nature of this body and human life. *Bhaja* means 'devotional adoration of God'. The name of God chosen for adoration is *Govinda* (one of the names of *Viṣṇu*).

Bhakta A devotee of God or of a Spiritual Master.

Bhaktaparādhīna God or the *Paramātmā,* the Supreme Soul, in the aspect of being dependent on the individual consciousness of the *bhakta.*

Bhakti Devotion and adoration of God, usually in a personalized form.

Bhakti Mārga Refers to the path [*mārga*] of devotion to God [*Bhakti*]. It is especially recommended to householders who may not have the time and the opportunities for treading the more difficult paths of *Jñāna* and *Yoga.*

Bhakti Yoga A spiritual path, based on service as well as devotional worship of God or Master, leading ultimately to Self-Realization but through the intermediate stage of God-Realization. Considered ideal for family people.

Bhāva Used in Hindu astrology to denote the houses, which are the various spheres of life. Thus, *karmabhāva* refers to the tenth house of action [*karma*].

Bhikṣāṭana The manifestation of God *Śiva* as the 'Supreme Mendicant'. Especially relevant to *sanyāsis* and devotees on the *Nivṛtti mārga* or the path of renunciation.

Bhukti A technical term in VA – also called the minor period or the sub-period in the SA – in the *Viṁśottarī daśa-bhukti* cyclical system of time.

Bhūminātha The name of the Deity (an aspect of *Śiva*) in Tiruchuzhi, the birthplace of *Śrī Ramaṇa Maharṣi.*

Brahma-jijñāsu A seeker of *Mokṣa* on the path of *Jñānayoga,* with a passion for knowing, understanding, and Self-Realization [*Brahma-jñāna*].

Brahman The one Absolute Reality of Awareness, both in its subjective aspect as *Ātmā* or Self and in its objective aspect as *Brahman,* the totality of the manifestation of the world. The term is often used in the Hindu *darśana* of *advaita Vedānta.*

Brihat Parāśara Horaśāstra A classical treatise in VA by *Maharṣi Parāśara.*

Bṛhaspati A *Vedic* Deity standing for the priest and teacher and identified with the planet Jupiter in VA and the SA.

Buddhikāraka Significator [*kāraka*] of intellect [*buddhi*] and analytical faculty in Hindu astrology, namely, Mercury.

Cakras The nerve plexuses along the spinal cord, standing for the various 'wheels' of consciousness and corresponding to the higher and subtler planes. In *Tantrayoga,* one meditates on these *cakrās* as visual patterns in order to awaken *Kuṇḍalinī.*

Candra Lagna A horoscope can be read with respect to the Moon sign [*candra rāśi*] as Asdt [*lagna*]. This would mean that in such a reading, the sign in which the Moon is placed is taken as the IH.

Caturviṁśāṁśa The D-24 divisional chart, which in VA gives additional information about the potential for higher education if the individual is in the spheres of *Artha* and *Kāma,* but signifies the potential for *Jñāna* and *Mokṣa* if the individual is in the spiritual spheres of *Dharma* and *Mokṣa.*

Dakṣiṇāmūrti One of the classical manifestations of *Śiva* as the silent teacher of *Mokṣa* – *mūrti* means manifestation; *Dakṣiṇāmūrti* would mean *Śiva's* manifestation in the Southern part [*dakṣiṇā*] of India.

Darśana Literally meaning a vision, stands for a philosophical system or world view that is arrived at as a result of mystic insights and experiences on the one hand and its intelligent and systematized formulation by the intuition of the illumined (see the entry *Prajñāna*) on the other.

Daśā-bhukti The major [*daśā*] and minor [*bhukti*] periods in the *Viṁśottarī daśā-bhukti* cyclical system of time – used in VA and the SA.

Daśāṁśa The D-10 divisional chart, in VA and the SA. It is used to estimate the measure of Divine grace for the XH significations of professional achievement, virtue in action and beneficial impact of the profession on society as a whole.

Daśās The major or main cyclical periods of the planets in VA and the SA, usually running for several years.

Dehātmabuddhi The perception or view [*buddhi*] that one (in essence the *Ātmā*) thinks that one is the body [*deha*]. It therefore refers to our primordial state of spiritual ignorance.

Deva A personification of one of the cosmic benefic life energies in the *Purāṇas,* and represented by a functional benefic planet (FB) in Hindu astrology.

Devatā A Divine being with a specific kind of Divine power. Used in this work to point to those who came like messengers of God, to help complete the work. In Hindu astrology the planets are viewed as '*Navagraha Devatās*', or the nine cosmic life energies of the Divine Mother.

Dharma The first goal of human life in traditional Hindu society, devoted to spiritual learning and understanding of the self and the world on the basis of a God-centred world view. Hindu male children studied for a period of fourteen years upto their twenty first year at the feet of a competent Master and his consort in order to get a good foundation in *Dharma.*

Dharmasaṁsthāpana An *Avatār* or an incarnation of the Hindu God *Viṣṇu* vanquishes evil forces hindering *Dharma,* and thus serves to re-establish [*saṁsthāpana*] the lost moral and spiritual excellences in human society through a new cycle of *yugas,* commencing with the most virtuous season of the new cycle.

Dharma Śāśtra Authoritative scriptures [*Śāśtras*] on how to lead a righteous life and uphold *Dharma.*

Dīkṣa Transmission of grace, usually by an adept or a Spiritual Master, through touch or a gaze.

Duhsthānas The so-called malefic houses [*sthānas*] in VA and the SA, which cover all the kinds of sufferings [*duhkha*] in human life: VIH, VIIIH, and XIIH.

Durgā Saptaśatī A Hindu scripture extracted from *Mārkaṇḍeya Purāṇa* in seven hundred verses, extolling the powers of the Divine Mother as *Durga* or *Caṇḍī.* Attributed to the period 900-500 BCE.

Dvaita The Hindu *darśana* that takes for granted the duality between the perceiving subject and the perceived object and builds a God-centred world view based on this experiential dualistic perception. A *dvaitin* is one who accepts this philosophical world view as true to him.

Dwāpara Yuga *Yuga* means age or cosmic cycle. In *Śrī Yukteśwar Giri's* model of the chronology of the *yugas,* in each great cosmic cycle [*mahāyuga*] of 24,000 years, a certain segment of time has the quality of *Dwāpara,* during this period, the bull of *Dharma* stands on only two of its four feet. During such a *yuga, Dharma* or virtue, is reduced to fifty percent of its original presence.

Gaṇeśa Etymologically, 'the Lord of all the manifested forms' and the essence of all the gods in the Hindu pantheon. Also, the precursor to the fullness of God as Godhead [*Parabrahma*]. In this work, understood as the *sāttvic* and timeless witness consciousness of 'I AM', which is the foundation for the manifestation of the world or *Brahman.* In mythological [*Purāṇic*] terms, the eldest born of *Śiva* and his consort *Śakti.*

Garbhagṛha The *sanctum sanctorum* or innermost shrine of a Hindu temple where the Deity, as a formful aspect of God, is enshrined. Also used in the context of the divisional charts, wherein each divisional chart corresponding to a house of the *rāśi* chart is interpreted to be the *garbhagṛha* of that particular house.

Gṛhasthāśrama *Gṛhasthā* means householder, and *āśrama* here means stage of life. Thus, *gṛhasthāśrama* means the householder's life, in the mundane spheres of *Artha* and *Kāma.*

Guṇas Three fundamental 'modes' of the Divine Mother's *Śakti* but occurring always as a triad of three sub-manifestations, *sattva, rajas,* and *tamas. Sattva* is compassionate, peaceful, and intelligent; conducive to learning, gentleness, and a spiritual life. *Rajas* is active, restless, and aggressive. *Tamas* is indolent, lethargic, and inert. Every created entity, whether man, insect, or atom, is constituted of this triad. Usually, one 'mode' predominates as the innate characteristic of that created entity.

Guru A God-Realized or Self-Realized Spiritual Master in the Hindu tradition, who acts as an embodiment of the Divine Light leading us from darkness to Light and who enjoys full freedom to expound the truth of the Self or God in a manner s/he thinks will be beneficial to followers. The *Guru* is not obliged to adhere exclusively to any one tradition [*sampradāya*], as it is with an *ācārya.*

Gurukulāśrama An *āśrama* of a Spiritual Master or a *Ṛṣi* and his family. Usually a peaceful abode and a seat or centre for spiritual learning where disciples go and stay periodically or for many years in order to learn *Dharma* and the *Vidyās* at the feet of the Spiritual Master.

Hasta Nakṣatra One of the twenty seven *nakṣatras* in the zodiac, situated in the sixth sign Virgo [*Kanya*].

Hora Stands for hour or time. *Horaśāstra* is a discipline (doctrine) on time, namely, Hindu astrology.

Hṛdayakamalavāsa The personal God, who, in mystic experiences, may be felt in the lotus [*kamala*] of the heart [*hṛdaya,* the very centre of our feeling nature], which is therefore taken to be His abode [*nivāsa*].

Icchā Śakti The energy of the Divine Mother carrying the blessings of will, desire, aspiration, or intention.

Iṣṭadevatā A personal formful aspect of God, generally with specific Divine attributes that the individual and/or family worship throughout life. *Iṣṭa* means that which is beloved to us; *devatā* means Deity.

Īśvara In *dvaita, Īśvara* [God] is the supreme controller. In *advaita,* when the Absolute Reality is perceived from a state of *avidyā* or spiritual ignorance, the personal self [*jīvātmā*] experiences Absolute Reality as *Īśvara* or God, that is, as the Supreme Being other than itself.

Janma Lagna A horoscope can be read with respect to the birth sign [*janma rāśi*] as Asdt [*lagna*]. This would mean that in such a reading, the sign in which the Asdt is placed is taken as the IH.

Janmanakṣatra Punarvasu The star [*nakṣatra*] in which one's natal Mo is placed at the time of one's birth [*janma*] is called the *Janmanakṣatra.* At the time of the *Maharṣi's* birth, his natal Moon was placed in the seventh *nakṣatra Punarvasu,* in the third sign Gemini of the natural zodiac.

Jīvanmukta One who has received the blessings of *Mokṣa* or who has lost the personal self (personality and individuality) permanently while still inhabiting a human body.

Jīvanmukti *Mokṣa,* Liberation or permanent freedom from seperative existence or the personal self (personality and individuality), while still inhabiting the human body.

Jīvātmā The personal self that thinks and experiences itself as the human body and the personality without realizing that it is itself the *Paramātmā* or the Self.

Jñāna The wisdom of Self-Realization, meaning discriminative knowledge with a capacity to set apart Truth [*Sat*] from illusion [*māyā*].

Jñāna Mārga The path [*mārga*] of enquiry, understanding, learning, and finally, Realization [*Jñāna*] – about both the personal self [*jīvātmā*] as well as the Self [*Paramātmā*].

Jñāna Śakti The Divine Mother's energy [*Śakti*], which is intrinsically *sāttvic* and highly favourable for a life of understanding, wisdom, compassion, and Self-Realization.

Jñāna Yoga *Yoga* is Self-Realization; *Jñānayoga* is Self-Realization through learning, understanding, contemplation, and enquiry, but the final breakthrough is always the result of Divine grace.

Jñāni One who is Self-Realized from the point of view of *advaita Vedānta.*

Jyotir Vidyā *Vidyā* is a Hindu discipline of learning that is spiritual and God-centred; *Jyotirvidyā* was the original name for Hindu astrology [*Jyotiṣa*], but encompassing its erstwhile sister discipline of Hindu astronomy as well.

Jyotiṣa Hindu astrology in modern times, but in former times encompassing Hindu astronomy as well.

Jyotiṣācārya A sanctified Hindu teacher [*ācārya*] of *Jyotirvidyā* or *Vedic* astrology, usually within a well-established and well-defined traditional (or modern) framework or school of learning.

Kaivalya In *Patañjali's Yogasūtras, Kaivalya* is the final state of Self-Realization, the state of Absolute Aloneness, which is also the state of Absolute Oneness.

Kali Yuga *Yuga* means age or cosmic cycle. In *Śrī Swāmi Yukteśwar Giri's* model of the chronology of the *yugas,* in each great cosmic cycle [*mahāyuga*] of 24,000 years, a certain segment of time has the quality of *Kali* [darkness, ignorance, stagnation], with *Dharma* or virtue correspondingly minimized to twenty five percent of its original presence. Thus, in this *mahāyuga,* Hindu India experienced this darkest period of *Kaliyuga* between 701 BCE and 1699 CE, spanning some 2,400 years.

Karma, Karma Bhāva In Hindu philosophy, *karma* refers to action and the fruits thereof, but in the context of astrology, *karma* applies to the XH [*karmabhāva*], which is the house [*bhāva*] of action and is an *Artha* house of profession.

Karma Yoga The path of action [*karma*]. It becomes a spiritual path only when the fruits of action are renounced or offered to God rather than desired and selfishly enjoyed by the *jīvātmā.* This spiritual approach is followed by those Hindus who are usually householders and who enter into selfless action for the welfare of the world, and in this way, evolve into beings worthy of *Mokṣa.*

Kavach An astrological protective shield, usually in the form of a metal tablet. On it, the energies of the FBs are engraved in numerical form [*yantras*] during an auspicious *muhurta,* and the *kavach* is worn during another auspicious *muhurta,* in order to enhance God's grace in life. A *kavach* is usually prescribed by traditional *Vedic* astrologers. SA astrologers however, use the SA model of the *kavach,* which was designed for the first time by Prof. V. K. Choudhry.

Kālakāla A manifestation of *Śiva* as the slayer of death, and thus, as the giver of Immortality.

Kāla Puruṣa The God of time in VA and the SA. *Kāla* means time; *Puruṣa* means Supreme Spirit or the Self.

Kālīmātā *Kālī* is a special manifestation of the Divine Mother [*Mātā*], usually in malefic [*krūra*] form.

Kāma The third goal of human life, pertaining to marriage, family life, pleasure seeking, aesthetic enjoyment, and refinement. One of the four goals of life in a traditional Hindu society.

Kāminī-kāñcana-tyāga Renunciation [*tyāga*] of all association with women [*kāminī*] as well as wealth [*kāñcana* means gold].

Ketu The south node of the Moon, one of the nine *Navagrahas,* but not a physical planet.

Ketu Daśa The main period [*daśa*] corresponding to the planet *Ketu,* lasting for seven years.

Kriyā Śakti The energy of the Divine Mother present in the lords of the *Artha* Hs, the IIH, VIH, and XH. This energy is necessary for success and achievement in worldly life [*Pravṛtti mārga*].

Krūra Malefic, corresponding to the FMs (in opposition to *soumya,* benefic, corresponding to the FBs).

Kuṇḍalinī The coiled up and hidden energy of the Divine Mother lying dormant in the nerve plexus at the bottom of the spine, *Mūlādhāra cakra.*

Lagna The IH of the horoscope called the Ascendent (Asdt). The MEP (Most Effective Point) of the *lagna* [Asdt] corresponds to that point of the natural zodiac that is rising on the horizon at the place of birth, at the time of birth. The MEP is the heart of the *lagna* [Asdt], whereas the *lagna per se* refers to the zodiacal sign that contains the MEP.

Lakṣmī Sthānas The houses of the Divine Mother (the consort of the Hindu God *Viṣṇu*). These are the angular houses, the IH, IVH, VIIH, and XH. They contain the 'energy of becoming', and when these houses are strong, success comes more easily in life.

Liṅga The mythic symbol and Deity of the Hindus, signifying the formless aspect of Godhead, *Śiva,* and taking on, therefore, the 'formless geometry' of the *Śivaliṅga.*

Līlā Divine play of the *Śakti* or power of God in its joyous spontaneous unfoldment and Self-expression.

Lokakalyāṇa Saṁkalpa A determination and affirmation [*saṁkalpa*] for the welfare [*kalyāṇa*] of the world [*loka*].

Lokakalyāṇa Seva Service [*seva*] rendered for the welfare [*kalyāṇa*] of the world [*loka*]. A Hindu ideal in the sphere of *Dharma.*

Maharṣi A great [*Mahā*] Sage [*Ṛṣi*]. The greatness invariably came from the Sage's Self-Realization.

Mahā Nirvāṇa The passing away of a great soul. *Nirvāṇa* is the light of the individual consciousness being extinguished. *Mahānirvāṇa* is the withdrawal of the Self from its physical vehicle, resulting in 'death'.

Mahā Puruṣa A great [*mahā*] soul [*Ātmā*], usually with a great mission for the welfare of the world.

Mahātmā *Mahā* means great and *Ātmā* here means, soul or personage. Mrs. Annie Besant, one of the second line of founders of the worldwide Theosophical Movement, first referred to Gandhiji as the *Mahātmā.* Thereafter, this honorific title became inseparable from his name in the consciousness of the Indian people.

Manahkāraka The significator [*kāraka*] of *manas* or the feeling aspect of the human consciousness, namely, the Moon.

Manomayakośa The 'sheath of the mental body' or that aspect of the consciousness pertaining to feelings and the capacity to soak in feeling and empathy [*manomaya*]; *kośa* means sheath.

Mantra Jñāna Knowledge and understanding [*jñāna*] of *mantras,* or how to use focussed and empowered devotional, God-centred thoughts and feelings [*mantras*] to achieve various goals in life.

Mantra Sādhana The spiritual practice [*sādhana*] of regularly chanting a *mantra* with a view to achieving something specific.

Maṅgala Hārati *Maṅgala* means auspicious. *Hārati* is the daily ceremonial, circular waving of multiple ghee and oil lamps in front of the idol of God in Hindu temples and in Hindu homes (mornings and evenings at specified hours) to the tune of hymns and *mantras* expressing devotional adoration of God. This same form of Hindu ceremonial worship is also offered to Hindu living Masters and *Avatārs*. It often happens during such intense ceremonial invocation of God's grace that devotees experience an overwhelming devotional upsurge [*Bhakti*] or they might even have a *darśana* of God or Master. For the Hindus, this ceremony is sacred and all members of the community gathered become absorbed in their feeling towards God.

Maraṇa Vicāra An enquiry [*vicāra*] into the nature of death [*maraṇa*].

Mārga Spiritual path, also called *yoga.*

Mārkaṇḍeya The sixteen-year old virtuous son of a *Ṛṣi* who was rescued from death by *Śiva* in his aspect as *Kālakāla* or 'the slayer of death'.

Mātṛbhūteśvar The temple built over the *samādhi* of the *Maharṣi's* mother. A *Śivaliṅga* was installed over the *samādhisthal* to signify that the mother was the manifestation of *Śiva.*

Māyā Also called *mūla avidyā* [primordial ignorance] in *advaita Vedānta* and is an unavoidable aspect of the power of *Brahman* called *vikṣepa,* or 'projection of the world'. *Māyā* is the aspect of the power of God's manifestation that makes us perceive duality, whereas from the the state of *Mokṣa,* duality is seen to be an appearance only.

Mīnākṣi Sundareśwarar The names of the Hindu Deities *Pārvati* and *Śiva* at their abode in the *Mīnākṣi* temple in Madurai.

Mokṣa The fourth and the final goal of human life in ancient Hindu society, pertaining to the dissolution of the personal self, which results in Liberation from all sufferings.

Mokṣa Kāraka Usually the lord of the VIIIH or XIIH of *Mokṣa,* or either of the *Nirvāṇakārakas* [significators of *Nirvāṇa* or Liberation] Saturn and *Ketu.*

Mokṣa Nakṣatra In VA, the twenty seven *nakṣatras* are classified as *Dharma, Artha, Kāma,* and *Mokṣa nakṣatras. Hasta* is one of the seven *Mokṣa nakṣatras* in VA. The Asdt MEP of the *Maharṣi* is in the *Mokṣa nakṣatra Hasta.*

Mokṣa Pradāta One who bestows *Mokṣa — Aruṇācala Śiva* was the *Mokṣapradāta* for the boy *Ramaṇa.*

Mokṣa Yoga A close association through aspect or conjunction in Hindu astrology, between a *Mokṣakāraka* and an *asmitākāraka.*

Mouna The state of being silent without any oral expression as an aid to *pratyāhāra,* or withdrawal of the senses from their sense objects.

Mṛkaṇḍu A *Ṛṣi* and father of *Mārkaṇḍeya.*

Mṛtyuṁjaya Mantra *Mantra* has the syllables of *man* and *tra. Man* comes from *manana,* which means to think or dwell on, and *tra* comes from *trāṇa,* which means liberation from ignorance, or from whatever undesireable condition one may be in. Thus, *mantra* (which is always to be used with devotion, faith, and diligence) is intended to give not only liberation from our miseries but also fulfilment in all the four goals of life: *Dharma, Artha, Kāma,* and *Mokṣa. Mṛtyuṁjaya* is one of the names of Lord *Śiva.* It means one who secures victory [*jaya*] over death [*mṛtyuhu*] — meaning thereby that Lord *Śiva* can vanquish or negate death through His blessing of Immortality or *Mokṣa.*

Mumukṣu One seeking Liberation or *Mokṣa.*

Muruga The Tamil name for the younger son of *Śiva* and *Pārvati,* meaning charming. This Deity of the *Śaiva sampradāya* [Hindu *Śiva* tradition] represents the energy of Mars. Another name for *Muruga* is *Kārttikeya.*

Mūla Mantra *Mūla* means foundation or root. *Mūlamantra,* within the world view of a particular school of *yoga* or particular spiritual tradition, represented by a Spiritual Master or *āśrama,* is a foundational *mantra* and thus enjoys a unique position in the *sādhana* of devotees affiliated with that spiritual tradition. The *Mūlamantra* invoked at the end of this Pilgrimage is that of the Oneness Spiritual Movement, established by the Master *Śrī Śrī Bhagavān.*

Mūla Trikoṇa (MT) In VA and the SA, with the exception of the Sun and the Moon, each planet rules two signs in the zodiac. One of these two signs for each of the five planets is called the *Mūla Trikoṇa* sign [MTS]. When the ruling planet is placed in its own *Mūla Trikoṇa* sign, it becomes very strong. *Mūla* means foundational and *trikoṇa* means triangle.

Nakṣatra Means guardian of the night. The natural zodiac is divided either into twelve *rāśis* or signs, or into twenty seven *nakṣatras.* Each *nakṣatra* has an identifiable star pattern, which serves as a milestone in measuring the movements of the *Navagrahas* on the zodiacal belt.

Narasiṁha Swāmi In VA, the planet Me is taken to signify Lord *Viṣṇu's* consciousness. For individuals who have an Aries, Libra, or Aquarius Ascendant, the planet Me (because of its lordship over a malefic house), has the potential of becoming an *Iṣṭadevatā* of the *krūra* type, whenever it occupies the VH, without afflicting that house. In such cases, the *Iṣṭadevatā* corresponding to such a malefic Me, may be taken to be the *krūra* aspect of *Viṣṇu: Śrī Narasiṁha Swāmi.*

Navagrahas The *Sanskrit* name for the Deities corresponding to the nine planets in Hindu astrology. The *Navagrahas* represent the presence of *Īśvara* in the various spheres of life. The significance of planets in Hindu astronomy and Hindu astrology is entirely different. *Nava* means nine, *graha* means to possess or take hold of.

Navagraha Sannidhis The smaller shrines in all Hindu temples where Deities of the *Navagrahas* are worshipped.

Navāṁśa The most important divisional chart in VA and the SA. The D-9 chart, which is the *sanctum sanctorum* of the IXH.

Nayana Dīkṣa *Dīkṣa* is the transmission of spiritual grace, usually from a Master or even from an adept to a disciple, through a concentrated benevolent gaze — *nayana* means eye.

Nayanmars Considered to be sixty three in number and are the illustrious *Śiva*-Realized devotees of *Śiva*.

Nāḍi Non-physical channel or pathway along which the currents of *prāṇa* flow in the body.

Nirbīja Samādhi *Samādhi* is a state of consciousness, occurring as a meditational trance, in which the knower, the known (as the object meditated upon, the 'seed'), and the process of knowing, all become inseparably unified. *Nir* means without, *bīja* means seed. In *Patañjali's Yogasūtras, nirbīja samādhi* is understood to be more advanced than *sabīja samādhi.* Thus, it is the final round of meditational trance [*samādhi*] that is expected to deliver the fruit of *Mokṣa.* The Light of the *Puruṣa* in *sabīja samādhi* illuminates another chosen meditational object (the 'seed'), whereas in *nirbīja samādhi* the Light illuminates only Itself [*Puruṣa*] rather than another object, thereby producing Self-Realization. Thus, it is only through this final round of *nirbīja samādhi* that the Seer comes to be established in his own Self (see Taimni 123).

Nirguṇa Parabrahma Attributeless Godhead [*Parabrahma*] in *advaita Vedānta*.

Nirmohatvam State of freedom from delusion and attachment.

Nirvāṇa Buddhist term for Liberation, meaning the extinguishing of the light of individuality or I-am-ness.

Nirvāṇakāraka Term applied in VA to Saturn (Sa), which is the significator of the VIIIH of *Mokṣa.*

Nisañgatvam Detachment from all worldly things and concepts.

Niścalitatvam Stabilized in wisdom.

Nivṛtti Mārga The spiritual path away from worldly pursuits, intended for *Mumukṣus* and *Jijñāsus. Nir* means without, or negation; *vṛtti* means mode of life; *mārga* means path.

Nyāya Name of a Hindu *darśana* or world view that is primarily one of Hindu logic — the word also means principle.

Pacchaiamman Koil A shrine [*koil* in Tamil] to the Divine Mother [*Pacchaiamman*]at the northeastern corner of the foothills of *Aruṇācala.* The *Maharṣi* dwelt here when plague broke out in Tiruvannamalai in 1899.

Pañcabhūtas The five [*pañca*] primordial 'formful' elements [*bhūtas*] — space, air, fire, water, and earth.

Pañcāṁśa A divisional chart in Hindu astrology pertinent to the VH. In the SA, it may be used to estimate the measure of Divine grace for the VH significations of creative intelligence and capacity for spiritual learning, in the spheres of *Dharma* and *Mokṣa.*

Para Bhakti Supreme [*Para*] or highest form of devotion [*Bhakti*].

Parabrahma The Supreme unmanifest Source or Self or Godhead. *Para* means beyond; *Brahman* means the cosmic form of the *Ātmā.*

Paramaśiva Absolute Reality [*Paramaśiva*] in the *Śaiva sampradāya* [Hindu *Śaivite* tradition].

Paramātmā After Self-Realization, one learns that the personal self has been but a delusion and that one's essence [*Ātmā*] has been, in fact, the Supreme Self or the *Paramātmā.*

Parāśara The *Maharṣi* who created the system of *Vedic* astrology, now known by his name as the *Parāśara* system of *Vedic* astrology.

Parihāra The surmounting of *karmic* obstacles that block the flow of grace for all human activities. This is achieved through propitiatory charities to the creatures of God and is also known as remedial measures in Hindu/*Vedic* Astrology. The SA places a strong emphasis on the power of the remedial measures.

Parivrājaka Sanyāsi A renunciant [*sanyāsi*] who wanders from place to place [*parivrājaka*] without being anchored to a fixed abode. The reason for this mode of life is to keep all attachments to people and places from growing and developing.

Patañjali's Yogasūtras One of the scriptural sources of *yoga* as a means to *Kaivalya* or *Mokṣa.* A *Mokṣaśāstra* attributed to the *Maharṣi Patañjali* and assigned to the epoch 500-200 BCE.

Paurṇami The full moon day, when the Mo has maximum brightness. Also refers to one of the *tithis* or phases of the Moon in the Hindu lunar calendar.

Pātāla Liṅgam In the basement of the *Aruṇācaleśvara* temple in Tiruvannamalai, there was enshrined a *Śiva Liṅga* (and a *Naṅdi*) that belonged to a more hidden and denser plane of consciousness called *Pātāla loka.* The boy *Ramaṇa* spontaneously took refuge here and went into meditative trances.

Poṣa Kāraka Significator [*kāraka*] of nourishment [*poṣaṇa*], namely, the Moon, the planet of the Divine Mother.

Prajñāna Intuition of the illumined, according to *Śrī Ramaṇa Maharṣi.* Also, his own state after Self-Realization.

Praṇām This is a humble and respectful form of obeisance, offered to a God, Master, or elderly person by a devotee, disciple, or someone younger in years. The graceful gesture takes the form of bringing both palms symmetrically together into contact in front of the chest while bowing simultaneously. In a spiritual context, this is invariably an expression of one's devotion and gratitude. In polite Hindu society, this is also a customary way for people to greet each other – but in such a context, the bowing is mutually avoided.

Prasāda Usually a freshly prepared food item that is offered with devotion to a Deity, God, or *Guru* on a festive occasion or even on a daily basis. This offering is thereafter distributed to one and all in the congregation as a token of God's grace. Used in the Pilgrimage in this sense of 'grace'.

Praśna A question, in Horary astrology [*praśna śāstra*]. This is a specialized branch of Hindu astrology, which provides answers to questions through decipherment of the positions of the *Navagrahas* at the time of the question. Such an astrological solution to baffling questions is generally resorted to when the individual who has asked the question does not know his or her birth details.

Pravṛtti Mārga Life in the spheres of 'extroversion', namely, in *Artha* and *Kāma*. Its opposite is the *Nivṛtti mārga,* in which the worldly life of sensory enjoyment and attachment to wealth and family is renounced.

Prāṇa Subtle life energy that sustains all living beings. This is not the life-sustaining oxygen discovered by modern science, but a far subtler energy unknown to modern allopathic medicine because of its invisibility and subtle nature. *Prāṇa* is however the most important object of study in *yoga.*

Prāṇamayakośa The life [*prāṇa*] sheath [*kośa*] that wraps around, thereby concealing the Self or the *Ātmā.* The *pañcakośas* must be taken to be a convenient model for understanding the spiritual nature of humans. The IIIH of Hindu astrology and the planet Ma represent this sheath.

Prāṇa Śakti The subtle life [*prāṇa*] energy [*Śakti*] drawn into the body in the process of inhalation but distinct from oxygen, and which sustains the physical body. The strength of the IIIH and Ma decide the degree of vitality or *prāṇaśakti* of any given individual.

Punarvasu The seventh *nakṣatra* in the natural zodiac, with three *pādas* [quarters] lying in the sign Gemini and the last *pāda* lying in the sign Cancer. It is the *janma nakṣatra* of *Śrī Ramaṇa Maharṣi.*

Puṇya Spiritual merit or virtue, which accrues when one follows the cosmic moral order or *Dharma.*

Purāṇa Historical texts of the ancient Hindus dating back some five thousand years but certainly not in the sense of western chronological history. The 'history' of the Hindus, though not entirely faithful to space-time reality on account of its mythological, philosophical, and spiritual ingredients, has more inspirational and didactic value rather than as texts that portray purely historical events. *Purāṇa* means ancient.

Puruṣa In *Patañjali's Yogasūtras, Puruṣa* stands for the Absolute Reality, described in *advaita Vedānta* as *Parabrahma.*

Puruṣārthas The goals [*Artha*] of man [*puruṣa*] in Hindu society, namely *Dharma, Artha, Kāma,* and *Mokṣa.*

Pūrva Puṇya The result of spiritual merit [*puṇya*] from past [*pūrva*] lives. VA holds the VH to be the house of *pūrvapuṇya,* whereas the SA holds the IXH to be the house of *pūrvapuṇya.*

Rajas, Rajoguṇa, Rājasic One of the three aspects in the triune (three in one) manifestation of *Śakti,* which applies to all created forms in nature. *Guṇa* refers to the manifested quality. Depending upon which aspect of the triune manifestation becomes dominant, the individual acquires that *guṇa* as his/her temperament.

The aspect of *rajas,* manifests as endless craving, passion for life, thirst for action, restlessness, lust, haste, impatience, anger, aggression, greed, sense of division and duality, attraction and repulsion, etc. In Hindu astrology, this *rājasic* aspect of the triune manifestation of *Śakti* is represented by the planets Mars, Venus, Mercury, and by the cosmic malefic life energy called *Rāhu.*

Ramacharithramanas (***Śrī Rāmacaritamānasa***) *Magnum opus* in Hindi of the sixteenth-century Saint *Śrī Goswāmi Tulasidāsa.* The Saint's inspirational source must have been the original *Saṁskṛta Rāmāyaṇa* of *Śrī Vālmīki Maharṣi.*

The title means: The *Mānasa* lake brimming over with the exploits of *Śrī Rāma.* The *Mānasa* lake can only refer to the waters (feelings) of the Saint's own expansive consciousness, as the same was evidently suffused with a communion of the highest devotional intensity [*Bhakti*] with his beloved *Śrī Rāmachandra. Mahātmā* Gandhi considered this to be the best devotional work in the Hindi-speaking heartland of India. Pious Hindu families in North India still adore this great work and live by its timeless teachings.

Rāhu The north node of the Moon. The Moon's orbit when moving north from the southern side intersects the ecliptic. This point of intersection is known as *Rāhu* or the 'dragon's head'. The nodes cause eclipses in astronomy, but in astrology, they have profound *karmic* significations enveloping all aspects of human life.

Rāhu Daśā In the *Viṁśottarī daśā-bhukti* system of time used in VA and the SA, the main period of *Rāhu,* which lasts eighteen years.

Rājasic Kriyā Śakti The energy of the Divine Mother that is action-oriented in the outside world in its creative aspect. This energy drives the *Artha* Hs, namely, the IIH, VIH and XH.

Rāśis The zodiacal signs from Aries [*Meṣa*] to Pisces [*Mīna*].

Ribhu Gīta The Tamil *Śaivaite* classic on *advaita,* sourced in the *Sanskrit* classical epic *Śivarahasya* [The mysterious and esoteric knowledge of the God *Śiva*].

Ṛṣi Hindu Sage. In the ancient *Vedic* and Hindu societies, which were spiritual to the core, the Sages along with kings constituted the creative minority in the sense meant by the British historian Arnold J. Toynbee.

Ruci Taste, relish, appetite.

Rudra A *Vedic* Deity and aspect of *Śiva,* and the ruling Deity in the *nakṣatra Ārdra.* This *nakṣatra* can bring into manifestation a wrathful energy of the Divine, which is favourable for healing but is prone to first create a crisis and only then a fruitful transformation. This signification was fulfilled during *Ramaṇa Maharṣi's Mokṣa.*

Samādhi An introverted state of self-absorption, which may occur during deep meditation, in which the self-conscious subject becomes one with the object of meditation. This state is usually rapturous. There are many levels in *samādhi.* The word itself means gathering or bringing together (consciousness) into one whole essence.

Samādhisthal The place [*sthal*] where the *Maharṣi's* mortal remains were enshrined and which is within the precincts of *Śrī Ramaṇāśramam.*

Sampradāya Tradition and custom going back to some special lineage or system set up by a great Master or Sage.

Saṁkalpa Intention, willed and kept afire in consciousness for the purpose of bringing it to fruition.

Saṁsāra The endless cycle of birth-death-rebirth. Also used in the sense of worldly existence. Sometimes it is wrongly applied to family life, thereby creating the misperception that it is family life, that is the *Saṁsāra.*

Saṁskāras Latent impressions in human consciousness, which give us urges and inclinations to act and think in certain specific and enigmatic ways. The seed of these latent impressions could have been formed either during childhood in this life or can be traced to some former life.

Saṁskṛta The *Sanskrit* language. The word means: Perfected, refined, systematized, polished, and well synthesized.

Sanātana Dharma The eternal [*Sanātana*] religion [*Dharma*] of the Hindus, with beginnings in the *Vedas.*

Sandhi A transitional zone of 'narrow width' either in time, as at the expiry of one *yuga* and the commencement of the succeeding one, or in space, marking a transitional interface between two adjacent zones, such as that between two zodiacal signs. In the former case we speak of *yuga sandhi,* and in the latter case we speak of *rāśi sandhi.*

Sannidhi Exactly at the *sanctum sanctorum* of the Deity.

Satsaṅg Association with spiritual and wise people. *Sat* means truthful and spiritual; *saṅg* is association with.

Sattvaguṇa, Sattva, Sāttvic One of the three aspects in the triune (three in one) manifestation of *Śakti,* which applies to all created forms in nature. *Guṇa* refers to the manifested quality. Depending upon which aspect in the triune manifestation becomes dominant, the individual acquires that *guṇa* as his/her temperament. *Sattvaguṇa* alone, may be considered to be spiritual in nature, while the other two are definitely unspiritual.

The aspect of *sattva* manifests as peace, contentment, tranquility, love and compassion, intelligence, sensitivity, a sense of empathy and unity with the 'other', generosity, a humanitarian approach to life, freedom from a sense of division and duality, etc. However, in spite of all these spiritual blessings inherent in *sattvaguṇa,* it is nevertheless tainted by the presence of individuality or *asmitā.* In Hindu astrology, the Sun, Moon, and Jupiter represent the *sāttvic* nature. Among the houses, the IVH, VH, and the IXH are *sāttvic.* Strong *sāttvic* planets and houses make the spiritual life easier. *Sāttvic* is the adjectival form.

Satyāgraha *Mahātmā* Gandhi's spiritual ideal of 'tenaciously holding on to the truth' while observing the spiritual principle of *ahiṁsā* or non-violence. *Satya* is truth; *graha* means possession of or tenaciously holding on to.

Sādhana A system of spiritual practice that usually culminates in *siddhi,* or attainment.

Sāttvic Jñāna Śakti *Sāttvic* is the adjectival for of *sattva.* The auspicious spiritual energy [*Śakti*] of the Divine Mother that drives the *Dharma* houses in VA is called *Jñāna Śakti. Jñāna* is understanding and wisdom, which is especially needed for God Realization and Self-Realization.

Seva In Hindu society, even those married and in family life hold it to be a spiritual ideal to render some service [*seva*] for the betterment of society without expecting anything in return. This is an ideal very beloved to *karmayogis,* who may become *sevaks* attached to an *āśrama* or to a spiritual movement under the leadership of an adored Master.

Soumya As an adjective, the word means gentle or beneficial. Applicable to the *Navagrahas* when they act as FBs in a horoscope. The FMs, by contrast, are malefic or *krūra.*

Sthira, Sthiratva Used as an adjective signifying fixity, constancy, and stability. In Hindu astrology, *Vṛṣabha* [Taurus], *Siṁha* [Leo], and *Vṛścika* [Scorpio] and *Kumbha* [Aquarius] are *Sthira rāśis* [fixed signs]. *Sthiratva* is stability. There are four other *rāśis* which are of the *cara* [moving] type and yet four more of the *dwisvabhāva* [swinging, that is, dual-natured, with both fixed and moving characteristics] type.

Subramaṇya Swāmi The *Sanskrit* name for the Hindu Deity *Kārttikeya.* The Tamils know this Deity as *Muruga.*

Sūrya Lagna A horoscope can be read with respect to the Sun sign [*sūrya rāśi*] as Asdt [*lagna*]. This would mean that in such a reading, the sign in which the Sun is placed is taken as the IH.

Sūtra A succinctly expressed principle. Best thought of as an 'integrating string'. Just as a string passes through many beads and holds them together, so too the *sūtra* integrates and holds together diverse human experiences anchored to that principle.

In ancient Hindu society, the *sūtra* method was adopted, to facilitate easy memorization as that age did not have the luxury of the printed word. Because of great etymological precision and brevity of expression, *sūtras* were meant only for more advanced *sādhakas,* who already had a deep and detailed working knowledge of their discipline of learning. For this reason, a particular subject cannot be learnt by beginning with its *sūtras.*

Śaivite One for whom the Hindu God *Śiva* is the *Iṣṭadevatā* and the family Deity as well.

Śakti The dynamic aspect of *Śiva* (considered feminine), which creates all formful manifestations and thus stands for His Divine Power — in contrast to His timeless transcendental state of Divine Being (considered to be masculine). However, this *Śakti* aspect of *Śiva* is intrinsically inseparable from His unmanifest state of Divine Being. In Hindu astrology, this life energy of the Divine Mother is understood in terms of its three distinct manifestations: *Icchā, Kriyā,* and *Jñāna Śaktis.*

Śāstrās Authoritative Hindu works invested with spiritual and scriptural authority in all departments of learning.

Śiva The transcendent God of the Hindu world, especially dear to those on the path of Self-Realization and those on the *Nivṛtti mārga* as renunciants.

Śrī Signifies auspiciousness or glory or even the consort of Lord *Viṣṇu.* However, the word is also used as an honorific prefix to the names of Deities and eminent persons, thereby showing recognition of the Divine nature of that being. As *Sanātana Dharma* inculcates the recognition of Divinity in all human beings, this honorific prefix is freely applied to one and all, irrespective of their status in society.

Śrīmatī A respectful title or address applied to Hindu married women, meaning bearer of prosperity or grace [*Śrī*]. Other meanings are Divine, royal, charming, beautiful, and graceful.

Śrīmūrti Upāsana Regular disciplined worship [*upāsana*] of one's personal God or family Deity, portrayed in a mythical, anthropomorphic, or pictorial form [*Śrīmūrti*].

Śuddha Manas The state of pure [*śuddha*] consciousness [*manas*], which is devoid of dualistic perception, ignorance and comes into existence only with Self-Realization, as in the illustative example of *Śrī Ramaṇa Maharṣi.*

Tamas, Tamoguṇa, Tāmasic One of the three aspects in the triune (three in one) manifestation of *Śakti,* which applies to all created forms in nature. *Guṇa* refers to the manifested quality. Depending upon which aspect of the triune manifestation becomes dominant, the individual acquires that *guṇa* as his/her temperament.

The aspect of *tamas,* manifests as inertia, darkness of ignorance, sleep, slow motion, indolence, immobility, resistance to change, decay, dullness, stupidity, and stagnation. The life force is too feeble in this aspect. In Hindu astrology, the planet Saturn represents the aspect of *tamas,* especially when it is a functional malefic in the chart. *Tāmasic* is the adjectival form.

Tiruchuzhi The birthplace of *Śrī Ramaṇa Maharṣi.*

Tirumeninathar The prefix *Tiru* in Tamil is equivalent to the *Saṁskṛta Śrī,* which is applied as an auspicious and honorific title to saintly beings, holy places and things. Here, it refers to the Hindu God *Śiva's* manifestation as *Tirumeninathar. Meninathar* means, Lord and Master [*Nathar* in Tamil] of the body [*meni*].

Tiruvannamalai The township in which *Śrī Ramaṇāśramam* is located.

Tyāga Renunciation of all bondages in consciousness to name, fame, pleasure, and people.

Tyāgarāja King of renunciation — another name for the God *Śiva.* Also applied to *Śrī Ramaṇa Maharṣi* in the Pilgrimage.

Umāpati A *Śivācārya* [an *ācārya* or a spiritual teacher who exclusively teaches the truth of *Śiva* as the Absolute Reality] of the fourteenth century, who, in his compositions, had described the manifestation of God *Śiva* as *Kālakāla.*

Umā Sahasram An erudite and poetic composition on the Divine Mother *Umā* [the consort of *Śiva*] in one-thousand verses [*sahasram*] by *Vāśiṣṭa Gaṇapati Muni.* It was completed in a record time of three weeks. During the last sitting, the *Muni,* in the physical presence of *Śrī Ramaṇa Maharṣi* had dictated more than two-hundred verses to his disciples within the short span of four hours.

Upadeśa Spiritual guidance.

Upaniṣads The *Upaniṣads* are considered to be the crown of the *Vedas* and contain the insights, Realizations, and mystic perceptions of Absolute Reality of the ancient *Ṛṣis,* who were liberated beings just like *Śrī Ramaṇa Maharṣi.*

Vairāgya Detachment from all worldly attachments and cravings.

Vanaprasthāśrama Refers to the third stage of life in ancient Hindu society. Its purpose was to make the transition from a full involvement in worldly life [*Gṛhasthāśrama*] to spiritual seclusion and renunciation [*Sanyāsāśrama*] smooth, without any sense of shock. It took the form of withdrawal from all worldly responsibilities, by retreating [*prastha*] into the woods [*vana*], as this afforded the necessary solitude and peaceful environment for pursuing the contemplative life as a prelude to complete renunciation. *Āśrama* here means stage of life.

Vāhana Vehicle used by Hindu Gods. The mouse is the *vāhana* of God *Gaṇeśa.*

Vāk *Sanskrit* name for speech or the spoken word.

Vāśiṣṭa Gaṇapati Muni The illustrious disciple of *Śrī Ramaṇa Maharṣi,* known for his profound learning of the *Vedas,* his *tapas* [meditations], his prodigious memory, and for being a champion of a *Vedic* renaissance.

Vedas Has its origin in the *Saṁskṛta* verb *vid,* to know. Thus, *Vedas,* insofar as its esoteric spiritual dimension is concerned, refers to knowledge of a certain mystical or *yogic* nature. Such knowledge must have become available to Sages and *Yogis* when they either plumbed the depths of their consciousness during meditations or when they received the blessings of God, in the form of intutive revelations.

In terms of content and chronology, *Vedas* are the well-preserved corpus of ancient *Sanskrit* compositions, which have been recognized to be the oldest wellspring of religious *sūktas* [hymns] as well as of historical records of the *Vedic Aryans.* Some *Vedic* scholars hold the view that the classification of the *Vedas,* into four distinct Parts, *Ṛg, Yajur, Sāma,* and *Atharva,* date back to 3700 BCE (see *Vedic Aryans* 216). The oldest among the *Vedas* is the *Ṛg Veda,* which consists of some 10 books, covering 1028 *sūktas* [hymns] and 10,552 *mantras.* Hinduism, which is world's oldest living religion, stands firmly upon the bedrock of the *Vedas.*

Vedācārya A teacher [*ācārya*] of the *Vedas,* usually adhering to some specific *Vedic* tradition or *Vedic* school of learning.

Vedānta The 'ultimate end' of the *Vedic* and the Hindu scriptures (*Upaniṣads,* principally), which deal with the Absolute Reality as a non-dual experience.

Vedānta Pañcadaśi An *advaitic* text by *Vidyāraṇya Swāmī,* belonging to *circa* 1400 CE.

Vedic Ṛṣis Self-Realized or God-Realized Sages and Spiritual Masters, like *Śrī Ramaṇa Maharṣi* and other ancient or modern Masters, who created and structured the *Vedas* through direct Realization of Absolute Reality.

Veṣa The personal self (personality) that wears various masks [*veṣa*] for its survival and is itself a mask on the *Paramātmā.*

Vidyā Specifically refers to 'knowledge', as the Hindus used that term, in the context of their spiritual world view. Thus, any God-centred system of knowledge created by Hindu *Ṛṣis.*

Vigraha An anthropomorphic form of a sacred Deity, usually in granite, marble, or bronze.

Vijñānamayakośa The 'sheath' of wisdom (in another phraseology, a level or plane of consciousness), which gives direct perception and insights of wisdom.

Viṁśāṁśa The D-20 divisional chart that reflects devotional [*Bhakti*] potential.

Viṁśottarī Daśa The subjective astrological time for each individual is the *Viṁśottarī* (120 year) *daśa* (major cycle) system of time. This is reflected through the *Navagrahas* in each individual's life.

Virūpākṣa Cave A cave on *Aruṇācala* hill that was the *Maharṣi's* abode between 1899 and 1916. It was named after the saint *Virūpākṣa Deva,* who used it as his abode in the thirteenth century.

Viṣṇu The Immanent God of the Hindu world, represented by the planet Me in VA. He is the God who preserves and nurtures existence.

Viṣṇu Sthānas The IH, VH, and IXH of the horoscope are called *Viṣṇu sthānas,* also known as *Dharma* houses. The VH and IXH are *sāttvic* in nature, and when they are strong in a horoscope or when there are good benefic planets in these houses, the individual has the blessings to abide in the state of 'being' rather than the state of 'becoming'. *Viṣṇu sthānas* are the houses of 'being' while the angular houses are *Artha* houses of 'becoming'.

Vivekacūḍāmaṇi A renowned work by *Ādi Śaṅkarācārya* (788-820 CE), who is considered by many to be the father of Hinduism of the first millennium. *Viveka* means discrimination, of Absolute Reality [*Parabrahma*] from all appearances and illusions [*māyā*] that surround us in our worldly life. *Cūḍāmaṇi* is the crest jewel that is poetically endowed with this power of discrimination. The work is in 580 sublime verses in the form of a dialogue between a Self-Realized Master [*Guru*] and an earnest disciple, and culminates in the beatific Self-Realization of the disciple. The *Sanskrit* work was translated by *Śrī Ramaṇa Maharṣi* into his mother tongue Tamil during his *Virūpākṣa* years.

Yantra A representative geometrical form or symbol of a planetary Deity, which is worshipped for receiving God's grace in a particular sphere of life.

Yoga A very comprehensive term, sometimes referring to a Hindu *darśana* and sometimes to the final goal of life, *Mokṣa,* which is the union, or *yoga,* of the *jīvātmā* [individual] and *Paramātmā* [God]. Also refers to Self-Realization, which is sought through various paths such as *Bhakti, Jñāna, Karma, Tantra, Dhyāna,* etc.

Yogācārya A teacher [*ācārya*] qualified to guide disciples in their quest for Self-Realization through one or the other paths of *yoga.*

Yoga Sādhana Disciplined practice [*sādhana*] of one or the other systems of *yoga.*

Yoga Sūtras See under *Patañjali's Yogasūtras* and *Yogaśāstra* as well as under *Sūtra.*

Yoga Śāstra Scriptures that comprehensively deal with the path of *yoga,* whose final goal is *Mokṣa. Patañjali's Yogasūtras* are a typical example of a *Yogaśāstra.*

Yogi One who leads life as enjoined in the *Yogaśāstras.* Also one who is Self-Realized on the path of *yoga.*

Yuga A cosmic cycle of time, of the order of thousands of years, governing the rising and falling of civilizations, as understood by the Hindu Sages.

For further details, contact:
Yogi Impressions Books Pvt. Ltd.
1711, Centre 1, World Trade Centre,
Cuffe Parade, Mumbai 400 005, India.

Fill in the Mailing List form on our website
and receive, via email, information on
books, authors, events and more.
Visit: www.yogiimpressions.com

Telephone: (022) 61541500, 61541541
Fax: (022) 61541542
E-mail: yogi@yogiimpressions.com

Join us on Facebook:
www.facebook.com/yogiimpressions

CPSIA information can be obtained
at www.ICGtesting.com
Printed in the USA
BVOW09s1832011117
499243BV00001B/40/P

9 788188 479405